Visit classzone and get connected

Online resources for students and parents

ClassZone resources provide instruction, practice, and learning support.

eEdition Plus Online

This online version of the text features *Animated Grammar*, practice activities, and video and audio clips.

@Home Tutor

The *@Home Tutor* provides leveled interactive practice with audio, video, and *Animated Grammar* to help all students prepare successfully for tests.

Animated Grammar

This entertaining animated tutor helps students learn Spanish grammar in a fun and lively way.

Get Help Online

Downloadable activity pages provide additional review and practice for struggling students.

Cultura Interactiva

Textbook culture pages introduce students to the rich culture of the Spanish-speaking world.

Flashcards

Online flashcards provide an interactive review of vocabulary and pronunciation with audio prompts and clip art.

WebQuests and Self-Check Quizzes

 CLASSZONE.COM

Animated Grammar

 McDougal Littell

MW01180785

NEW YORK EDITION

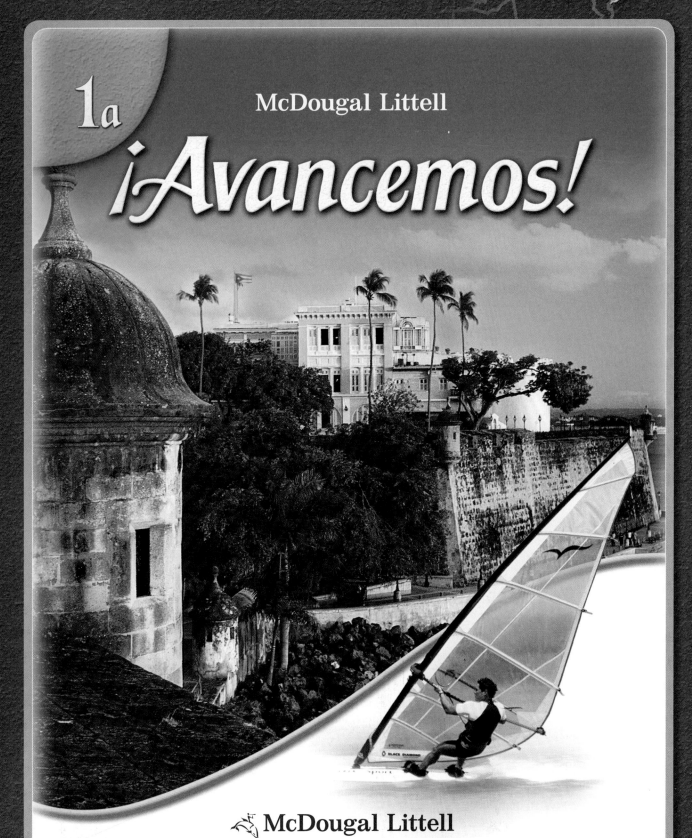

1a

McDougal Littell

¡Avancemos!

McDougal Littell
A DIVISION OF HOUGHTON MIFFLIN COMPANY
Evanston, Illinois • Boston • Dallas

Cover Photography

Front cover
View toward La Fortaleza, San Juan, Puerto Rico, © Steve Dunwell/The Image Bank/Getty Images
Inset: Windsurfing in Puerto Rico, © Mark Bacon/Latin Focus.com

Back cover
Level 1a: View toward La Fortaleza, San Juan, Puerto Rico, © Steve Dunwell/The Image Bank/Getty Images
Level 1b: View of Buenos Aires through the Puente de la Mujer, © Rodriguez Joseph/Gallery Stock Limited
Level 1: Monumento a la Independencia on the Paseo de la Reforma at night, Mexico City, Mexico, © Panoramic Images/Getty Images
Level 2: Cibeles Fountain and Palacio de Comunicaciones at night, Madrid, Spain, © Doug Armand/Getty Images
Level 3: Plaza de la Constitución at night, Santiago, Chile, © David Noton/Masterfile
Level 4: Templo II, Tikal, Guatemala, © P. Pet/zefa/Corbis

New York Edition Photography and Illustration Acknowledgments
The following acknowledgments supersede those found on Roman numeral pages up through **xix** in the Créditos on page R35.

Unless otherwise noted, all photos in this section are by Jorge Albán/McDougal Littell/Houghton Mifflin Co. **x** *top* Guy Jarvis/School Division/Houghton Mifflin Co.; *bottom left* Jaime Puebla/AP Images; *bottom right* Alberto Martin/Agencia EFE; **xi** *bottom left* Gregory Bull/AP Images; *bottom right* Jennifer Szymaszek/AP Images; **xii–xiii** *all* Ann Summa/McDougal Littell/Houghton Mifflin Co.; **NYS2** *top left* Jorge Albán/McDougal Littell/Houghton Mifflin Co.; *all others* © Rubberball; **NYS3** *top center* © Rubberball; *top right* © PhotoDisc; **NYS5** *Fernanda & Constantino* Jorge Albán/McDougal Littell/ Houghton Mifflin Co.; *Urbina* © PhotoDisc; *all others* © Rubberball; **NYS6** *center right* © PhotoDisc; **NYS7** *top right inset* © PhotoDisc; *top left inset* © Elnur/Shutterstock; *bottom right inset* © PhotoSpin; *bottom left inset* © Artville; **NYS9** *watch* © PhotoObjects/Jupiterimages Corporation; *medicine* © Artville; *steak* © Comstock; *bread* © PhotoDisc; *books* © PhotoSpin; *shoes* © Elnur/Shutterstock.

Copyright © 2008 by McDougal Littell, a division of Houghton Mifflin Company. All rights reserved.

Acknowledgments for the remainder of copyrighted material are on page R35 and constitute an extension of this page.

Warning: No part of this work may be reproduced or transmitted in any form or by any means, electronic or mechanical, including photocopying and recording, or by any information storage or retrieval system without the prior written permission of McDougal Littell unless such copying is expressly permitted by federal copyright law. With the exception of not-for-profit transcription in Braille, McDougal Littell is not authorized to grant permission for further uses of copyrighted selections reprinted in this text without the permission of their owners. Permission must be obtained from the individual copyright owners as identified herein. Address inquiries to Supervisor, Rights and Permissions, McDougal Littell, P.O. Box 1667, Evanston, IL 60204.

ISBN-10: 0-618-98057-1
ISBN-13: 978-0-618-98057-4

1 2 3 4 5 6 7 8 9 WMW 10 09 08 07

Internet: www.mcdougallittell.com

About the Authors

Estella Gahala   Estella Gahala received degrees in Spanish from Wichita State University, French from Middlebury College, and a Ph.D. in Educational Administration and Curriculum from Northwestern University. A career teacher of Spanish and French, she has worked with a wide variety of students at the secondary level. Her workshops and publications focus on research and practice in a wide range of topics, including culture and language learning, learning strategies, assessment, and the impact of current brain research on curriculum and instruction. She has coauthored twelve basal textbooks. Honors include the Chevalier dans l'Ordre des Palmes Académiques and listings in *Who's Who of American Women, Who's Who in America,* and *Who's Who in the World.*

Patricia Hamilton Carlin   Patricia Hamilton Carlin completed her M.A. in Spanish at the University of California, Davis, where she also taught as a lecturer. Previously she earned a Master of Secondary Education with specialization in foreign languages from the University of Arkansas and taught Spanish and French at the K–12 level. Patricia currently teaches Spanish and foreign language/ESL methodology at the University of Central Arkansas, where she coordinates the second language teacher education program. In 2005, she was awarded the Southern Conference on Language Teaching's Outstanding Teaching Award: Post-Secondary. Her professional service has included the presidency of the Arkansas Foreign Language Teachers Association and the presidency of Arkansas's DeSoto Chapter of the AATSP.

Audrey L. Heining-Boynton   Audrey L. Heining-Boynton received her Ph.D. in Curriculum and Instruction from Michigan State University. She is a professor of Education and Romance Languages at The University of North Carolina at Chapel Hill, where she teaches educational methodology classes and Spanish. She has also taught Spanish, French, and ESL at the K–12 level. Dr. Heining-Boynton served as the president of ACTFL and the National Network for Early Language Learning. She has been involved with AATSP, Phi Delta Kappa, and state foreign language associations. In addition, she has published over forty books, articles, and curricula.

Ricardo Otheguy   Ricardo Otheguy received his Ph.D. in Linguistics from the City University of New York, where he is currently professor of Linguistics at the Graduate Center. He is also director of the Research Institute for the Study of Language in Urban Society (RISLUS) and coeditor of the research journal *Spanish in Context.* He has extensive experience with school-based research and has written on topics related to Spanish grammar, bilingual education, and Spanish in the United States. He is coauthor of *Tu mundo: Curso para hispanohablantes* and *Prueba de ubicación para hispanohablantes.*

Barbara J. Rupert   Barbara Rupert completed her M.A. at Pacific Lutheran University. She has taught Level 1 through A.P. Spanish and has implemented a FLES program in her district. Barbara is the author of CD-ROM activities for the *¡Bravo!* series. She has served as president of both the Pacific Northwest Council for Languages (PNCFL) and the Washington Association for Language Teaching. In 1996, Barbara received the Christa McAuliffe Award for Excellence in Education, and in 1999, she was selected Washington's "Spanish Teacher of the Year" by the Juan de Fuca Chapter of the AATSP.

Carl Johnson, Senior Program Advisor   Carl Johnson received degrees from Marietta College (OH), the University of Illinois, Université Laval, and a Ph.D. in Foreign Language Education from The Ohio State University. He has been a lifelong foreign language educator, retiring in 2003 after 27 years as a language teacher (secondary and university level), consultant, and Director of Languages Other Than English for the Texas Department of Education. He has completed many publications relating to student and teacher language proficiency development, language textbooks, and nationwide textbook adoption practices. He also served as president of the Texas Foreign Language Association, Chair of the Board of the Southwest Conference on Language Teaching, and president of the National Council of State Supervisors of Foreign Languages. In addition, he was named Chevalier dans l'Ordre des Palmes Académiques by the French government.

Rebecca L. Oxford, Learning Strategy Specialist   Rebecca L. Oxford received her Ph.D. in educational psychology from The University of North Carolina. She also holds two degrees in foreign language from Vanderbilt University and Yale University, and a degree in educational psychology from Boston University. She leads the Second Language Education and Culture Program and is a professor at the University of Maryland. She has directed programs at Teachers College, Columbia University; the University of Alabama; and the Pennsylvania State University. In addition, she initiated and edited *Tapestry,* a series of student textbooks used around the world. Dr. Oxford specializes in language learning strategies and styles.

Contributing Writers

Louis G. Baskinger
New Hartford High School
New Hartford, NY

Jacquelyn Cinotti-Dirmann
Duval County Public Schools
Jacksonville, FL

Consulting Authors

Dan Battisti
Dr. Teresa Carrera-Hanley

Bill Lionetti
Patty Murguía Bohannan
Lorena Richins Layser

Teacher Reviewers

Sue Arandjelovic
Dobson High School
Mesa, AZ

Susan K. Arbuckle
Mahomet-Seymour High School
Mahomet, IL

Kristi Ashe
Amador Valley High School
Pleasanton, CA

Shaun A. Bauer
Olympia High School, *retired*
Orlando, FL

Sheila Bayles
Rogers High School
Rogers, AR

Robert L. Bowbeer
Detroit Country Day Upper School
Beverly Hills, MI

Hercilia Bretón
Highlands High School
San Antonio, TX

Adrienne Chamberlain-Parris
Mariner High School
Everett, WA

Mike Cooperider
Truman High School
Independence, MO

Susan B. Cress
Sheridan High School
Sheridan, IN

Michèle S. de Cruz-Sáenz, Ph.D.
Strath Haven High School
Wallingford, PA

Lizveth Dague
Park Vista Community High School
Lake Worth, FL

Parthena Draggett
Jackson High School
Massillon, OH

Rubén D. Elías
Roosevelt High School
Fresno, CA

Phillip Elkins
Lane Tech College Prep High School
Chicago, IL

Maria Fleming Álvarez
The Park School
Brookline, MA

Michael Garber
Boston Latin Academy
Boston, MA

Marco García
Derry University Advantage Academy
Chicago, IL

David González
Hollywood Hills High School
Hollywood, FL

Raquel R. González
Odessa Senior High School
Odessa, TX

Neyda González-Droz
Ridge Community High School
Davenport, FL

Becky Hay de García
James Madison Memorial
 High School
Madison, WI

Fatima Hicks
Suncoast High School, *retired*
Riviera Beach, FL

Gladys V. Horford
William T. Dwyer High School
Palm Beach Gardens, FL

Pam Johnson
Stevensville High School
Stevensville, MT

Richard Ladd
Ipswich High School
Ipswich, MA

Patsy Lanigan
Hume Fogg Academic Magnet
 High School
Nashville, TN

Kris Laws
Palm Bay High School
Melbourne, FL

Elizabeth Lupafya
North High School
Worcester, MA

David Malatesta
Niles West High School
Skokie, IL

Patrick Malloy
James B. Conant High School
Hoffman Estates, IL

Brandi Meeks
Starr's Mill High School
Fayetteville, GA

Kathleen L. Michaels
Palm Harbor University High School
Palm Harbor, FL

Linda Nanos
Brook Farm Business Academy
West Roxbury, MA

Nadine F. Olson
School of Teaching and Curriculum
 Leadership
Stillwater, OK

Pam Osthoff
Lakeland Senior High School
Lakeland, FL

Nicholas Patterson
Davenport Central High School
Davenport, IA

Daniel N. Richardson
Concord High School, *retired*
Concord, NH

Rita E. Risco
Palm Harbor University High School
Palm Harbor, FL

Miguel Roma
Boston Latin Academy
West Roxbury, MA

Lauren Schultz
Dover High School
Dover, NH

Nona M. Seaver
New Berlin West Middle/High School
New Berlin, WI

Susan Seraphine-Kimel
Astronaut High School
Titusville, FL

Mary Severo
Thomas Hart Middle School
Pleasanton, CA

Clarette Shelton
WT Woodson High School, *retired*
Fairfax, VA

Irma Sprague
Countryside High School
Clearwater, FL

Mary A. Stimmel
Lincoln High School
Des Moines, IA

Karen Tharrington
Wakefield High School
Raleigh, NC

Alicia Turnier
Countryside High School
Clearwater, FL

Roberto E. del Valle
The Overlake School
Redmond, WA

Todd Wagner
Upper Darby High School, *retired*
Drexel Hill, PA

Ronie R. Webster
Monson Junior/Senior High School
Monson, MA

Cheryl Wellman
Bloomingdale High School
Valrico, FL

Thomasina White
School District of Philadelphia
Philadelphia, PA

Jena Williams
Jonesboro High School
Jonesboro, AR

Program Advisory Council

Louis G. Baskinger
New Hartford High School
New Hartford, NY

Linda M. Bigler
James Madison University
Harrisonburg, VA

Flora María Ciccone-Quintanilla
Holly Senior High School
Holly, MI

Jacquelyn Cinotti-Dirmann
Duval County Public Schools
Jacksonville, FL

Desa Dawson
Del City High School
Del City, OK

Robin C. Hill
Warrensville Heights High School
Warrensville Heights, OH

Barbara M. Johnson
Gordon Tech High School, *retired*
Chicago, IL

Ray Maldonado
Houston Independent School
  District
Houston, TX

Karen S. Miller
Friends School of Baltimore
Baltimore, MD

Dr. Robert A. Miller
Woodcreek High School
  Roseville Joint Union High School
  District
Roseville, CA

Debra M. Morris
Wellington Landings Middle School
Wellington, FL

María Nieto Zezas
West Morris Central High School
Chester, NJ

Rita Oleksak
Glastonbury Public Schools
Glastonbury, CT

Sandra Rosenstiel
University of Dallas, *retired*
Grapevine, TX

Emily Serafa Manschot
Northville High School
Northville, MI

NEW YORK REVIEWERS

New York Program Advisors

Louis G. Baskinger
New Hartford High School
New Hartford, NY

Cherie Bluth
Farmingdale High School
Farmingdale, NY

Elizabeth Bossong
Vestal Senior High School
Vestal, NY

Robert Hughes
Martha Brown Middle School, *retired*
Fairport, NY

New York Reviewers

Joseph T. Baker
LaGuardia Arts High School
New York, NY

Deborah A. Carlson
Sweet Home Middle School
Amherst, NY

Annamaria Falzarano
Greece Central School District
Rochester, NY

Joyce Jackson-Kalinoski, PhD
Jamesville-DeWitt Middle School
Jamesville, NY

Dr. Elaine Margarita
Jericho Schools
Jericho, NY

Frank D. Marino, Jr.
Great Hollow Middle School
Nesconset, NY

Paula Nurse
North Tonawanda High School
North Tonawanda, NY

NEW YORK STANDARDS—Checkpoint A

Standard 1: Communication Skills

NY1.1 Listening and speaking are primary communicative goals in modern language learning. These skills are used for the purpose of socializing, providing and acquiring information, expressing personal feelings and opinions, and getting others to adopt a course of action.

Students can:

- Comprehend language consisting of simple vocabulary and structures in face-to-face conversation with peers and familiar adults.
- Comprehend the main idea of more extended conversations with some unfamiliar vocabulary and structures as well as cognates of English words.
- Call upon repetition, rephrasing, and nonverbal cues to derive or convey meaning from a language other than English.
- Use appropriate strategies to initiate and engage in simple conversations with more fluent or native speakers of the same age group, familiar adults, and providers of common public services.

NY1.2 Reading and writing are used in languages other than English for the purposes of socializing, providing and acquiring information, expressing personal feelings and opinions, and getting others to adopt a course of action.

Students can:

- Understand the main idea and some details of simple informative materials written for native speakers.
- Compose short, informal notes and messages to exchange information with members of the target culture.

Standard 2: Cultural Understanding

NY2 Effective communication involves meanings that go beyond words and require an understanding of perceptions, gestures, folklore, and family and community dynamics. All of these elements can affect whether and how well a message is received.

Students can:

- Use some key cultural traits of the societies in which the target language is spoken.

NEW YORK

CONTENTS
New York Student Edition

Liberty Island, New York © Christopher Hill/Alamy

Celebraciones

NEW YORK EDITION

Cultura INTERACTIVA   Explora las celebraciones del mundo hispano

NY2 Cultural Understanding

El Día de los Muertos,
Santiago Sacatepéquez, Guatemala

Online at CLASSZONE.COM

Cultura INTERACTIVA   *pp. C2–C3, C4–C5, C6–C7, C8–C9, C10–C11, C12–C13, C14–C15, C16–C17, C18–C19, C20–C21, C22–C23, C24–C25*

New Year's Eve, Madrid, Spain

Nueva York
¡Hola!

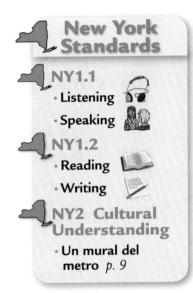

New York Standards

NY1.1
- Listening
- Speaking

NY1.2
- Reading
- Writing

NY2 Cultural Understanding
- Un mural del metro *p. 9*

Did you get it?
Student Self-Check
pp. 5, 9, 11, 15, 17, 19, 21, 24

A performer wearing the colors of the Puerto Rican Flag

Dominican dancers in colorful costumes

Estados Unidos

Un rato con los amigos

¿Recuerdas?
• weather expressions *p. 37*

Did you get it?
Student Self-Check
pp. 35, 37, 41, 43, 47, 50

Online at CLASSZONE.COM

Video/DVD
Vocabulario
pp. 32–34, 60–62
Telehistoria
pp. 36, 42, 48 64, 70, 76

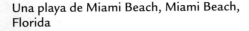

Una playa de Miami Beach, Miami Beach, Florida

Paseo del Río, San Antonio, Texas

New York Standards

NY1.1
• Listening
• Speaking

NY1.2
• Reading
• Writing

NY2 Cultural Understanding
• **Comida mexicana y Tex-Mex** *p. 65*
• **El arte en Texas** *p. 75*
• **Saludos desde San Antonio y Miami** *p. 80*
• **Platos tradicionales de México y Cuba** *p. 82*
• **Me gusta...** *p. 86*

 ¿Recuerdas?
• **ser** *p. 63*
• snack foods *p. 67*
• **gustar** with an infinitive *p. 69*
• after-school activities *p. 71*

 Did you get it?
Student Self-Check
pp. 63, 65, 69, 71, 75, 78

UNIDAD 2

México
¡Vamos a la escuela!

New York Standards

NY1.1
- Listening
- Speaking

NY1.2
- Reading
- Writing

NY2 Cultural Understanding
- Explora México *p. 90*
- Uniformes escolares *p. 102*
- Los murales en México *p. 109*
- Una escuela bilingüe en México *p. 114*

¿Recuerdas?
- after-school activities *p. 103*
- days of the week *p. 105*

PARA Y PIENSA Did you get it?
Student Self-Check
pp. 97, 99, 103, 105, 109, 112

Online at CLASSZONE.COM

Cultura INTERACTIVA
pp. 90–91 148–149

Animated Grammar
pp. 100, 106, 117 128, 134, 145

@HomeTutor VideoPlus
pp. 98, 104, 110 126, 132, 138

Video/DVD

Vocabulario
pp. 94–96, 122–124

Telehistoria
pp. 98, 104, 110 126, 132, 138

La fuente de San Miguel en el Zócalo,
Puebla, México

El patio de una escuela secundaria,
México

Lección 2

Tema: *En la escuela*

New York Standards

¿Recuerdas?

Did you get it?

Puerto Rico
Comer en familia

NEW YORK EDITION

New York Standards

NY1.1

• Listening
• Speaking

NY1.2
• Reading
• Writing

NY2 Cultural Understanding
• **Explora Puerto Rico** *p. 152*
• **La cocina criolla** *p. 164*
• **La Plaza de Colón** *p. 170*
• **¡A comprar y a comer!** *p. 176*

 ¿Recuerdas?
• **gustar** with an infinitive *p. 159*
• snack foods *p. 161*
• the verb **estar** *p. 169*
• telling time *p. 173*

 PARA Y PIENSA **Did you get it?**
Student Self-Check
pp. 159, 161, 165, 167, 171, 174

Online at CLASSZONE.COM

Cultura INTERACTIVA
pp. 152–153 210–211

Animated Grammar
pp. 162, 168, 179 190, 196, 207

@HomeTutor VideoPlus
pp. 160, 166, 172 188, 194, 200

Video/DVD
Vocabulario
pp. 156–158, 184–186
Telehistoria
pp. 160, 166, 172 188, 194, 200

La Plaza de Colón en el Viejo San Juan,
San Juan, Puerto Rico

Una familia come en casa,
San Juan, Puerto Rico

Lección 2

Tema: *En mi familia* 182

New York Standards

NY1.1
- Listening
- Speaking

NY1.2
- Reading
- Writing

NY2 Cultural Understanding
- **Las elecciones en Puerto Rico** *p. 193*
- **Los retratos** *p. 199*
- **La quinceañera** *p. 204*
- **Instrumentos de Puerto Rico y Perú** *p. 206*
- **¿Qué comemos?** *p. 210*

¿Recuerdas?
- the verb **tener** *p. 189*
- numbers from 11 to 100 *p. 189*
- after-school activities *p. 191*
- describing others *p. 192*

Did you get it?
Student Self-Check
pp. NYS5, 187, 189, 193, 195, 199, 202

UNIDAD 4

España
En el centro

NEW YORK EDITION

New York Standards

NY1.1
- Listening
- Speaking

NY1.2
- Reading
- Writing

NY2 Cultural Understanding
- **Explora España** *p. 214*
- **El arte surrealista de España** *p. 229*
- **Climas diferentes** *p. 233*
- **Las memorias del invierno** *p. 238*

 ¿Recuerdas?
- numbers from 11 to 100 *p. 221*
- the verb **tener** *p. 223*
- after-school activities *p. 223*

 Did you get it?
Student Self-Check
pp. 221, 223, 227, 229, 233, 236

Online at CLASSZONE.COM

Cultura INTERACTIVA
pp. 214–215 272–273

Animated Grammar
pp. 224, 230, 241 252, 258, 269

@HomeTutor VideoPlus
pp. 222, 228, 234 250, 256, 262

 Video/DVD
Vocabulario
pp. 218–220, 246–248
Telehistoria
pp. 222, 228, 234 250, 256, 262

Una tienda de ropa, Madrid, España

El Teatro de la Comedia en la calle Príncipe, Madrid, España

Lección 2

Tema: ¿Qué hacemos esta noche? 244

**UNIT 4
WRAP-UP**

Comparación cultural

 ¿Recuerdas?
• present tense of **-er** verbs *p. 249*
• the verb **ir** *p. 251*
• direct object pronouns *p. 259*
• **tener** expressions *p. 261*

 PARA Y PIENSA **Did you get it?**
Student Self-Check
pp. NYS9, 249, 251, 255, 257, 261, 264

Recursos

TOPIC SUPPORT

Liberty Island, New York © Christopher Hill/Alamy

Presentación de VOCABULARIO

¡AVANZA! **Goal:** Learn about the families of Marisol's friends and what some of their family members do for a living. Then practice what you have learned to talk about professions.

Expand the vocabulary in Unit 3 Lesson 2

A ¡Hola! Me llamo Marisol. Te presento a unas personas de las familias de mis amigos.

la enfermera | el hombre de negocios | la médica | el bombero

B La madre de Soledad es **enfermera** y el padrastro de José es **hombre de negocios.** La tía de Miguel es **médica** y el tío es **bombero.**

Topic Support

C En la familia de Emiliano hay una **dentista,** una **mujer de negocios** y un **abogado.**

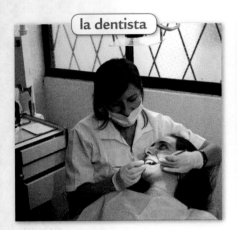

la dentista

la mujer de negocios

el abogado

el policía

D El padre de Sara tiene **una profesión** muy importante. Es **policía.**

¡A responder!

Escucha las palabras. Indica la foto con la profesión que se menciona.
(Listen to the words. Point to the photo with the profession that is mentioned.)

❈ Práctica de VOCABULARIO

1 | Ellos también

Escribir
Hablar

Indica que estas personas también tienen la misma profesión.
(Say that these people have the same occupation.)

> modelo: Mi padre es médico. (mi madre)
> Mi madre es médica también.

1. La tía de Ana es abogada. (el tío de Ana)
2. El primo de Carlos es hombre de negocios. (mi prima)
3. Mi abuela es enfermera. (mi padrastro)
4. El tío de Nora es dentista. (la madrastra de Nora)
5. Mi hermano es bombero. (mi hermana)
6. La tía de David es policía. (el abuelo de David)

Expansión
Write sentences describing the professions of both people using **son**.

2 | Una familia trabajadora

Leer
Escribir

Hernán le escribe un correo electrónico a Carolina. Completa el párrafo con las palabras apropiadas. *(Fill in the blanks.)*

enfermero	médica
dentista	abogado
bombera	mujer de negocios

A: Carolina

Asunto: Mi familia

Hola, chica. ¿Qué hace mi familia? Bueno, todas las personas en mi familia son muy trabajadoras. Mi padre es __1.__ . Él va a la corte[1] todos los días. Mi madre es __2.__ . Trabaja en una oficina en la ciudad de Nueva York. A ella le gustan las matemáticas. Tengo dos hermanos y dos hermanas. Pedro y Pilar trabajan en un hospital. Él es __3.__ y ella es __4.__ . Mi hermano Andrés es __5.__ . Si tienes problemas con los dientes[2], debes hablar con él. Mi hermana Amanda ayuda[3] a las personas… ¡y a los gatos que están en los árboles[4]! Ella es __6.__ . Yo soy trabajador también. No trabajo pero estudio mucho.

Hasta pronto,

Hernán

[1] court   [2] teeth   [3] helps   [4] trees

3 | ¿Qué hacen?

Hablar

Pregúntale a otro(a) estudiante qué hacen las siguientes personas.
(Ask a partner what the following people do for a living..)

modelo:

A ¿Qué hace Fernanda?

B Ella es dentista.

Fernanda

Raimundo

la señorita Moreno

Magdalena

el señor Urbina

la señora Lopez

Constantino

Topic Support

4 | ¿Y en tu familia?

Hablar

Habla con otro(a) estudiante sobre las profesiones de los miembros de tu familia o la familia de un amigo(a). *(Talk about what people in your family do for a living.)*

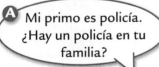
A Mi primo es policía. ¿Hay un policía en tu familia?

B No, pero mi tía es bombera.

Expansión
Take notes and present your partner's family to the class.

PARA Y PIENSA

Did you get it?
1. Name two occupations in Spanish that require you to work outside.
2. Name three occupations in Spanish that require you to work with patients.

❈ Presentación de VOCABULARIO

¡AVANZA! **Goal:** Learn about some of the specialty shops and neighborhood merchants in Enrique's neighborhood. Then practice what you have learned to talk about shops where you live.

Expand the vocabulary in Unit 4 Lesson 2

A Hola, soy Enrique. Vivo en Madrid. Aquí hay muchas tiendas.

la carnicería

el carnicero

B El señor Cruz trabaja en **la carnicería** en la calle Leñeros. Él es **carnicero.** Hay una **joyería** en el centro. El señor Rodríguez trabaja allí. Es **joyero.** El señor Martín es **cartero.** Él no trabaja en una tienda; trabaja en **el correo**.

la joyería

el joyero

el cartero

Topic Support

C Mi tía trabaja en **una zapatería** en la calle Estrecho. Ella es **zapatera**. Hay **una panadería** al lado del parque. La señora Aznar es **la panadera**. ¡Vende pan muy rico!

la zapatería

la panadería

D Mi padre es **farmacéutico** en **la farmacia** de la calle Alvarado. Mi madre trabaja en **la librería** cerca de mi escuela. Ella es **librera**. Le gusta mucho leer.

la farmacia

la librería

Más vocabulario

abrir *to open*

mandar cartas
    to send letters

la medicina *medicine*

repartir cartas
    to deliver letters

¡A responder!

Escucha las oraciones. Señala con el pulgar hacia arriba si la oración es lógica o con el pulgar hacia abajo si es ilógica. *(Listen to the sentences. Make a thumbs-up sign if the sentence is logical or a thumbs-down sign if it is illogical.)*

❋Práctica de VOCABULARIO

1 Analogías

Escribir

Completa las analogías. *(Complete the analogies.)*

correo	carne	farmacia	medicina
librería	panadero	repartir	abrir

modelo: joyero : *joyería* :: zapatero : **zapatería**

1. zapatos : *zapatería* :: libros : _____

2. camarero : *servir* :: cartero : _____

3. librería : *librero* :: panadería : _____

4. enfermera : *hospital* :: farmacéutica : _____

5. joyero : *relojes* :: carnicero : _____

6. comprar una entrada : *ventanilla* :: mandar una carta : _____

7. zapatero : *zapatos* :: farmacéutico : _____

8. bueno : *malo* :: cerrar : _____

2 ¿Quién lo dice?

Hablar

Identifica la persona que dice lo siguiente. *(Identify the person who most likely says the following.)*

A Aquí tiene la cuenta, señor.

B un(a) camarero(a)

1. Tengo mucha carne para vender.

2. Necesitas tomar la medicina por la mañana.

3. ¿No le gustan los zapatos rojos?

4. Perdón. No vendo libros en inglés.

5. Dos kilos de pollo... ¿algo más?

6. Tengo una carta para usted.

7. El reloj cuesta cincuenta dólares.

8. Sí, tenemos pan para hacer sándwiches.

> **Expansión**
> Write sentences telling where each person works.

Topic Support

3 | ¿Dónde puedo comprarlo?

Hablar

Di que necesitas comprar las siguientes cosas. Tu compañero(a) te va a decir dónde puedes comprarlo. *(Say that you need to buy the following items and your partner will tell you where you can buy them.)*

modelo:

A Necesito comprar bistec.

B Puedes comprar bistec en una carnicería.

1.

2.

3.

4.

5.

6.

Expansión
Tell your partner who he or she needs to talk to at each of the places.

4 | ¡A jugar! Las Charadas

Hablar

Túrnense para representar las acciones de una professión sin usar palabras. Tus compañeros(as) deben adivinar qué profesión es. *(Play charades. Act out an occupation for others to guess.)*

modelo: *Pretends to roll out dough, make loaves, and put them in a hot oven.*

A ¡Carnicero!

B No, no es carnicero.

C ¡Panadero!

¡Sí, es panadero!

PARA Y PIENSA

Did you get it? Say what you do in the following places:
1. el correo 2. la librería 3. la farmacia

En resumen

Vocabulario *Expanded vocabulary for Unit 3 Lesson 2*

Talk About Occupations

el (la) abogado(a)	*lawyer*	el (la) enfermero(a)	*nurse*	la mujer de negocios	*businesswoman*
el (la) bombero(a)	*firefighter*	el hombre de negocios	*businessman*	el (la) policía	*police officer*
el (la) dentista	*dentist*	el (la) médico(a)	*doctor*		

Vocabulario *Expanded vocabulary for Unit 4 Lesson 2*

Talk About Shopping

Speciality shops		Merchants	
la carnicería	*butcher shop*	el (la) carnicero(a)	*butcher*
la farmacia	*pharmacy*	el (la) farmacéutico(a)	*pharmacist*
la joyería	*jewelry store*	el (la) joyero(a)	*jeweler*
la librería	*bookstore*	el (la) librero(a)	*bookseller*
la panadería	*bakery*	el (la) panadero(a)	*baker*
la zapatería	*shoe store*	el (la) zapatero(a)	*shoemaker*

Other words and phrases

abrir	*to open*
el (la) cartero(a)	*mail carrier*
el correo	*post office*
mandar cartas	*to send letters*
la medicina	*medicine*
repartir cartas	*to deliver letters*

PARA Y PIENSA **Self-Check Answers**

Answers may vary but can include:

p. NY5 1. el (la) bombero(a), el (la) policía. 2. el (la) enfermero(a), el (la) médico(a), el (la) dentista.

p. NY9 1. Mando cartas en el correo. 2. Compro libros en la librería. 3. Compro medicina en la farmacia.

Repaso inclusivo

1 | Draw a map of a new downtown

Hablar

Work in a small group to draw a map of a new downtown. Discuss what specialty shops you will include and where they are going to be located. After you draw the map and label each building, present it to the class. Be prepared to explain why you organized your downtown as you did.

2 | Write a brochure

Escribir

Create a brochure for your school's Career Fair. Choose six occupations to include in your **¿Qué quieres ser de grande?** brochure. Write a brief description of what a person in each profession does, and describe someone in your community who has the same occupation. You might want to include drawings or pictures from magazines.

NEW YORK

SKILL SUPPORT

Liberty Island, New York © Christopher Hill/Alamy

Skill Support

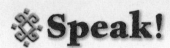 Speak!

Why?
Speaking allows you to interact with other people, express your concerns and dreams, share your experiences and ideas, negotiate, persuade, report, explain, and complain. Speaking develops both language learning abilities and social skills.

What?
You'll speak about a wide range of topics in a variety of realistic situations. You'll also be involved in simple face-to-face conversations with classmates and teachers. Your goal is to be able to start a conversation, respond to simple statements, ask for information, and express your own thoughts so that fluent or native speakers used to interacting with Spanish learners can understand.

How?
In ¡Avancemos! you will use a variety of conversational strategies to clarify and continue a conversation. Here are some that will help you communicate effectively:

• If you don't know a word, describe it using words you do know. An example of this strategy, called circumlocution, is to say "the person who cleans the school" instead of "janitor."

• Make sure you understand what your partner says. If you don't, say **Repite, por favor** or **No comprendo.**

• Use appropriate intonation, such as raising the pitch to indicate a question.

• Monitor yourself. If you hear errors, stop and correct yourself. It's okay to do so.

• Use gestures and facial expressions to help convey meaning.

• Don't be anxious about pronunciation; perfect pronunciation is not necessary for effective communication.

• Take your time. First think about what you want to say, then practice saying it smoothly and naturally.

The Bottom Line

Don't be afraid to make mistakes. You learn faster when you are willing to take chances. So relax, don't worry about how you sound, and speak!

Informal Speaking

Informal speaking is what you do in daily classroom activities. *¡Avancemos!* provides you with many opportunities for creative oral expression. These activities are labeled **Hablar** and take place with a partner or in a small group. The following rubric shows you how your teacher might assess your oral performance in the classroom.

DIMENSION	4	3	2	1
Initiation	*The student:* Eagerly initiates speech, utilizing appropriate attention-getting devices. Easily asks questions and speaks spontaneously.	Is willing to initiate speech, utilizing appropriate attention-getting devices. Asks questions and speaks evenly.	Sometimes initiates speech, using attention-getting devices. Sometimes asks questions and speaks hesitantly.	Is reluctant to initiate speech and struggles to ask questions. Speech is halting.
Response	Almost always responds appropriately to questions/statements.	Frequently responds appropriately to questions/statements.	Sometimes responds appropriately to questions/statements.	Rarely responds appropriately to questions/statements.
Conversational Strategies	Clarifies and continues conversation, using all or some of the following strategies: • Circumlocution • Survival strategies • Intonation • Self-correction • Verbal cues	Uses all or some strategies, but may need occasional prompting.	Uses some strategies and needs frequent prompting to further the conversation.	Uses few strategies. Relies heavily on conversation partner to sustain conversation. Rarely responds even with frequent prompting.
Vocabulary	• Incorporates a variety of old and new vocabulary. • Uses idiomatic expressions appropriate to topic. • Speaks clearly and imitates accurate pronunciation.	• Utilizes a variety of old and limited new vocabulary. • Attempts to use idiomatic expressions appropriate to topic. • Speaks clearly and attempts accurate pronunciation.	• Relies on basic vocabulary. • Speech is comprehensible in spite on mispronunciations.	• Uses limited vocabulary. • Mispronunciations impede comprehensibility.
Structure	Makes few errors in the following areas: • Verbs in utterances when necessary with appropriate subject/verb agreement • Noun and adjective agreement • Correct word order and article adjectives • Errors do not hinder comprehensibility.	Makes several errors in structure which do not affect overall comprehensibility.	Makes several errors which may interfere with comprehensibility.	Makes utterances which are so brief that there is little evidence of structure and comprehensibility is impeded.
Cultural Appropriateness	Almost always uses/interprets cultural manifestations when appropriate to the task (e.g., greeting, leave taking, gestures, proximity, etc.).	Frequently uses/interprets cultural manifestations when appropriate to the task.	Sometimes uses/interprets cultural manifestations when appropriate to the task.	Rarely uses/interprets cultural manifestations when appropriate to the task.

Skill Support

Formal Speaking

Formal speaking consists of specific communication tasks in which your partner assumes a specific role. Each task achieves a communication function, such as socializing, providing and obtaining information, expressing personal feelings, or persuading.

¡Avancemos! prepares you for formal speaking by including role-play activities throughout the lessons, especially in **Todo junto** and **Repaso inclusivo.** Moreover, in each **Todo junto** there is a speaking strategy designed to help you accomplish the task.

At the end of the year you may take a formal speaking test which consists of four communication tasks performed by you and your teacher. Each task will be a conversation of four interactions in which you will play the role of yourself and the teacher will assume a specific role. You will receive credit for each comprehensible and appropriate statement or question. To receive full credit, you need to show evidence from each of the following categories:

- **Comprehensibility** may be demonstrated by, but is not limited to, the statement or question making sense to native speakers who know no English but are used to foreigners trying to speak their language.

- **Appropriateness** may be demonstrated by, but is not limited to, the statement or question contributing to the completion of the task.

- **Fluency** may be demonstrated by, but is not limited to, the ability to sustain the conversation, spontaneity, efficiency of task completion, intonation, pronunciation, and exclusive use of the target language.

- **Complexity** may be demonstrated by, but is not limited to, the ability to initiate and direct conversation, risk taking, creativity, choice and variety of vocabulary and grammatical structures.

- **Accuracy** may be demonstrated by, but is not limited to, use of correct grammatical structures, use of self-correction strategies, and cultural appropriateness.

Try It!

Choose one task from each category.

Socializing

- *(Teacher initiates)* I am your friend. I will ask you to go to the store with me, and we will talk about what we will buy. I will start the conversation.

- *(Student initiates)* I am your friend. We are both going to a party, and we are talking about how to get there. You start the conversation.

- *(Teacher initiates)* You are visiting Costa Rica. I am a Costa Rican teenager. We have just met. Tell me about your family. I will start the conversation.

Providing/Obtaining Information

- *(Student initiates)* I am a doctor. Because you do not feel well, you have come to my office. You start the conversation.

- *(Teacher initiates)* I am your friend. I have met the new student in our school. You would like to know about that person. I will start the conversation.

- *(Student initiates)* I am a clerk in your hotel in Argentina. You want to know where to buy something you need. You start the conversation.

Expressing Personal Feelings

- *(Teacher initiates)* I am your friend. You have just returned from a weekend trip. We will discuss what you think about it. I will start the conversation.

- *(Teacher initiates)* I am your classmate. We have just heard that we have a new teacher. We will talk about how we feel about this. I will start the conversation.

- *(Student initiates)* I am your friend. You are moving to a new school district. Tell me how you feel about that. You start the conversation.

Persuasion

- *(Student initiates)* I am your friend. We made plans to eat at a local restaurant tomorrow afternoon. You prefer a different restaurant. Try to convince me to go to the other restaurant. You start the conversation.

- *(Student initiates)* I am your Spanish teacher. Your best friend's birthday is Friday. Try to convince me to have a class party to celebrate. You start the conversation.

- *(Student initiates)* I am your friend. You want to see your favorite movie for the third time. Try to convince me to go with you. You start the conversation.

Skill Support

New York

❖ Listen!

You can get a lot of information by listening: instructions from your teacher, news from your friends, announcements over the loudspeakers, and information from the radio and television. Listening is an important skill that allows you to understand what others are saying and to stay connected to the community and the world.

What?

You'll be listening to simple statements and questions in face-to-face conversations with peers and familiar adults. You'll also learn to understand the main idea of longer messages and conversations that contain some unfamiliar words.

How?

¡Avancemos! will help you develop listening skills by providing many opportunities to hear various speakers in real-life situations.

Every time you see this icon  you will be engaged in active listening. You will also be given listening strategies with each **Telehistoria.** Here are some examples of effective listening strategies:

• Listen for cognates, words that sound like English words and share the same meaning.

• Think about what you already know about the subject to guess the meaning of unknown phrases.

• Use visual cues, such as pictures and facial expressions.

• Listen for intonation to find out how the speakers feel.

• Listen for key words to determine a specific piece of information.

The Bottom Line

Like all skills, listening takes practice and time. The important thing to remember is that it's okay not to understand every word you hear.

Try It!

Try these three listening activities.

1. For the following question, you will hear background information in English. Then you will hear a passage in Spanish twice, followed by a question in English. Choose the best answer from the choices below.

   To whom is Enrique talking?

   (1) his cousin

   (2) his classmate

   (3) his teacher

   (4) his grandmother

2. For the following question, you will hear background information in English. Then you will hear a passage in Spanish twice, followed by a question in Spanish. Choose the best answer from the choices below.

   ¿Qué venden en Coqueta?

   (1) todo para la escuela

   (2) comida international

   (3) regalos para mujeres

   (4) ropa para hombres

3. For the following question, you will hear background information in English. Then you will hear a passage in Spanish twice, followed by a question in Spanish. Choose the picture that best answers the question.

   What sport does the guest athlete play professionally?

   (1)   (2)

   (3)   (4)

Read!

Why?   Reading allows you to get information from written materials, socialize with peers, and appreciate the different cultures of the Spanish-speaking world through literature, song lyrics, and recipes.

What?   You'll read a variety of written materials such as posters, postcards, e-mails, journals, brochures, menus, charts, surveys, ads, articles from newspapers and magazines, and poems. Your goal is to understand the main idea as well as some details of simple texts written for native speakers.

How?   There are a lot of activities in *¡Avancemos!* labeled **Leer** that will give you reading practice. *¡Avancemos!* also has a reading section called **Lectura** which explores topics of interest to young people and a section called **Lectura cultural** with readings that highlight cultural diversity. These sections include strategies that will help you become a successful reader. You will also find reading strategies in each **Telehistoria**. To better understand what you read, you'll rely on visual cues, prior knowledge, and cognates. Some other strategies include:

- Find the main idea by scanning or glancing over the text before reading it carefully.

- Use the title to help you predict the contents of the reading.

- Rely on the context (surrounding words and sentences) and what you already know about the subject to guess the meanings of unfamiliar words.

- Use charts and other visual organizers to record and organize the information in the text.

- Predict the content and purpose of the reading based on visual cues, such as pictures and diagrams.

The Bottom Line

Developing good reading skills in Spanish will not only open your eyes to a whole new world of ideas, it will also help you become a better reader in English.

Try It!

Try these three reading activities.

① Answer the question in English based on the reading. Select the best answer from the choices below.

PÁGINA SOCIAL

FIESTA QUINCEAÑERA

Ana Beatriz Reyes Blanco celebra los quince años el día sábado 10 de marzo. Su padre, el distinguido doctor Hugo Reyes Pérez, invita a toda la familia a una fiesta con cena en el Club Social. ¡Le deseamos muy feliz cumpleaños a la señorita Reyes!

NACIMIENTO

Roberto Cabrera Moreno y Angélica Salazar de Cabrera están muy contentos de anunciar el nacimiento de su primer hijo, José Antonio. José Antonio nació sin complicaciones el 5 de marzo a las catorce horas en la Clínica Santa Teresita.

¡FELIZ CUMPLEAÑOS!

La Escuela Valdivia le desea muchas felicidades a nuestra directora, doña Pilar de Urrutia, quien cumple ochenta años el día domingo 11 de marzo. Los maestros y los estudiantes planean una fiesta en el gimnasio en honor a esta persona tan inteligente, trabajadora y generosa.

REUNIÓN DE FAMILIA

La familia Iriarte invita a todos los primos Iriarte a compartir un desayuno el día sábado 10 de marzo en el salón principal del Hotel Bungavilla. Después del desayuno, celebramos el cumpleaños del abuelo Pedro, quien no admite tener setenta años.

1. According to the society news, who is eighty years old?

(1) Ana Beatriz Reyes

(3) José Antonio Cabrera

(2) Pilar de Urrutia

(4) Pedro Iriarte

Skill Support

2 Answer the question in Spanish based on the reading. Select the best answer from the choices below.

HOTEL LUX

Hotel Lux tiene el confort de un apartamento pero con todos los servicios de un hotel.

· Estamos cerca del Jardín Botánico y a diez minutos de la playa.

· Tenemos 30 apartamentos completos con sala, comedor, cocina moderna, baño grande y con uno o dos cuartos. En los apartamentos hay todos los muebles necesarios, televisor, lector de DVD y conexión a Internet.

· En el segundo piso tenemos restaurante, gimnasio y sala de conferencias. La tarifa incluye también desayuno completo con jugo, café, cereales, huevo, pan y frutas.

Visite nuestro sitio Web para más información o llame 234-0009.

---

2. Hotel LUX es para familias que

    (1) quieren comprar un apartamento   (3) están de vacaciones

    (2) quieren una casa con jardín   (4) buscan muebles nuevos

3 Answer the question in Spanish based on the reading. Select the best answer from the choices below.

Querida abuela,

¿Cómo estás? ¿Te gustó tu fiesta de sorpresa? ¿Estuvo rico el pastel que preparó mi tía Zulema? Perdón que no fui pero tuve que quedarme en cama todo el fin de semana. Estoy mucho mejor. Estoy sentada frente la computadora y el médico dice que mañana puedo volver a clases.

Abuelita, me gustaría invitarte a salir el próximo sábado. Podemos ir al museo de arte y luego al cine. ¿Qué te parece?

Tu nieta favorita,
Adriana

---

3. Adriana no fue a la fiesta de la abuela porque

    (1) trabajó el fin de semana   (3) no le gustan los pasteles

    (2) se fue de vacaciones   (4) se enfermó

❖ Write!

Why?

Writing allows you to communicate with others, express your ideas, personal feelings and opinions, and persuade others to take a course of action. Writing in Spanish, like writing in English, is a skill worth practicing.

What?

You'll compose short, informal notes and messages to exchange information with Spanish-speaking people in everyday life situations. You'll fill out forms for the use of common public services, such as school enrollment forms, and you'll write short messages on familiar topics based on personal experience.

How?

The writing process in any language is similar: brainstorm, organize, draft, and revise. In *¡Avancemos!* you will have the opportunity to write whenever you see  . Some of the tasks include writing e-mails, personal journal entries, and blogs. The **Lectura y escritura** sections provide you with specific strategies for writing in Spanish. In **Todo junto**, an open-ended writing activity includes a model and a rubric so you know exactly what to do to succeed. Become a better writer with these strategies:

- Take some time to brainstorm and jot down any ideas about the topic that you have.

- Organize your ideas using charts, mind maps, or timelines.

- In your planning stage, consider your audience and what the purpose of your writing is.

- Ask a peer to check your writing and make any necessary corrections.

- Use adverbs **(primero, luego, también)** and linking words **(porque, pero, cuando)** to make your writing flow naturally.

The Bottom Line

Everyone can improve their writing skills. The more writing you do, the more confident and skilled you'll become.

The following rubric will help you understand what you need to do in order to write something that is organized and easy to understand.

DIMENSION	4	3	2	1
Purpose/Task	*The student:* Satisfies the task, connects all ideas to task/purpose, and exhibits a logical and coherent sequence of ideas throughout.	Satisfies the task; connections are implied with few irrelevancies.	Satisfies the task. Connections may be unclear with some irrelevancies.	Makes at least one statement which satisfies the task. Remaining statements are irrelevant to the task.
Vocabulary	Utilizes a wide variety of vocabulary which expands the topic in the statement/question to include nouns, verbs, and/or adjectives as appropriate to the task.	Utilizes a variety of vocabulary relevant to the topic in statements/ questions to include nouns, verbs, and/or adjectives as appropriate to the task.	Utilizes vocabulary, some of which is inaccurate or irrelevant to the task.	Utilizes limited vocabulary, most of which is inaccurate or irrelevant to the task.
Structure/ Conventions • Subject/verb agreement • Noun/adjective agreement • Correct word order Spelling	Exhibits a high degree of control of structure/ conventions: • Subject/verb agreement • Noun/adjective agreement • Correct word order • Spelling • Errors do not hinder overall comprehensibility of the passage.	Exhibits some control of structure/conventions: • Subject/verb agreement • Noun/adjective agreement • Correct word order • Spelling • Errors do not hinder overall comprehensibility of the passage.	Exhibits some control of structure/conventions: • Subject/verb agreement • Noun/adjective agreement • Correct word order • Spelling • Errors do hinder overall comprehensibility of the passage.	Demonstrates little control of structure or conventions, or errors impede overall comprehensibility of passage.
Word count	Uses 30 or more comprehensible words in target language that contribute to the development of the task.	Uses 25-29 comprehensible words in target language that contribute to the development of the task.	Uses 20-24 comprehensible words in target language that contribute to the development of the task.	Uses 15-19 comprehensible words in target language that contribute to the development of the task.

Try It!

Choose two of the following writing tasks.

You should write your response entirely in Spanish and use at least 30 words. Place names and brand names written in Spanish count as one word. Numbers, unless written as words, and names of people do not count as words.

1. You have logged onto a chat room, and a Spanish-speaking friend wants to know more about your family. In Spanish, write a note describing the family members in your household, either real or imaginary. You may wish to include:

   - how many people live with you
   - their names and ages
   - their relationship to you
   - what they look like
   - what their personalities are like
   - their likes and dislikes
   - comparisons between family members

2. You are hosting a birthday party for your cousin. There are a lot of things to do so you enlist the help of a friend. In Spanish, write your friend an e-mail explaining everything that needs to be done. You may wish to include:

   - the household chores you need help with
   - the food you will serve
   - things you still need to buy
   - what you will wear
   - some fun activities you plan for the party
   - what guests should bring to the party

3. Your Spanish-speaking pen pal is going to come and spend the summer with you. In Spanish, write a note to your pen pal about summer plans. You may wish to include:

   - what the weather will be like
   - the clothes he or she should bring
   - the sports you can play together
   - the places you will visit and what you will do there
   - what your daily routine will be like

La Telehistoria

VIDEO DVD

Hi! My name is Alicia. My family and I live in Miami, Florida. My favorite thing to do is play soccer. At the Pan-American Youth Games, my team took second place. I made a lot of great friends from all over the world. I also met Trini Salgado, the best soccer player ever!

I got a T-shirt like hers, but I never got her to autograph it. She is always traveling to different countries, so maybe I can send my shirt to some of my soccer friends to try to get it signed.

Follow along in the *¡Avancemos!* Telehistoria to find out what happens to Alicia's T-shirt as it travels from country to country.

Trini Salgado

En Parque de l

Próximo Sábado 15 de Ju

Sandra - San Antonio ✓
Pablo - México
Rodrigo - Puerto Rico ✓
Maribel - España ✓
Manuel - Ecuador ✓
Mario - República Dominicana ✓
Florencia - Argentina ✓
Jorge - Costa Rica ✓

Level 1a

1 San Antonio

Sandra

2 Mexico

Pablo

3 Puerto Rico

Rodrigo

4 Spain

Maribel

Level 1b

5 Ecuador

Manuel

6 Dominican Republic

Mario

7 Argentina

Florencia

8 Costa Rica

Jorge

Key Words to Know

el autógrafo   autograph

la camiseta   T-shirt

el jugador (la jugadora) de fútbol   soccer player

Why Study Spanish?

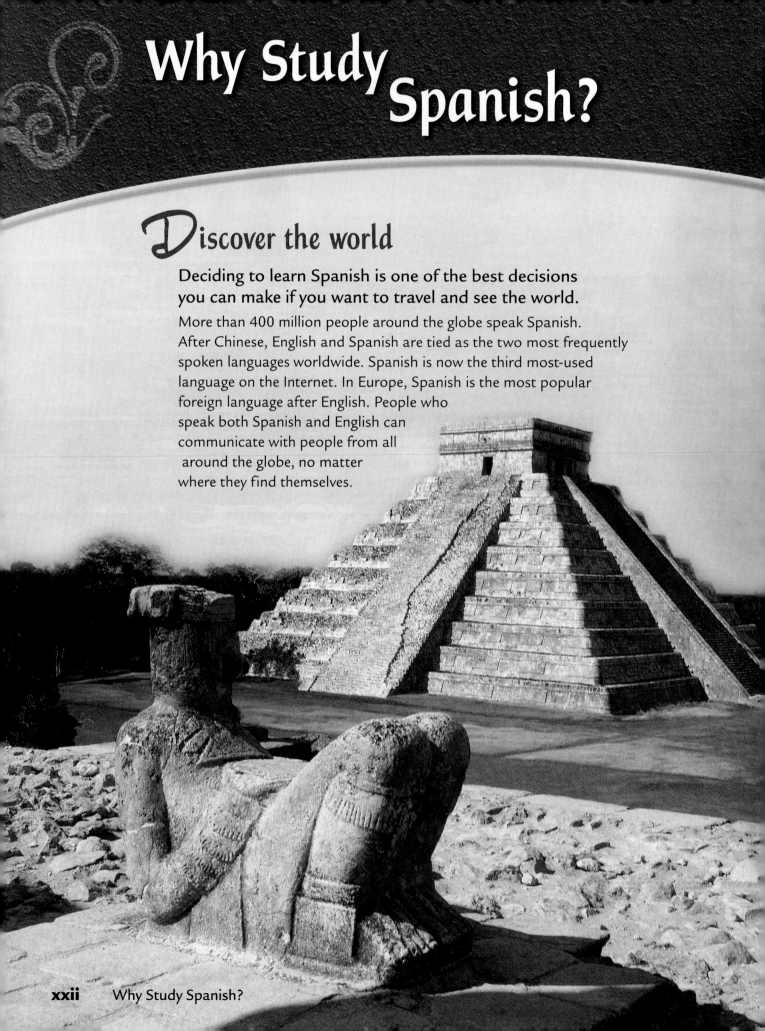

Discover the world

Deciding to learn Spanish is one of the best decisions you can make if you want to travel and see the world.

More than 400 million people around the globe speak Spanish. After Chinese, English and Spanish are tied as the two most frequently spoken languages worldwide. Spanish is now the third most-used language on the Internet. In Europe, Spanish is the most popular foreign language after English. People who speak both Spanish and English can communicate with people from all around the globe, no matter where they find themselves.

Explore your community

Inside the United States, Spanish is by far the most widely spoken language after English.

There are currently about 30 million Spanish-speakers in the U.S. When you start to look and listen for it, you will quickly realize that Spanish is all around you—on the television, on the radio, and in magazines and newspapers. You may even hear your neighbors speaking it. Learning Spanish will help you communicate and interact with the rapidly growing communities of Spanish-speakers around you.

 # Experience a new perspective

Learning a language is more than just memorizing words and structures.

When you study Spanish, you learn how the people who speak it think, feel, work, and live. Learning a language can open your eyes to a whole new world of ideas and insights. And as you learn about other cultures, you gain a better perspective on your own.

 # Create career possibilities

Knowing Spanish opens many doors.

If you speak Spanish fluently, you can work for international and multinational companies anywhere in the Spanish-speaking world. You can create a career working as a translator, an interpreter, or a teacher of Spanish. And because the number of Spanish-speakers in the U.S. is growing so rapidly, being able to communicate in Spanish is becoming important in almost every career.

What is Vocabulary?

Building Your Spanish Vocabulary

Vocabulary is a basic building block for learning a foreign language. By learning just a few words, you can start to communicate in Spanish right away! You will probably find that it is easier to understand words you hear or read than it is to use them yourself. But with a little practice, you will start to produce the right words in the right context. Soon you will be able to carry on conversations with other Spanish-speakers.

How Do I Study Vocabulary?

First Steps

· Read all of the new words in **blue** on the Vocabulary presentation page in your textbook.

· Point to each word as you say it out loud.

Be Creative

· Make flashcards with your new vocabulary words. You could also draw pictures of the words on the back of the flashcards.

· Group vocabulary words by theme. Add other words that fit the categories you've learned.

· Imagine a picture of the word.

· Create a rhyme or song to help you remember the words.

Make It Personal

· Use vocabulary words to write original sentences. Make them funny so you'll be sure to remember!

· Label everyday items in Spanish.

· Create reminders for difficult words. Put note cards inside your locker door, or on your mirror at home.

· See it, and say it to yourself! For example, if you are learning colors and clothing words, think of the Spanish word to describe what your friends are wearing.

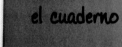
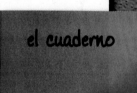

el cuaderno

Practice Makes Perfect

· Say your vocabulary words out loud and repeat each word several times.

· Write each word five times, keeping its meaning in mind.

· Use Spanish words with your classmates outside of class—if you're having lunch in the cafeteria, use the words you know for food. Greet your classmates in the hallway in Spanish!

Create Your Own System

· Practice a little bit every day. Many short sessions are better than one long one.

· Focus on the words that are the hardest for you.

· Find a buddy. Quiz one another on the vocabulary words.

· Keep a vocabulary notebook and update it regularly.

· Use the study sheets in the back of your workbook to review vocabulary.

What is Grammar?

Some people think of grammar as the rules of a language, rules that tell you the "correct" way to speak a language. For instance, why do you say *big red house,* not *red big house*? Why do you say *how much money do you have* instead of *how many money*? If English is your first language, you probably don't think about the rule. You make the correct choice instinctively because it *sounds right.* Non-native speakers of English have to learn the rules. As you begin your study of Spanish, you will need to learn the grammar rules of Spanish.

Why Should I Study Grammar?

Grammar helps you to communicate.

For instance, using the past tense or future tense makes it clear when something happens (*I did my homework* versus *I will do my homework.*) Using subject pronouns lets you know who is performing the action. (*I gave the book to her* versus *She gave the book to me.*) Using correct grammar when speaking Spanish will help you communicate successfully with native speakers of Spanish.

 # How Do I Study Grammar?

Read the English Grammar Connection before each grammar explanation.

Think about how you use the same type of grammar in English. Understanding your own language will help you to better understand Spanish.

> **English Grammar Connection:** A **verb tense** is the form of the verb that shows *when* an action is happening. The **present tense** shows that an action is happening *now*. The Spanish present-tense verb form **estudiamos** can be expressed in English in three different ways: *we study, we are studying,* or *we do study.*
>
> We **study** Spanish.   **Estudiamos** español.
>
> ← present-tense verb   ← present-tense verb

Practice the new forms that you are learning.

Completing the practice activities in your student book and workbook will help you to learn the correct way to say things.

Use the Spanish you know as often as you can.

After all, that's how you learned to speak English, by hearing and speaking it every day.

What Is Culture?

To communicate with people from Spanish-speaking countries in a meaningful way, you need to know something about their culture. Vocabulary and grammar will help you learn what words to say and how to put them together, but culture will give you a better understanding of "how, when, and why to say what to whom."

What exactly is culture?

Culture includes . . .

Art
History
Traditions
Relationships
Music
Holidays
Food
Architecture
Pastimes

and more!

How can I learn about another culture?

- Read the **Comparación cultural** information to find out more about the cultures that you are studying.
- Think about the answers to the questions in the **Comparación cultural.**
- Think about the perspectives and practices that shape and influence the culture.
- Compare your own culture with the cultures you are studying.

El mundo

OCÉANO ÁRTICO

Mar de Siberia
Oriental

Bahía
de
Baffin

GROENLANDIA
(DINAMARCA)

RUSIA

Mar de Beaufort

Alaska
(EE.UU.)

Mar de Bering

Bahía
de
Hudson

Mar del
Labrador

CANADÁ

ESTADOS UNIDOS

OCÉANO ATLÁNTICO

REP. DOMINICANA

Golfo de
México

ISLAS
BAHAMAS

PUERTO RICO (EE.UU.)

Islas Hawai
(EE.UU.)

CUBA

HAITÍ

SAN CRISTÓBAL Y NEVIS

MÉXICO

JAMAICA

ANTIGUA Y BARBUDA

GUADALUPE (FRANCIA)

BELICE

DOMINICA

Mar Caribe

MARTINICA (FRANCIA)

ISLAS
MARSHALL

OCÉANO PACÍFICO

GUATEMALA
EL SALVADOR
HONDURAS
NICARAGUA

COSTA
RICA

PANAMÁ

SANTA LUCÍA

GRANADA

SAN VICENTE Y GRANADINAS
BARBADOS

TRINIDAD Y TOBAGO

VENEZUELA

NAURU

KIRIBATI

COLOMBIA

GUAYANA
FRANCESA
(FRANCIA)

ISLAS
SALOMÓN

ISLAS
TUVALU

Islas Galápagos
(Ecuador)

ECUADOR

GUYANA

SURINAM

SAMOA

VANUATÚ

Samoa
Americana
(EE.UU.)

PERÚ

BRASIL

FIDJI

TONGA

BOLIVIA

NUEVA
CALEDONIA
(FRANCIA)

PARAGUAY

NUEVA
ZELANDA

CHILE

URUGUAY

ARGENTINA

Islas Malvinas
(R.U.)

OCÉANO ÁRTICO

Mar de Laptev

Mar de Kara

Mar de Barents

Mar de Noruega

ISLANDIA

1 DINAMARCA   9 ESLOVENIA
2 HOLANDA   10 CROACIA
3 BÉLGICA   11 BOSNIA Y HERZEGOVINA
4 LUXEMBURGO   12 SERBIA Y MONTENEGRO
5 SUIZA   13 ALBANIA
6 REPÚBLICA CHECA   14 MACEDONIA
7 ESLOVAQUIA   15 BULGARIA
8 HUNGRÍA

RUSIA

Mar de Ojotsk

SUECIA   FINLANDIA

NORUEGA

REINO UNIDO
IRLANDA

Mar del Norte

ESTONIA
LETONIA
LITUANIA
BIELORRUSIA

Mar Báltico

ALEMANIA   POLONIA
UCRANIA
MOLDAVIA

KAZAKSTÁN

MONGOLIA

Mar de Aral

COREA DEL NORTE
Mar de Japón
COREA DEL SUR   JAPÓN

FRANCIA   AUSTRIA
ANDORRA
PORTUGAL   ESPAÑA
GIBRALTAR (R.U.)
Islas Canarias (Esp.)

RUMANIA
ITALIA
GRECIA
MALTA
TÚNEZ

Mar Negro
GEORGIA
Mar Caspio
TURQUÍA   ARMENIA
AZERBAIYÁN

UZBEKISTÁN
KIRGUISTÁN
TURKMENISTÁN
TADJIKISTÁN

CHINA

BHUTÁN

TAIWÁN

OCÉANO PACÍFICO

Trópico de Cáncer

MARRUECOS
Mar Mediterráneo
CHIPRE   LÍBANO
SIRIA   IRAQ
ISRAEL   JORDANIA
EGIPTO   BAHREIN
ARABIA SAUDITA
KUWAIT   QATAR
IRÁN
E.Á.U
OMÁN
AFGANISTÁN
PAQUISTÁN
NEPAL
BANGLADESH
INDIA
MYANMAR
LAOS
TAILANDIA
VIETNAM
CAMBOYA
FILIPINAS
GUAM (EE.UU.)
MICRONESIA

SAHARA OCCIDENTAL
CABO VERDE   MAURITANIA
MALÍ   NÍGER
CHAD   SUDÁN
ARGELIA
LIBIA

ERITREA
YEMEN
JIBUTI
ETIOPÍA
SOMALIA

Mar Arábigo
Golfo de Bengala
Mar de China
BRUNEI
MALASIA
PALAU

SENEGAL
GAMBIA   GUINEA
GUINEA BISSAU
SIERRA LEONA
LIBERIA
BURKINA FASO
COSTA DE MARFIL
GHANA
BENIN
NIGERIA
TOGO
CAMERÚN
GUINEA ECUATORIAL
GABÓN
REP. CENTRO-AFRICANA
CONGO
REP. DEM. DEL CONGO
UGANDA
KENIA
RUANDA
BURUNDI
TANZANÍA

ISLAS MALDIVAS
SRI LANKA
SEYCHELLES

SINGAPUR
INDONESIA

Ecuador 0°

PAPUASIA NUEVA GUINEA

SANTO TOMÉ Y PRÍNCIPE
CABINDA (ANGOLA)
ANGOLA
ZAMBIA
NAMIBIA   ZIMBABWE
BOTSWANA
MALAWI
MOZAMBIQUE
MADAGASCAR
COMORES
MAURICIO

OCÉANO ÍNDICO

TIMOR ORIENTAL

AUSTRALIA

Trópico de Capricornio

30°S

SUDÁFRICA   LESOTHO
SUAZILANDIA

0   1,000   2,000 millas
0   1,000   2,000 kilómetros

N
O   E
S

ANTÁRTIDA

60°S

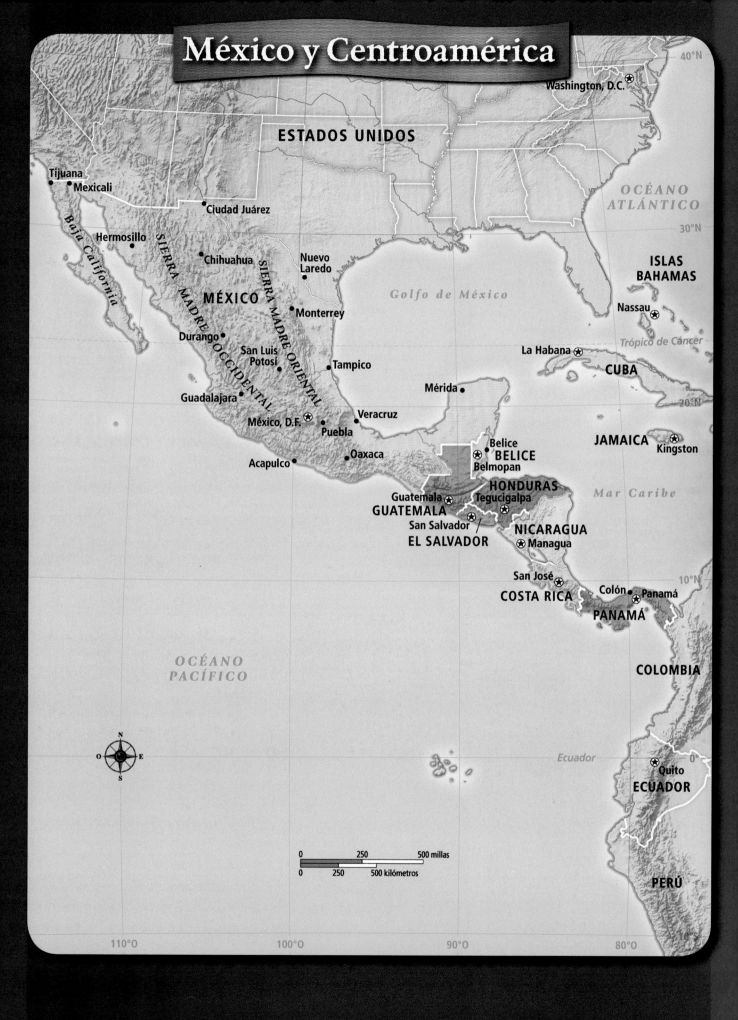

México y Centroamérica

Washington, D.C. ⊛

ESTADOS UNIDOS

OCÉANO
ATLÁNTICO

40°N

30°N

Tijuana
Mexicali
Ciudad Juárez

Hermosillo

**ISLAS
BAHAMAS**

Nassau ⊛

SIERRA MADRE OCCIDENTAL

Chihuahua

Nuevo
Laredo

Golfo de México

Trópico de Cáncer

MÉXICO

SIERRA MADRE ORIENTAL

Monterrey

La Habana ⊛

CUBA

Durango

San Luis
Potosí

Tampico

Mérida

20°N

Guadalajara

México, D.F. ⊛

Veracruz

JAMAICA

Kingston ⊛

Puebla

Baja California

Acapulco

Oaxaca

Belice
BELICE
Belmopan ⊛

Mar Caribe

HONDURAS
Tegucigalpa ⊛

Guatemala ⊛
GUATEMALA

San Salvador
EL SALVADOR

NICARAGUA
⊛ Managua

San José ⊛

Colón
COSTA RICA
Panamá

PANAMÁ

10°N

COLOMBIA

OCÉANO
PACÍFICO

N
O · E
S

Ecuador

0°

Quito ⊛

ECUADOR

PERÚ

10°S

0   250   500 millas
0   250   500 kilómetros

110°O   100°O   90°O   80°O

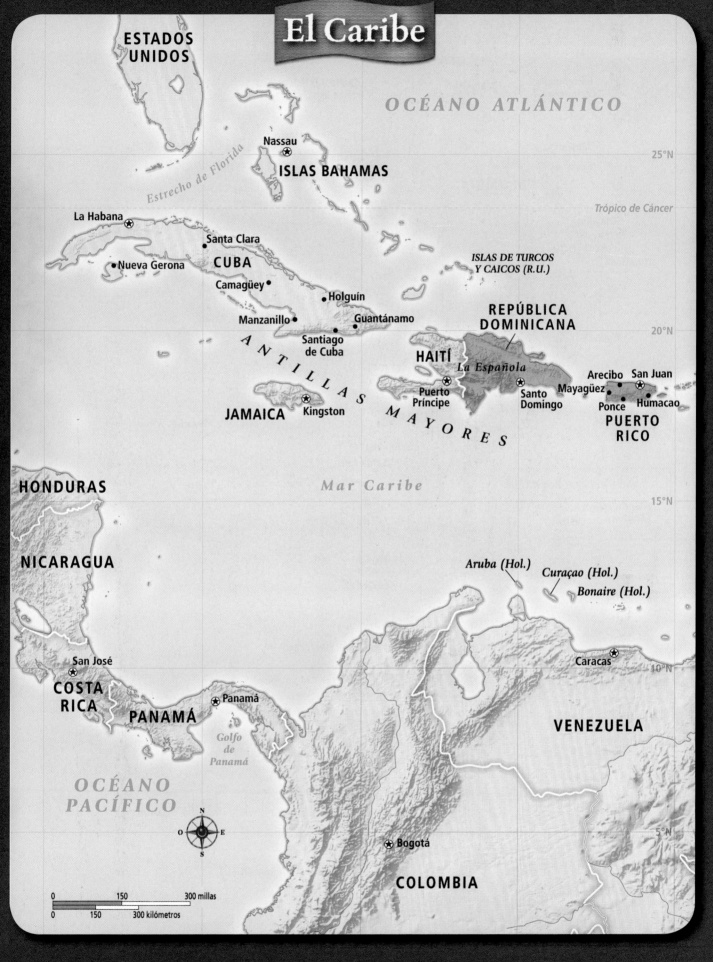

El Caribe

ESTADOS UNIDOS

OCÉANO ATLÁNTICO

25°N

Estrecho de Florida

Nassau ⭑

ISLAS BAHAMAS

Trópico de Cáncer

La Habana ⭑
Santa Clara •
Nueva Gerona •

CUBA

Camagüey •
Holguín •
Manzanillo •
Guantánamo •
Santiago de Cuba •

ISLAS DE TURCOS Y CAICOS (R.U.)

REPÚBLICA DOMINICANA

20°N

HAITÍ
La Española

Arecibo •
San Juan •
Mayagüez •
Humacao •
Ponce •

A N T I L L A S   M A Y O R E S

Puerto Príncipe ⭑
Santo Domingo ⭑

PUERTO RICO

JAMAICA
Kingston •

Mar Caribe

15°N

HONDURAS

NICARAGUA

Aruba (Hol.)
Curaçao (Hol.)
Bonaire (Hol.)

San José •

Caracas ⭑
10°N

COSTA RICA

PANAMÁ
⭑ Panamá

VENEZUELA

Golfo de Panamá

OCÉANO PACÍFICO

N
O ⎯ E
S

5°N

⭑ Bogotá

COLOMBIA

0   150   300 millas
0   150   300 kilómetros

Sudamérica

Mar Caribe

OCÉANO ATLÁNTICO

Barranquilla
Cartagena
Maracaibo
Caracas
TRINIDAD Y TOBAGO
Puerto España

Lago Maracaibo
Río Orinoco

VENEZUELA

Medellín
Manizales
Bogotá
Cali

COLOMBIA

Georgetown
Paramaribo
GUYANA
SURINAM
Cayena
GUAYANA FRANCESA (FRANCIA)

Río Negro

Ecuador 0°

Otavalo
Quito
ECUADOR
Guayaquil
Cuenca

Río Amazonas

Río Madeira
Río Tapajós
Río Xingú
Río Tocantins

PERÚ

Trujillo

C O R D I L L E R A

Callao
Lima

Lago Titicaca

BOLIVIA
La Paz
Cochabamba
Santa Cruz
Sucre

BRASIL

10°S

Río São Francisco

Brasilia

D E

GRAN CHACO

PARAGUAY
Asunción

L O S

Salta
San Miguel de Tucumán
Resistencia

20°S

Trópico de Capricornio

CHILE

OCÉANO PACÍFICO

Islas Galápagos (Ecuador)

Bogotá
COLOMBIA
Quito
ECUADOR
PERÚ

0   200   400 millas
0 200 400 kilómetros

Córdoba

URUGUAY

30°S

Valparaíso
Santiago

Mendoza
Rosario
Buenos Aires
La Plata
Montevideo

OCÉANO ATLÁNTICO

OCÉANO PACÍFICO

Concepción

ARGENTINA

Temuco

P A M P A S

Mar del Plata

Bahía Blanca

40°S

A N D E S

P A T A G O N I A

N
O   E
S

0   250   500 millas
0   250   500 kilómetros

Estrecho de Magallanes

Islas Malvinas (R.U.)

50°S

Tierra del Fuego

Cabo de Hornos

100°O   90°O   80°O   70°O   60°O   50°O   40°O   30°O   20°O

España

OCÉANO ATLÁNTICO

FRANCIA

MAR CANTÁBRICO

La Coruña

ASTURIAS

CANTABRIA

Bilbao

PAÍS VASCO

LOS PIRINEOS

ANDORRA

GALICIA

CORDILLERA CANTÁBRICA

León

Pamplona

NAVARRA

CATALUÑA

CASTILLA-LEÓN

LA RIOJA

Valladolid

Río Duero

Zaragoza

Barcelona

ARAGÓN

E S P A Ñ A

Salamanca

Río Ebro

SIERRA DE GUADARRAMA

MADRID

Madrid

PORTUGAL

ISLAS BALEARES

Menorca

EXTREMADURA

CASTILLA-LA MANCHA

Palma

Mallorca

Valencia

Río Guadiana

Lisboa

COMUNIDAD VALENCIANA

Ibiza

Córdoba

MURCIA

Río Guadalquivir

MAR MEDITERRÁNEO

Sevilla

ANDALUCÍA

Granada

SIERRA NEVADA

Málaga

N
O   E
S

Gibraltar (R.U.)

Estrecho de Gibraltar

Ceuta (España)

Melilla (España)

OCÉANO ATLÁNTICO

MARRUECOS

ÁFRICA

CAMERÚN

Malabo

GUINEA ECUATORIAL

Golfo de Guinea

Bata

GABÓN

Ecuador 0°

2°N

10°E   12°E   14°E

0   50   100 millas
0   50   100 kilómetros

ISLAS CANARIAS (España)

OCÉANO ATLÁNTICO

La Palma

Santa Cruz de Tenerife

Las Palmas

Tenerife

Gran Canaria

ÁFRICA

28°N

0   25   50 millas
0   25   50 kilómetros

18°O   16°O   14°O

0   50   100 millas
0   50   100 kilómetros

46°N

44°N

42°N

38°N

36°N

Las celebraciones

The following lessons about holidays are provided for your personal enjoyment. You may choose to read them on your own, or your teacher may present them throughout the year.

Countries in the Spanish-speaking world often share the same celebrations and holidays. The celebrations are a result of a long history of traditions that reflect the mix of primarily Spanish, indigenous, and African cultures. Holidays celebrating religious events and beliefs are often similar between countries. Other holidays commemorate events or people that are important to a particular region. Many holidays, though celebrated on the same day, have traditions and customs that differ between countries.

As you read the pages of Celebraciones, you will discover how the Spanish-speaking world celebrates important holidays and how they compare to your own traditions.

Contenido

FERIA DE MÁLAGA

La Feria de Málaga celebrates King Ferdinand and Queen Isabella's triumphant entrance into the coastal city of Málaga on August 19, 1487. The pair claimed the city for the crown of Castile, an event this Spanish city has been celebrating for over 500 years. The *Feria de Málaga* now lasts for nine days and takes place in two parts of the city. Each day at noon the downtown fills with fairgoers. In the *Real*, a separate fairground, participants in *flamenco* dress or riding clothes ride on horseback or in horse-drawn carriages, or stroll, in a tradition known as *el paseo*. This daytime *feria* unfolds against a backdrop of music, singing, and dancing and ends at 6:00 p.m., when everyone goes home to rest. The celebration starts again at night in the *Real* and continues into the early morning hours. For this nightly *feria*, people gather in public and private *casetas*, to enjoy concerts, theatrical presentations, music, dance, and food. The last night of the *feria* ends with a city-sponsored concert followed by a spectacular fireworks display.

Feria de caballos More than a thousand riders and over a hundred horse-drawn carriages and carts participate in *el paseo*.

Música callejera Musicians play in the streets during the *feria*. Here a *panda*, or group, plays *verdiales*, traditional music that features guitars, tambourines, and tiny cymbals.

Una caseta offers free samples of *paella,* a rice and seafood dish that is a regional specialty from the coastal cities of Spain.

Una entrada a la feria Riders pass in front of one of the decorative entrances to a street in the historic downtown of Málaga.

Bailando flamenco Fairgoers perform folkloric dances such as *flamenco* and *sevillanas* in the streets, plazas, and *casetas,* wherever there is music.

Vocabulario para celebrar

los caballos	horses
las carretas	horse-drawn carriages
las casetas	small houses or tents
la feria	fair
el paseo	a walk, stroll, or ride

Comparación cultural

1. Does your town or city celebrate its beginnings or inauguration as a community, or is there a special "town day"? What events take place during the celebration?

2. What events in your community or region are similar to those of the *Feria de Málaga*? Describe them and then compare them to the *Feria de Málaga*.

Día de la Independencia

El Día de la Independencia falls in September for many of the Spanish-speaking countries in the Americas. Mexico celebrates on September 15 and 16, with the *Grito de la Independencia*, music, fireworks, and parades. The first *Grito* occurred at dawn on September 16, 1810, when Padre Miguel Hidalgo de Costilla called to the people of Dolores to rise up against the Spanish crown. That rebellion led to the Mexican War of Independence.

Just two days later, on September 18, 1810, Chile declared its independence from Spain. Today Chile celebrates the date during a week of *fiestas patrias* that include parades, rodeos, dance competitions, and special foods.

Eleven years later, on September 15, 1821, a large part of Central America also proclaimed its independence from Spain, becoming El Salvador, Nicaragua, Guatemala, Costa Rica, and Honduras. These countries celebrate their independence on the 14 and 15 with a focus on students: parades, assemblies, and sports competitions.

México

El Grito de la Independencia On the night of September 15, the president of Mexico commemorates *el Grito* by ringing a bell, proclaiming *¡Que viva México!*, and waving the Mexican flag from a balcony above the Zócalo. Crowds gather below to participate in the *Grito*.

Cultura INTERACTIVA *See these pages come alive!*
ClassZone.com

Fiestas patrias Costa Rican schoolchildren, dressed in colors of their country, dance in a parade.

Guatemala

Costa Rica

El recorrido de la antorcha Runners carrying a flaming torch start in Guatemala and end in Costa Rica. All along the route, uniformed schoolchildren wait expectantly for the torch to pass.

Vocabulario para celebrar

la antorcha	torch
la banda	band
las fiestas patrias	patriotic holidays
el grito	shout
el recorrido	run, journey
proclamar	to declare

Comparación cultural

1. Compare the way your town or city celebrates Independence Day with the celebrations in Mexico and Central America. How are they similar? Are there any differences?

2. How do you celebrate Independence Day? Do you participate in community events or have a special tradition?

El 12 de Octubre

El 12 de Octubre has many different meanings in the Spanish-speaking world. For some people it is *el Día de Colón,* the day Christopher Columbus arrived in the Americas. For some, it is *el Día de la Hispanidad,* a day to celebrate one's connection with all other Spanish-speaking people, regardless of their country. And for others, it is *el Día de la Raza,* a day when indigenous people come together as a community and celebrate their heritage. Other Spanish speakers celebrate their mixed heritage of indigenous, African, and European cultures. How you celebrate depends very much on you and your family's origin and on the community where you live. For all Spanish-speaking groups, *el 12 de octubre* marks a key turning point in the lives and cultures of the people in Spain and those living in the Americas.

Vocabulario para celebrar

Cristóbal Colón	Christopher Columbus
el Día Nacional	National Day
la hispanidad	the cultural community of Spanish speakers
la raza	race

México

Día de la Raza Indigenous groups gather in Mexico City dressed in their community's traditional outfits, some wearing pre-Columbian clothing and headdresses.

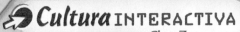

Chile

Día de la Raza A woman from the Pehuenche indigenous community gathers with other indigenous groups in downtown Santiago.

Nueva York

Día de la Hispanidad High school students carry flags representing all the American countries as they march in a parade down Fifth Avenue.

España

Día Nacional de España The Spanish government celebrates with a parade in Madrid.

Comparación cultural

1. How do you celebrate October 12 in your community or school? Is it similar to or different from the celebrations in Spanish-speaking countries? How so?

2. What does October 12 mean to you? Which of the Spanish names for the holiday has the most meaning for you? How would you rename the holiday to celebrate your heritage?

¡Día de los Muertos!

Las mojigangas People parade through the Pilsen-Little Village neighborhood of Chicago. Some carry *mojigangas*, giant papier-mâché puppets typically carried in Mexican processions.

On Día de los Muertos families visit the cemeteries and gravesites of their loved ones. They clean the sites and leave flowers and candles and, in many countries, they bring entire meals with special drinks and traditional breads to share with the deceased. Displays are set up next to the gravesite that include flowers, hand-crafted skeletons, colorful paper cutouts, candy skulls, personal items, and photos. Family members pass the night sharing food and conversation as they keep vigil for their ancestors.

The celebration of *Día de los Muertos* spans two days, November 1 and 2. Also known as *Día de los Difuntos*, the traditions originate in the centuries-old religious holiday *Día de Todos los Santos*. In the Americas, this holiday coincided with pre-Columbian festivals that celebrated the harvest, the new year, and honored the dead. The mix of cultures and traditions resulted in the celebration *Día de los Muertos*.

México

Las calaveras A display of dressed-up skulls and skeletons on a street in Mexico City

Ecuador

El pan de muertos This bread is made only for *Día de los Muertos*. In Ecuador, these breads are called *guaguas de pan*. *Guagua* is the Quechua word for "baby" and refers to the bread's shape. The *guaguas* are served with *colada morada*, a warm, purple-colored drink made from blueberries and raspberries.

México

El papel picado These tissue paper cutouts are a common holiday decoration. To celebrate *Día de los Muertos*, the cutouts form images of skeletons.

Guatemala

Los barriletes Guatemalans celebrate by flying *barriletes*, or colorful kites, to which they attach messages for the deceased. The town of Santiago Sacatepéquez celebrates with a *barrilete* contest.

Vocabulario para celebrar

las calaveras	skulls
el cementerio	cemetery
los difuntos	deceased
el esqueleto	skeleton
el pan de muertos	special bread made for *Día de los Muertos*
el papel picado	paper cutouts
los santos	saints

Comparación cultural

1. Does your family or community have a special day or specific traditions to remember the deceased? How are they similar to or different from the traditions of *Día de los Muertos*?

2. Centuries ago in Europe, the night of October 31, before All Saint's Day, was known as "All Hallowed's Eve." According to ancient beliefs, on this night the dead join the world of the living. Today we call this night Halloween. How would you compare the celebrations of Halloween and *Día de los Muertos*?

Las Navidades

Las Navidades are celebrated throughout the Spanish-speaking world with family gatherings and special meals. Celebrations start in mid-December and, in some countries, extend to January 6.

Many families gather the night of December 24, or *la Nochebuena,* to share a special meal of traditional foods and drinks that vary depending on the country. *Tamales, empanadas,* and *buñuelos* are served in many countries. In Spain, there is turkey, or *pavo,* and *turrón.* In Argentina and Chile, where it is summer, people eat cold foods and salads.

The tradition of giving and receiving gifts also forms a part of *las Navidades.* In some countries, families exchange gifts at midnight on *la Nochebuena,* while in others children receive gifts the morning of December 25, and in other countries the gifts appear the morning of January 6. Often gifts are given primarily to children.

Panamá

Un desfile navideño The holiday parade in Panama City takes place in mid-December.

México

La noche de rábanos On the night of December 23, elaborate carvings made from radishes, or *rábanos,* are on display in Oaxaca's central plaza. The figures include people, animals, and even entire scenes. This unique tradition has been celebrated for over 100 years.

Argentina

Las empanadas Dancers dress as *empanadas* in Buenos Aires. These meat-filled pies are especially enjoyed during *las Navidades.*

Perú

El Día de los Reyes Magos In Peru, Argentina, the Dominican Republic, Paraguay, and Spain, children receive presents on January 6 from *los Reyes Magos*. In anticipation, children leave out a snack for the Three Kings, carrots or grass for the camels, and a pair of empty shoes for the gifts.

España

Un desfile navideño Circus elephants take part in Madrid's holiday parade on January 5. In Spain, parades on January 5 or 6 celebrate the arrival of *los Reyes Magos*.

Vocabulario para celebrar

la Nochebuena	Christmas Eve
los Reyes Magos	Three Kings
la rosca de reyes	sweet bread eaten on January 6
el turrón	almond nougat candy
los villancicos	seasonal children's songs

Comparación cultural

1. Do you and your family celebrate a holiday in December? If so, compare the traditions of your family to the traditions of *las Navidades*.

2. What special meals and foods do you associate with certain holidays? Describe the foods you traditionally enjoy on a holiday you celebrate.

3. What time of the year do you give or receive gifts and for what reason?

¡Año Nuevo!

Perú

La buena suerte In Lima, people believe touching a Chinese Lion brings happiness, good luck, and prosperity in the New Year. Ten percent of Peru's population is of Chinese descent.

España

La medianoche In Madrid, people gather in the Puerta del Sol, holding bags of 12 grapes as they wait for the 12 strokes of midnight from the Puerta del Sol clock, the city's official timekeeper.

El Año Nuevo celebrates the arrival of the New Year and *la Nochevieja* says goodbye to the old. In much of the Spanish-speaking world, traditions include making a toast, exchanging a kiss or hug, or eating twelve grapes—one for each stroke of midnight—to ensure your wishes come true for the New Year. Other good luck traditions include wearing yellow or red, eating a tablespoon of lentils, or carrying a suitcase around the block if you hope to take a trip. To wish someone a happy New Year, say *¡Feliz año nuevo!* or *¡Próspero año nuevo!*

On *Nochevieja*, there are also traditions for saying goodbye to the old year. Some people dress in masks representing *el año viejo*. Others build satirical figures called *los años viejos* that represent famous people or politicians. Adorned with poems or messages that poke fun at *el año viejo*, and filled with shavings and firecrackers, these figures are lit on fire at midnight, to burn and explode on street corners, as a final *despedida*, or farewell, to the old year.

Colombia

Paseo de los años viejos In Popayán, families and neighbors take their *año viejo* figures out for a final ride before the *Nochevieja* celebration. Later on, at midnight, they will burn the figures.

Guatemala

Baile de los Gigantes In Antigua, people celebrate the New Year with the folkloric "Dance of the Giants." These giant heads, or *cabezudos*, are similar to costumes used since the medieval period in Spain.

Vocabulario para celebrar

el Año Nuevo	New Year
el brindis	toast
las doce uvas	twelve grapes
las lentejas	lentils
la medianoche	midnight
la Nochevieja	New Year's Eve

Comparación cultural

1. How do you celebrate the New Year? Does your family or community have any special traditions? Are any of the traditions similar to the ones in Spanish-speaking countries? How are they similar or different?

2. If you were to build an *año viejo* representing the past year, what figure or event would you portray? Explain your choice.

¡Carnaval!

Carnaval marks a period of festivity prior to the beginning of Lent. Lent was, and for some still is, a 40-day period of solemnity and fasting with the removal of meat from the diet being a key feature. You can see the word *carne* (meat) in *Carnaval*; traditionally, this was the last chance to eat meat before the Lenten fast. Today, *Carnaval* often resembles a lively, multi-day party.

Falling in either February or March, *Carnaval* is typically celebrated during the five days that precede Ash Wednesday, the first day of Lent. In some countries, *Carnaval* lasts longer, overlapping other local celebrations. In many regions, traditions such as throwing water and eggs can start over a month before the actual holiday. The planning for the next year's parades, parties, and dance groups often starts as soon as the current *Carnaval* ends!

España

Disfraces Elaborate costumes are central to the *Carnaval* celebration. This costume, entitled "África soy yo," appeared in Las Palmas, in the Canary Islands.

Carnaval Revelers dance in Encarnación, site of the largest celebration in Paraguay.

Paraguay

C14 Celebraciones

México

Cascarones Breaking *cascarones* on the heads of friends and other party-goers is a *Carnaval* tradition. The sprinkling of confetti from these hollowed-out eggs is said to bring good luck, as seen here in Mazatlán.

Bolivia

Máscaras are a *Carnaval* tradition dating back to medieval Spain. This masked dancer is from the parade in Oruro, where some 40,000 folkloric dancers and musicians participate.

Bailarines folklóricos Dancers from the Mestizaje dance group perform in Barranquilla. The Colombian government proclaimed this city's *Carnaval* celebration, which combines indigenous, African, and European traditions, a National Cultural Heritage. UNESCO declared it a "Masterpiece" for its cultural uniqueness.

Colombia

Vocabulario para celebrar

los bailarines	dancers
la banda	musical band
Carnaval	Carnival
los cascarones	confetti-filled eggs
el disfraz	costume
las máscaras	masks

Comparación cultural

1. The ways in which *Carnaval* is celebrated in the Spanish-speaking world differ depending on the region. Why do you think the celebrations have evolved differently?

2. Compare the traditions of *Carnaval* to any holiday that you celebrate. Which one(s) are similar? How are they similar?

marzo

Las Fallas

Las Fallas is a weeklong festival in March that engulfs the city of Valencia, Spain. Tens of thousands of visitors from all over the world come to the city to experience *Las Fallas,* a week of pageants, music, flowers, and creative displays. Each day, the deafening explosions of thousands of firecrackers, *la mascletà,* fills the city at 2:00 p.m. and each night's celebration ends in fireworks.

The main characters of the celebration are the *ninots,* gigantic figures built of wood, plaster, and cardboard. The largest are up to several stories tall. Neighborhood organizations build these enormous figures during the preceding year. Then, during the week of *Las Fallas,* they display them in intersections, parks, and plazas throughout the city. The public visits the more than 400 *fallas* and votes for their favorite one. On the last night at midnight, all but the favorite are burned in enormous bonfires. Then one final, brilliant display of fireworks explodes over the city.

Los ninots These gigantic figures poke fun at well-known people or current events from the preceding year.

Las falleras During the festival, women dress in traditional outfits that include lace dresses, veils, jewelry, and colorful sashes.

Una falla iluminada Thousands of visitors come at night to see the illuminated *fallas*. This display was entered into a special contest, *la Sección Especial*, where a committee judges the *fallas* for creativity, gracefulness and charm, originality, and lighting.

La Cremà At midnight on the last night, the *fallas* are burned throughout the city. At the same time there are huge displays of colorful fireworks, which include explosions of roman candles and thousands of firecrackers.

Vocabulario para celebrar

La Cremà	burning of the *fallas*
las fallas	displays of figures
los falleros	celebrants of *Las Fallas*
los fuegos artificiales	fireworks
la mascletà	rhythmic explosion of large and small firecrackers
los ninots	large papier-mâché figures
quemar	to burn

Comparación cultural

1. Fireworks are a major part of *Las Fallas*. Does your community or region have fireworks displays? When and for what reasons?

2. Are there any other traditions in the festival of *Las Fallas* that are similar to traditions you follow in your community? What are they? Are they part of a specific celebration or season?

Semana Santa

La Semana Santa is one holiday during the year where in most Spanish-speaking countries entire towns, businesses, schools, and government close for at least four days, Thursday through Sunday. People that have relocated to other places often go back to their hometowns. Others take advantage of the long break to go to the countryside or beach. Entire communities come together for *Semana Santa* celebrations. In some places, religious processions fill the streets each day of the week from Palm Sunday to Easter; in others, Thursday and Friday are the most important days. Most *Semana Santa* traditions are hundreds of years old and originated in Spain, but many now have a unique twist due to the mix of cultures in each country.

México

Vestidos blancos Girls from San Miguel de Allende dress in white for the procession on *Viernes Santo*. In this town, the celebrations extend for two weeks, ending on *el Domingo de Pascua* with an explosion of papier-mâché figures in the center of town.

El Salvador

Alfombras de aserrín Rugs traditionally made of colored sawdust or sand, flowers, and fruits cover the streets where processions will pass in Sonsonate. Artisans also now use modern industrial paints and sprays.

abril

Cultura INTERACTIVA *See these pages come alive!*
ClassZone.com

Ecuador

La fanesca Ecuadorians eat *fanesca*, a bean and grain soup with a fish base, only during *Semana Santa*. The soup is traditionally served with *bolitas de harina* (fritters), *plátano verde* (fried green plantain), fresh cheese, and *ají*, a spicy sauce.

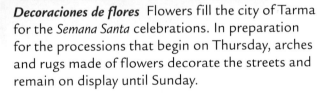

Perú

Decoraciones de flores Flowers fill the city of Tarma for the *Semana Santa* celebrations. In preparation for the processions that begin on Thursday, arches and rugs made of flowers decorate the streets and remain on display until Sunday.

Vocabulario para celebrar

las alfombras	rugs
las flores	flowers
las procesiones	processions
Semana Santa	Holy Week

México

Una procesión Young boys carry streamers during the processions in Cadereyta.

Comparación cultural

1. What holidays do you celebrate with special parades or processions? What kinds of decorations do people use?

2. In what kind of event would most of the people in your community participate? Compare the event to *Semana Santa*.

Celebraciones **C19**

¡Cinco de Mayo!

Cinco de Mayo has become a popular celebration thoughout the United States. However, not everyone who celebrates this uniquely Mexican holiday knows its origin. To find the reason, you must travel back to the year 1862 in Mexico. On May 5, in the town of Puebla de los Ángeles, the Mexican army, joined by farmers and townspeople, fought against the French and forced them to retreat. The Mexicans were led by General Ignacio Zaragoza and the town was later renamed Puebla de Zaragoza in his honor. Although the French went on to occupy Mexico City and assume a short-lived role in Mexico's government, *Cinco de Mayo* became a national holiday symbolizing Mexican unity.

A *Cinco de Mayo* celebration in Mexico includes dancing, music, and reenactments of the battle. In many parts of the U.S. where there is a large Mexican or Mexican-American community, you will often find *Cinco de Mayo* celebrations.

Mariachis y bailarines Folkloric dancers and musicians perform throughout the day in the Plaza Olvera during the *Cinco de Mayo* celebrations.

México

Reconstrucción de la batalla
A reenactment of the historic battle in Puebla commemorates Mexico's victory over the French.

Vocabulario para celebrar

los bailarines	dancers
la batalla	battle
el ejército	army
los franceses	French
los músicos	musicians
la reconstrucción	reenactment

Washington, D.C.

Bailarín folklórico A dancer performs in a traditional Mexican costume at the White House.

Comparación cultural

1. Do you know of a *Cinco de Mayo* celebration in your community or region? If so, how or where is it celebrated?

2. What important battles or historic events are celebrated in your community or state? How are they celebrated? Are they local or national holidays? Compare one of these holiday celebrations with the *Cinco de Mayo* celebrations.

junio

Inti Raymi

Inti Raymi, or the "Festival of the Sun," falls on June 21 or 22, the date of the southern hemisphere's winter solstice, the shortest day of the year. Indigenous communities throughout the Andean highland countries of South America celebrate the winter solstice with ceremonies designed to bring the Sun back and shorten the longest night. Incan in origin, *Inti Raymi* honored the sun as the source of light, heat, and life, and celebrated the start of a new planting season. The name *Inti Raymi* comes from the Quechua language: *inti* means "sun" and *raymi* means "festival." The largest festival takes place in Cuzco, Peru, the ancient capital of the Incan civilization and empire. In Cuzco, *Inti Raymi* has grown into a major tourist attraction. Thousands of people visit the city to enjoy the performances by folkloric groups and to watch the theatrical presentation of the Incan ceremony, the focal point of the celebration.

Perú

Presentación cultural de Inti Raymi
In Cuzco, professional actors and actresses interpret the roles of the Incan emperor and others.
Above: A woman carries offerings.
Right: The Incan emperor passes through the streets of Cuzco to the ruins of the Incan fortress, Sacsayhuaman.

Ecuador

Indígenas ecuatorianas A dance group from the Paktarinmi cultural organization forms a "sacred circle" with grains of corn, a pre-Incan rite. In Ecuador, which lies on the equator, this date is considered the summer solstice, rather than the winter.

Vocabulario para celebrar

el aymara	language of indigenous group from Bolivia and Peru
los incas	Incas, an ancient South American people
el quechua	language common to many South American indigenous groups and adopted and spread by Incas
el sol	sun

Bolivia

Los aymaras In the pre-Columbian ruins of Tihuanaku, an Aymara priest blows on a shell to celebrate the winter solstice, which marks the new year. The Aymara are one of two dominant indigenous groups in Bolivia, comprising 25 percent of the population. The other group, Quechua, makes up 30 percent.

Comparación cultural

1. In North America, June 21 is the summer solstice, or the longest day of the year, and December 21 is the winter solstice, or the shortest day of the year. What important holidays or events occur during this time of year?

2. In ancient civilizations, the appearance of the sun and moon were important events that helped mark the passing of time and the seasons. If you were to celebrate the winter or summer solstice, what would you include in your celebration?

Día de Simón Bolívar

Simón Bolívar, known as *El Libertador,* envisioned a united South America, a union for which he fought, but never attained. Despite this, he was instrumental in bringing about much of South America's independence from Spain and became one of its most revered leaders. His birthday is a national holiday in Venezuela, Ecuador, and Bolivia, and many cities and towns have plazas or monuments in his honor.

Born on July 24, 1783, in Caracas, Venezuela, Simón Bolívar strongly believed in freedom from Spanish rule and worked toward that goal as a political leader, writer, and military commander. With his troops, he liberated present-day Venezuela, then Colombia. He was then named president of Gran Colombia, a federation comprised of what is now Venezuela, Colombia, Panama, and Ecuador. He went on to lead his troops into Peru, aiding in the final defeat of Spain. For two more years, Bolívar maintained his leadership, writing the constitution of Bolivia, a country named in his honor. By 1827, his dream of unification dissolved amidst growing rivalries between the South American military leaders. Three years later Bolívar died, on December 17, 1830.

Colombia

Monumento a Simón Bolívar This monument marks the location of the Battle of Boyacá, where Bolívar's forces defeated the Spanish resulting in the liberation of Gran Colombia. To celebrate the anniversary of the battle, students form the colors of the Colombian flag.

Bolívares Venezuela's currency carries both Bolívar's name and image.

Venezuela

Ecuador

Líder de la Batalla de Pichincha Each year, the city of Quito commemorates the Battle of Pichincha, where Simón Bolívar sent troops under the command of Antonio José de Sucre to defeat the Spanish in one of the crucial battles in the fight for independence.

Simón Bolívar (1830), *José Gil de Castro* José Gil de Castro, renowned painter of Chilean society and of the independence leaders, painted this portrait of Bolívar in the early 1800s.

Venezuela

Vocabulario para celebrar

la batalla   battle
la independencia
      independence
El Libertador
      the liberator

Plaza de Bolívar This statue of Bolívar is located in the Plaza Bolívar, the historic, political, and commercial center of Caracas.

Comparación cultural

1. What famous leader in U.S. history would you compare with Simón Bolívar? Why? What do both leaders have in common?
2. What U.S. holidays are in honor of famous leaders? How are they celebrated? What other ways do we honor our important leaders?

Tema:

¡Hola!

¡AVANZA!

Let's get started

- greet people and say goodbye
- introduce yourself and others
- ask and say how to spell names
- say where you are from
- exchange phone numbers
- say what day of the week it is
- describe the weather
- respond to classroom instructions

A performer wearing the colors of the Puerto Rican flag

Dominican dancers in colorful costumes

Nueva York   New York City has the largest Hispanic population of any city in the nation. During its annual Hispanic Day Parade, colorful floats, bands, costumed dancers, and flags from Spanish-speaking countries fill Fifth Avenue. *What cultural celebrations are there in your area?*

Online SPANISH CLASSZONE.COM

Featuring...

Cultura INTERACTIVA

Animated Grammar

@HomeTutor

And more...
• Get Help Online
• Interactive Flashcards
• Review Games
• WebQuest
• Self-Check Quiz

A view of Lower Manhattan from the East River

New York, New York

Nueva York
uno

1

Hola, ¿qué tal?

Goal: Learn how various Spanish speakers greet each other. Then practice what you have learned to greet and say goodbye to others. *Actividades 1–3*

A

Hola. ¿Cómo estás?

Bien. ¿Y tú?

Mal.

AUDIO

B **Juan:** ¡Hola, Miguel! ¿Qué tal?
Miguel: Hola, ¿qué pasa?

C **Juan:** ¡Hasta luego, Ana!
Ana: Hasta luego.

D **Srta. Daza:** Adiós.
Sr. Ortega: Adiós, señorita.

E **Sr. Martínez:** Buenos días, señora Ramos. ¿Cómo está usted?
Sra. Ramos: Regular. ¿Y usted?
Sr. Martínez: Más o menos.

F **Juan:** Buenas tardes. ¿Cómo estás?
Esteban: Muy bien.

G **Sra. Acevedo:** Hola, **buenas noches.**
Diana: Buenas noches, señora.

H **Sr. García:** Buenas noches, Diana.
Diana: **Hasta mañana, señor** García.

¡A responder! Escuchar

Listen to these people greeting and saying goodbye. Wave toward the front of the room if you hear a greeting or toward the back of the room if you hear a goodbye.

1 | Muy bien

Leer | Complete each expression.

1. ¿Cómo está...
2. Buenas...
3. ¿Qué...
4. Muy bien...
5. Hasta...

a. tal?
b. mañana.
c. usted?
d. tardes.
e. ¿Y usted?

2 | ¿Cómo estás?

Escribir | Create a conversation to complete the speech bubbles of this cartoon strip.

NOMBRES DE CHICOS

Alejandro	Juan
Andrés	Luis
Carlos	Manuel
Cristóbal	Mateo
Daniel	Miguel
David	Nicolás
Eduardo	Pablo
Esteban	Pedro
Felipe	Ramón
Guillermo	Ricardo
Jaime	Roberto
Jorge	Tomás
José	Vicente

NOMBRES DE CHICAS

Alejandra	Juana
Alicia	Luisa
Ana	María
Bárbara	Marta
Carmen	Natalia
Carolina	Patricia
Cristina	Raquel
Diana	Rosa
Elena	Sofía
Emilia	Susana
Florencia	Teresa
Gabriela	Verónica
Isabel	Yolanda

Manuel

Isabel

Nota

¿**Cómo estás?** and ¿**Cómo está usted?** both mean *How are you?*

¿**Cómo estás?** and ¿**Y tú?** are familiar phrases used with:

- a person your own age
- a relative
- a person you call by his or her first name

Other familiar greetings: ¿**Qué tal?** and ¿**Qué pasa?**

¿**Cómo está usted?** and ¿**Y usted?** are formal phrases used with:

- a person you don't know
- someone older
- a person with whom you want to show respect

3 | Buenos días

Hablar

According to the time of day, greet your partner as if he or she were the following people. Use a formal greeting or a familiar greeting depending on whom you address.

modelo: Sr. (Sra.) Vargas / 7 a.m.

A Buenos días, señor (señora) Vargas. ¿Cómo está usted?

B Muy bien.

1. your best friend / 10 p.m.
2. the school principal / 2 p.m.
3. Sr. (Srta.) López / 7 p.m.
4. your mother/father / 9 a.m.
5. Sr. (Sra.) Santos / 4 p.m.
6. your brother/sister / 9 p.m.
7. your coach / 11 a.m.
8. your Spanish teacher / 10 a.m.

AUDIO

Pronunciación   La letra h

In Spanish, the letter **h** is always silent.

Listen and repeat.

ha	he	hi	ho	hu
hace	helado	hispano	hola	humano

¡Hola, Hugo!

Hasta mañana, Héctor.

PARA Y PIENSA

Did you get it?
1. Tell a friend good morning.
2. Ask a friend how he or she is.
3. Say goodbye to your teacher.

Get Help Online
ClassZone.com

¡Mucho gusto!

Goal: Notice how certain speakers introduce themselves and others. Then practice what you have learned to make introductions. *Actividades 4–7*

AUDIO

A **Esteban:** Hola. **Me llamo** Esteban.
　　　　　　¿Y tú? **¿Cómo te llamas?**
　　Diana: Me llamo Diana.
　Esteban: **Encantado,** Diana.
　　Diana: **Igualmente.**

B **Diana:** **Te presento a** Esteban.
　　　Ana: **Encantada.**
　Esteban: Igualmente.

C **Srta. Machado:** **Perdón.**
　　　　　　　　¿Cómo se llama?
　　Srta. Daza: Me llamo
　　　　　　　　Raquel Daza.

D **Srta. Machado:** Le presento a Ana Vega.
　　Sr. Ortega: **Mucho gusto.**
　　　　Ana: **El gusto es mío.**

E ¿Quién es? ¿Es Raúl?

No. Es Juan.

F ¿Cómo se llama?

Se llama Diana.

G **Rosa:** ¿Se llama Miguel?
Esteban: **Sí.** Se llama Miguel Luque.

¡A responder! Escuchar

Listen to four people make introductions. Point to yourself if you hear someone introducing themselves. Point to the person next to you if you hear someone introducing someone else.

4 | ¿Cómo te llamas?

Leer | Choose the correct response to each question or statement.

1. ¿Quién es?
   a. Es Hugo.
   b. Encantado.
   c. Me llamo Carlos.
2. Encantada.
   a. Le presento a Sergio.
   b. ¿Y tú?
   c. Igualmente.
3. Te presento a Joaquín.
   a. ¿Cómo se llama?
   b. Mucho gusto.
   c. Igualmente.

4. ¿Cómo te llamas?
   a. Perdón.
   b. Me llamo Isabel.
   c. Bien.
5. Me llamo Gabriel.
   a. Igualmente.
   b. Encantado.
   c. El gusto es mío.
6. Mucho gusto.
   a. Buenas tardes.
   b. ¿Quién es?
   c. El gusto es mío.

5 | Conversación

Leer
Escribir | Complete the conversation with the correct words.

Carlos: Hola. Me __1.__ Carlos. ¿ __2.__ te llamas?

Beatriz: Me __3.__ Beatriz.

Carlos: __4.__ , Beatriz.

Beatriz: __5.__ .

6 | Mucho gusto

Hablar | Work in a group of four. Introduce yourself to each member of the group.

Nota

¿Cómo te llamas? and **¿Cómo se llama?** both are used to ask *What is your name?*
Te presento a... and **Le presento a...** both mean *I'd like you to meet...*

¿Cómo te llamas? and **Te presento a...** are familiar phrases used with:

- a person your own age
- a relative
- a person you call by his or her first name

¿Cómo se llama? and **Le presento a...** are formal phrases used with:

- a person with whom you want to show respect
- a person you don't know
- someone older

7 | Te presento a...

 Hablar

Work in a group of three. Take turns introducing each other.

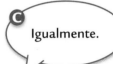

A Te presento a Tomás.

B Encantado(a), Tomás.

C Igualmente.

Comparación cultural

Un mural del metro

How can artists give back to their neighborhood through their work? Artist Manuel Vega moved with his family from Puerto Rico to **New York** at a young age. He created a series of mosaic murals called *Sábado en la Ciento Diez* that decorate the walls of the 110th Street subway station, located in East Harlem where he grew up. These works depict neighborhood scenes inspired by Vega's childhood. This mosaic shows a woman and child in front of a local store.

Sábado en la Ciento Diez
(1996), Manuel Vega

Compara con tu mundo *What childhood memory would you paint if you were creating a neighborhood mural? Compare it with the scene in Vega's mural.*

PARA Y PIENSA

Did you get it? Complete each statement.

1. Me llamo...   a. a Maricela.
2. Te presento...   b. gusto, señor.
3. Mucho...   c. Walter.

Get Help Online
ClassZone.com

El abecedario

AUDIO

A (a) — **a**lfombra

B (be, be grande) — **b**ate

C (ce) — **c**ine

D (de) — **d**inero

E (e) — **e**ntrada

F (efe) — **f**ruta

G (ge) — **g**ato

H (hache) — **h**elado

I (i) — **i**glú

J (jota) — **j**abón

K (ka) — **k**arate

L (ele) — **l**ápiz

M (eme) — **m**ochila

N (ene) — **n**ariz

Ñ (eñe) — **ñ**u

O (o) — **o**reja

P (pe) — **p**atines

Q (cu) — **q**ueso

R (ere) — **r**egalo

RR (erre) — guita**rr**a

S (ese) — **s**ofá

T (te) — **t**iza

U (u) — **u**vas

V (uve, ve chica) — **v**entana

W (doble uve, doble ve) — **w**afle

X (equis) — **x**ilófono

Y (i griega) — **y**ogur

Z (zeta) — **z**apato

¡A responder! Escuchar

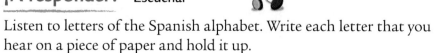

Listen to letters of the Spanish alphabet. Write each letter that you hear on a piece of paper and hold it up.

8 | Lista

Escuchar
Escribir

Listen to someone dictate an invitation list for a party. Write down each name as it is spelled.

> **modelo:** You hear: de, a, ene, i, e, ele
>   You write: Daniel

9 | Me llamo...

Hablar

Work in a group of three. Ask each person his or her name and write down the name as he or she spells it.

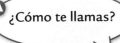

A ¿Cómo te llamas?

B Me llamo Shawna, S - H - A - W - N - A. (ese, hache, a, doble uve, ene, a)

10 | ABC

Hablar

Spell aloud the following things for a partner. He or she will write the word. Then verify that your partner spelled the word correctly.

your middle name   **your favorite singer**   **the name of your town**

the name of your school   **your favorite sports team**   **¿?**

AUDIO

Pronunciación   Las vocales

In Spanish, the vowels are **a, e, i, o,** and **u.** Each vowel is always pronounced the same way. Spanish vowels are always short and crisp.

Listen to and repeat these words.

a → as in *father*	**encantada**	**mal**	**mañana**
e → as in *hey*	**menos**	**señor**	**presento**
i → sounds like *meet*	**igualmente**	**adiós**	**bien**
o → as in *woke*	**hola**	**noches**	**cómo**
u → sounds like *boot*	**usted**	**mucho**	**tú**

PARA Y PIENSA

Did you get it? Recite the Spanish alphabet.

 **Get Help Online** ClassZone.com

¿De dónde eres?

¡AVANZA! **Goal:** Look at the Spanish-speaking world and how Spanish speakers say where someone is from. Then practice what you have learned to ask where people are from. *Actividades 11–13*

AUDIO

Alicia, ¿de dónde eres?

Soy de **Estados Unidos.** Soy de la Florida.

Soy de **Estados Unidos.** ¿De dónde es usted?

Sr. Costas

Alicia

Isabel **es de la República Dominicana.**

Pablo es de **México.**

Marisol es de **Puerto Rico.**

Susana es de **Costa Rica.**

Fernando es de **Ecuador.**

Mariano es de **Argentina.**

Enrique es de **España.**

Los países hispanohablantes

1. **Estados Unidos**
2. **México**
3. **Cuba**
4. **República Dominicana**
5. **Puerto Rico**
6. **Guatemala**
7. **Honduras**
8. **El Salvador**
9. **Nicaragua**
10. **Costa Rica**
11. **Panamá**
12. **Venezuela**
13. **Colombia**
14. **Ecuador**
15. **Perú**
16. **Bolivia**
17. **Paraguay**
18. **Chile**
19. **Argentina**
20. **Uruguay**
21. **España**
22. **Guinea Ecuatorial**
23. **Filipinas**
24. **Guam**

Color Key

Spanish is the official language.   Spanish is spoken.

¡A responder!   Escuchar

For each statement you hear, point to the person in the photo to whom it refers.

11 | Es de...

Indicate where each person is from, according to the number on the map.

modelo: Guillermo / ⑦

Guillermo es de **Uruguay.**

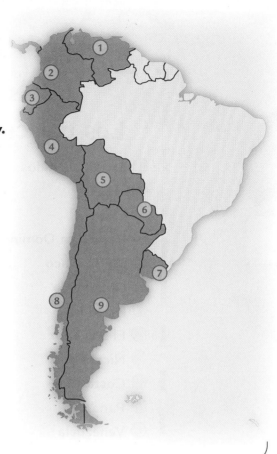

1. Andrea / ⑤
2. Tomás / ⑧
3. Nicolás / ④
4. Sofía / ②
5. Verónica / ③
6. Mateo / ⑨
7. Consuelo / ①
8. Pablo / ⑥

12 | ¿De dónde eres?

Ask a partner where he or she is from. Your partner will answer with the country listed.

modelo: Colombia

1. Venezuela
2. Panamá
3. México
4. Uruguay
5. España
6. Estados Unidos
7. El Salvador
8. Nicaragua

A ¿De dónde eres?

B Soy de Colombia.

Nota

When you are speaking, one way to change a statement into a question is to simply raise the intonation of your voice.

Beto es de Paraguay.   **¿Beto es de Paraguay?**

Answer simple yes/no questions with **sí** (*yes*) or **no** (*no*).

¿Eres de California?   **No. Soy de Nueva York.**

In written Spanish, all questions begin with an upside-down question mark (¿) and end with a question mark (?).

13 | ¿Eres de Honduras?

Hablar Ask a partner if he or she is from the country indicated. He or she will answer according to the number.

modelo: ① / ⑩

A ¿Eres de **México**?

B No. Soy de **Panamá**.

Estudiante A
1. ⑨   4. ⑩
2. ④   5. ⑤
3. ⑥   6. ⑧

Estudiante B
1. ③   4. ⑩
2. ④   5. ⑤
3. ②   6. ⑦

PARA Y PIENSA

Did you get it? Match each question with the correct response.

1. ¿De dónde eres?   a. Es de Puerto Rico.
2. ¿De dónde es Hugo?   b. Soy de Colombia.
3. ¿Eres de México?   c. Sí, soy de México.

Get Help Online
ClassZone.com

Lección preliminar
quince   **15**

Mi número de teléfono

Goal: Learn how to say the numbers from zero to ten and how to exchange phone numbers. Then use what you have learned to say your home (or cellular) phone number. *Actividades 14–16*

AUDIO

0 cero
1 uno   2 dos   3 tres
4 cuatro 5 cinco 6 seis
7 siete 8 ocho   9 nueve
10 diez

¿Cuál es tu número de teléfono?

Es 7-6-4-9-0-8-1.

Perdón. ¿Cuál es su número de teléfono?

Mi número de teléfono es 2-5-3-7-1-0-9.

¡A responder! Escuchar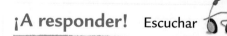

Listen to these numbers. If you hear an even number, raise your right hand. If you hear an odd number, raise your left hand.

14 | Matemáticas

Hablar
Escribir

Give the answers to the following math problems using words.

modelo: 2 + 4
        seis

1. 8 − 3   **3.** 3 + 6   **5.** 1 + 9   **7.** 6 − 5   **9.** 10 − 8

2. 4 + 4   **4.** 7 − 7   **6.** 5 − 2   **8.** 7 + 0   **10.** 1 + 3

15 | Teléfono

Hablar

Work in a group of five. Whisper a phone number to the person at your right. He or she will repeat it to the person at his or her right, and so on. Verify that the phone number you gave was repeated accurately.

A Mi número de teléfono es cinco - dos - uno - nueve - ocho - siete - uno.

B Cinco - dos - uno - nueve - ocho - siete - uno.

C Cinco - dos - uno...

16 | ¿Quién es?

Hablar

Work with a partner. Look at this Buenos Aires phone directory and read a phone number at random. Your partner will say whose phone number it is.

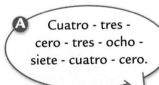

A Cuatro - tres - cero - tres - ocho - siete - cuatro - cero.

B Gianmarco Santander.

Santander Gemma
Lauerbach 3472 Pb 11- Capital Federal
Ciudad de Buenos Aires.................... 4301-9203

Santander Genoveva
Löschner 244- Capital Federal
Ciudad de Buenos Aires.................... 4921-4808

Santander Geraldo
López de Padilla 12 Pb 4- Capital Federal
Ciudad de Buenos Aires.................... 4704-5960

Santander Giancarlo
Filippozzi 9903 Pb Casa- Capital Federal
Ciudad de Buenos Aires.................... 4638-3123

Santander Gianmarco
Filippozzi 1099- Capital Federal
Ciudad de Buenos Aires.................... 4303-8740

Santander Gregorio
Sta Marta 374 Pb 7- Capital Federal
Ciudad de Buenos Aires.................... 4941-7819

PARA Y PIENSA

Did you get it? Say these phone numbers.
1. 6251-4209   **2.** 3708-9263   **3.** 4185-2760

Get Help Online
ClassZone.com

Los días de la semana

¡AVANZA! **Goal:** Learn to talk about the days of the week. Then practice what you have learned to say what day of the week it is. *Actividades 17–19*

AUDIO

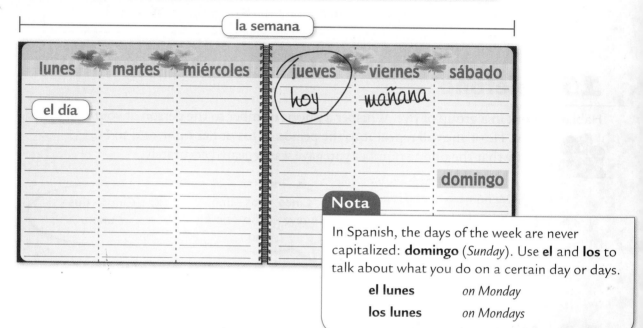

la semana

| lunes | martes | miércoles | jueves | viernes | sábado |

el día

hoy   mañana

domingo

Nota

In Spanish, the days of the week are never capitalized: **domingo** (*Sunday*). Use **el** and **los** to talk about what you do on a certain day or days.

| **el lunes** | *on Monday* |
| **los lunes** | *on Mondays* |

A **Ana:** ¿Qué día es hoy?
Rosa: Hoy es jueves.

B **Juan:** ¿Hoy es viernes?
Esteban: No. **Mañana es** viernes.

¡A responder! Escuchar

Listen to the days of the week. If you hear a day that you have Spanish class, stand up. If you hear a day that you don't have Spanish class, remain seated.

17 | Los días

Hablar
Escribir

Complete each list with the missing day of the week.

1. lunes, _____, miércoles, jueves
2. viernes, _____, domingo, lunes
3. _____, martes, miércoles, jueves
4. lunes, martes, miércoles, _____

5. _____, jueves, viernes, sábado
6. domingo, _____, martes, miércoles
7. sábado, _____, lunes, martes
8. martes, miércoles, jueves, _____

18 | ¿Lógico o ilógico?

Escuchar

Listen to these statements about the days of the week. Write **L** if the statement you hear is **lógico** (*logical*) or **I** if it is **ilógico** (*not logical*).

modelo: You hear: Hoy es viernes. Mañana es domingo.
You write: I

19 | ¿Qué día es?

Hablar

Ask a partner what day of the week it is. He or she will tell you what day of the week today is and what tomorrow is.

modelo: 6

A ¿Qué día es hoy?

B Hoy es **martes.** Mañana es **miércoles.**

1. 2
2. 12
3. 28
4. 15

5. 18
6. 3
7. 20
8. 16

PARA Y PIENSA

Did you get it?
1. Tell someone that today is Monday. Hoy es _____.
2. Ask what day tomorrow is. ¿Qué día es _____?

Get Help Online
ClassZone.com

¿Qué tiempo hace?

¡AVANZA! **Goal:** Learn how to describe the weather. Then practice what you have learned to describe a sunny day, a rainy day, and a windy day.
Actividades 20–22

AUDIO

¿Qué tiempo hace?

A **Luis:** Hace calor.

B **Natalia:** Hace sol.

C **Jorge:** Llueve.

D **Andrea:** Hace frío.

E **Diego:** Hace viento.

F **Mariana:** Nieva.

¡A responder! Escuchar

Listen to weather descriptions. Point to the photo of the person that corresponds to the description you hear.

20 | El tiempo

Escuchar

Listen to four meteorologists describe the weather in their region. Write the letter of the photo that corresponds to the weather description you hear.

a.    b.    c.    d.

21 | ¿Hace calor o hace frío?

Hablar

Work with a partner. Say whether it is cold or hot, according to the temperature given.

modelo: 32°F / 0°C
Hace frío.

1. 15°F / –9°C
2. 94°F / 35°C
3. 20°F / –6°C
4. 4°F / –16°C
5. 88°F / 32°C
6. 104°F / 40°C

22 | ¿Qué tiempo hace?

Hablar

Tell what city you are from, and ask a partner what the weather is like. He or she will give you the weather conditions for that city.

Buenos Aires	Bogotá	Madrid	México	Nueva York
86°	53°	45°	65°	30°

A Soy de la Ciudad de México. ¿Qué tiempo hace?

B Hace viento.

PARA Y PIENSA

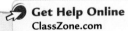

Get Help Online
ClassZone.com

Did you get it? Match each question with the correct response.

1. ¿Qué tiempo hace?
2. ¿Hace calor?
3. ¿Llueve?

a. No. Hace frío.
b. Hace viento.
c. No. Hace sol.

En la clase

¡AVANZA! **Goal:** Learn some useful phrases used by teachers and students. Then practice what you have learned to use classroom phrases with others. *Actividades 23–25*

AUDIO

Maestro, ¿cómo se dice *Wednesday*?

Se dice *miércoles*.

la clase

En la clase

Abran los libros (en la página...)	Open your books (to page . . .)
Cierren los libros.	Close your books.
¿Cómo se dice...?	How do you say . . .?
Se dice...	You say . . .
¿Cómo se escribe (tu nombre)?	How do you spell (your name)?
Se escribe...	It is spelled . . .
¿Comprendes?	Do you understand?
Levanten la mano.	Raise your hand.
Más despacio, por favor.	More slowly, please.
No sé.	I don't know.
¿Qué quiere decir...?	What does . . . mean?
Quiere decir...	It means . . .
Repitan, por favor.	Please repeat.
Saquen una hoja de papel.	Take out a piece of paper.
Siéntense.	Sit down.
¿Tienen preguntas?	Do you have questions?
¿Verdad?	Right?

Muchas gracias.

De nada.

el maestro de español

Otras instrucciones

Completa la conversación.   Complete the conversation.

Contesta las preguntas.   Answer the questions.

Escoge la palabra / la respuesta...   Choose the word / answer . . .

Escribe...   Write . . .

Escucha...   Listen . . .

Explica...   Explain . . .

Indica si es cierto o falso.   Indicate whether it is true or false.

Lee...   Read . . .

Pregúntale a otro(a) estudiante. Ask another student.

Trabaja con otro(a) estudiante. Work with another student.

Trabaja en un grupo de...   Work in a group of . . .

¡A responder!   Escuchar

Listen to each classroom instruction and respond appropriately.

23 | Instrucciones

Leer | Match each picture with the correct instruction.

1.

2.

a. Abran los libros en la página 7.
b. Levanten la mano.
c. Repitan, por favor.
d. Siéntense.

3.

4.

24 | ¿Qué dices?

Escribir Hablar | Indicate what you would say in each situation. Refer to the expressions on pages 22–23.

1. You want to thank your Spanish teacher.
2. Your teacher is speaking too fast.
3. You want to know how to say *book* in Spanish.
4. You want to know what **página** means.
5. You must admit that you don't have the answer to a question.
6. You wonder if your friend understands the lesson.

25 | ¿Cómo se dice?

Hablar | Ask a partner to say the following words in Spanish and how to spell them.

modelo: Tuesday

1. Spanish
2. week
3. Thank you very much.
4. male teacher
5. See you later.
6. Friday
7. It's raining.

PARA Y PIENSA

Did you get it? **1.** Ask how to say the word *please*.
2. Ask a friend if he or she understands.

Get Help Online
ClassZone.com

Vocabulario

Greet People and Say Goodbye

Greetings

Buenos días.	Good morning.
Buenas tardes.	Good afternoon.
Buenas noches.	Good evening.
Hola.	Hello./Hi.

Say Goodbye

Adiós.	Goodbye.
Buenas noches.	Good night.
Hasta luego.	See you later.
Hasta mañana.	See you tomorrow.

Say How You Are

¿Cómo estás?	How are you? (familiar)
¿Cómo está usted?	How are you? (formal)
¿Qué tal?	How is it going?
Bien.	Fine.
Mal.	Bad.
Más o menos.	So-so.
Muy bien.	Very well.
Regular.	Okay.
¿Y tú?	And you? (familiar)
¿Y usted?	And you? (formal)
¿Qué pasa?	What's up?

Make Introductions

¿Cómo se llama?	What's his/her/your (formal) name?
Se llama...	His/Her name is . . .
¿Cómo te llamas?	What's your (familiar) name?
Me llamo...	My name is . . .
Te/Le presento a...	Let me introduce you (familiar/formal) to . . .
El gusto es mío.	The pleasure is mine.
Encantado(a).	Delighted./Pleased to meet you.
Igualmente.	Same here./Likewise.
Mucho gusto.	Nice to meet you.
¿Quién es?	Who is he/she/it?
Es...	He/She/It is . . .

Say Which Day It Is

¿Qué día es hoy?	What day is today?
Hoy es...	Today is . . .
Mañana es...	Tomorrow is . . .
el día	day
hoy	today
mañana	tomorrow
la semana	week

Days of the week *p. 18*

Exchange Phone Numbers

¿Cuál es tu/su número de teléfono?	What's your (familiar/formal) phone number?
Mi número de teléfono es...	My phone number is . . .

Numbers from zero to ten *p. 16*

Other Words and Phrases

la clase	class
el (la) maestro(a) de español	Spanish teacher (male/female)
el país	country
Perdón.	Excuse me.
por favor	please
(Muchas) Gracias.	Thank you (very much).
De nada.	You're welcome.
el señor (Sr.)	Mr.
la señora (Sra.)	Mrs.
la señorita (Srta.)	Miss
sí	yes
no	no

Describe the Weather

¿Qué tiempo hace?	What is the weather like?
Hace calor.	It is hot.
Hace frío.	It is cold.
Hace sol.	It is sunny.
Hace viento.	It is windy.
Llueve.	It is raining.
Nieva.	It is snowing.

Say Where You Are From

¿De dónde eres?	Where are you (familiar) from?
¿De dónde es?	Where is he/she from?
¿De dónde es usted?	Where are you (formal) from?
Soy de...	I am from . . .
Es de...	He/She is from . . .

Spanish-speaking countries *p. 13*

Repaso de la lección

¡LLEGADA!

@HomeTutor
ClassZone.com

Now you can
- greet people and say goodbye
- introduce yourself and others
- ask and say how to spell names
- say where you are from

- exchange phone numbers
- say what day of the week it is
- describe the weather
- respond to classroom instructions

To review
- introductions pp. 6–7
- classroom instructions pp. 22–23

1 | Listen and understand

You will hear four separate conversations. Put the drawings in order according to what you hear.

a.  **b.**  **c.**  **d.**

To review
- greet people pp. 2–3
- introductions pp. 6–7
- weather p. 20

2 | Introduce yourself and others

Complete Enrique's e-mail message to his new e-pal.

Adiós	Hace	Hoy	calor

Hola	Soy	Cómo	tiempo	llamo

___1.___ ,

¿ ___2.___ estás? Me ___3.___ Enrique. ___4.___ de Panamá. ___5.___ es sábado y hace ___6.___ . ¿Qué ___7.___ hace en Estados Unidos? ¿ ___8.___ frío?

___9.___ ,

Enrique

---

3 | Say where you are from

To review
• origin pp. 12–13
• numbers p. 16

Look at these students' ID cards from the International Club.
Then complete the sentences that follow.

Club Internacional
NOMBRE:
Cristina Villaveces
PAÍS DE ORIGEN:
Venezuela
DOMICILIO:
332 Avenida de
las Américas
TELÉFONO:
241-0976
Cristina Villaveces

Club Internacional
NOMBRE:
Yolanda Hoyos
PAÍS DE ORIGEN:
Chile
DOMICILIO:
1902 Rúa Mayor
TELÉFONO:
397-2261
Yolanda Hoyos

Club Internacional
NOMBRE:
Alejandro Cruz
PAÍS DE ORIGEN:
México
DOMICILIO:
214 Paseo Suárez
TELÉFONO:
898-1035
Alejandro Cruz

Club Internacional
NOMBRE:
Guillermo Morales
PAÍS DE ORIGEN:
España
DOMICILIO:
38 Calle Toro, 3°D
TELÉFONO:
460-1853
Guillermo Morales

1. _____ es de España.
2. El número de teléfono es ocho - nueve - ocho - uno - cero - tres - cinco.
   Se llama _____ .
3. Se llama Cristina. El número de teléfono es _____ .
4. La señorita de Chile se llama _____ .
5. Se llama Guillermo. El número de teléfono es _____ .
6. _____ es de México.

4 | Answer personal questions

To review
• alphabet p. 10
• numbers p. 16
• days of the week
  p. 18

Answer these questions using complete sentences.

1. ¿Cómo te llamas?
2. ¿Cómo se escribe tu nombre?
3. ¿De dónde eres?
4. ¿Cuál es tu número de teléfono?
5. ¿Quién es el (la) maestro(a) de español? ¿De dónde es?
6. ¿Cómo se llama el libro de español?
7. ¿Qué día es mañana?
8. ¿Qué tiempo hace hoy?
9. ¿Cómo se dice *country* en español?

Get Help Online
ClassZone.com

Estados Unidos

Un rato con los amigos

Lección 1

Tema: **¿Qué te gusta hacer?**

Lección 2

Tema: **Mis amigos y yo**

Alaska

Islas Hawai

«¡Hola!

**Nosotras somos Alicia y Sandra.
Somos de Estados Unidos.»**

Chicago •
Filadelfia •
Nueva York

Estados Unidos

• San José
Denver •

Los Ángeles •
• Albuquerque

Phoenix •
Océano Atlántico

San Diego •
• Tucson
• Dallas

• El Paso
• Houston

San Antonio •
Miami •

Golfo de México

Cuba

México
Mar Caribe

Océano Pacífico
Honduras
Nicaragua

Costa Rica

Guatemala
El Salvador

Panamá

Población: 293.655.404

Población de ascendencia hispana: 41.322.070

Ciudad con más latinos: Nueva York
(más de 2.000.000)

**Ciudad con mayor porcentaje de
latinos:** El Paso, Texas (77%)

Comida latina: el sándwich cubano,
burritos, fajitas

El sándwich cubano

Gente famosa: Sandra Cisneros (escritora),
Gloria Estefan (cantante), Eva Mendes (actriz),
Eloy Rodríguez (bioquímico)

Hispanic teens gather for a celebration in Miami, Florida

◀ **La ascendencia hispana** The over 40 million Hispanics living in the United States trace their roots to more than 20 nations. From September 15 to October 15, Hispanic Heritage Month celebrates the diverse backgrounds and cultures of these Americans. *Do you know anyone from a Spanish-speaking country?*

La comunidad cubana de Miami The Cuban American community thrives in Miami's Little Havana. **Calle Ocho** is known for its Cuban restaurants, cafés, and shops, and the nearby Freedom Tower houses the Cuban American Museum. *How have people from other countries shaped your community?* ▶

Miami's Freedom Tower, home to the Cuban American Museum

Dancers in traditional dress during the Fiesta San Antonio

LA VILLITA
LITTLE VILLAGE of SAN ANTONIO

◀ **Las celebraciones** San Antonio is proud of its unique multicultural history. The **Fiesta San Antonio,** a ten-day celebration with food, music, and parades, honors the heroes of the Alamo and the Battle of San Jacinto. La Villita, the city's oldest neighborhood, hosts many of the festival events. *How do people celebrate history and culture where you live?*

Estados Unidos

Tema:

¿Qué te gusta hacer?

¡AVANZA!

In this lesson you will learn to

- talk about activities
- tell where you are from
- say what you like and don't like to do

using

- subject pronouns and **ser**
- **de** to describe where you are from
- **gustar** with an infinitive

♻ *¿Recuerdas?*

- weather expressions

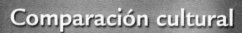

Comparación cultural

In this lesson you will learn about

- *Los Premios Juventud,* an awards show in Miami
- Cuban-American artist Xavier Cortada
- free-time activities of students at a Florida school

Compara con tu mundo

This group of teenagers is spending the day at a beach. In southern Florida, beaches are open year-round and are popular places to do many different activities. *Where do you like to go with your friends in your free time? What do you like to do?*

¿Qué ves?

Mira la foto

What is the weather like?

Do you think that these teenagers are friends?

What activities do they like to do?

Online SPANISH **CLASSZONE.COM**

Featuring...

Cultura INTERACTIVA

Animated Grammar

@HomeTutor

And more...
• **Get Help Online**
• **Interactive Flashcards**
• **Review Games**
• **WebQuest**
• **Self-Check Quiz**

Una playa de Miami Beach
Miami Beach, Florida

Presentación de VOCABULARIO

¡AVANZA!

Goal: Learn about what Alicia and her friends like to do. Then use what you have learned to talk about activities. **Actividades 1–2**

VIDEO
DVD

AUDIO

A ¡Hola! Me llamo Teresa. **Después de las clases, me gusta pasar un rato con los amigos.** Me gusta **escuchar música o tocar la guitarra.**

hablar por teléfono

escuchar música

leer un libro

Miguel   **Teresa**   **Alicia**

dibujar

tocar la guitarra

B ¡Hola! Me llamo Miguel. A mí me gusta **hablar por teléfono,
dibujar** y **estudiar.** Me gusta **pasear, pero** me gusta **más correr.**
A ti, ¿qué te gusta hacer?

estudiar

pasear

correr

C ¡Hola! Me llamo Alicia. A mí me gusta **montar en bicicleta** y
jugar al fútbol. También me gusta **andar en patineta.**

montar en bicicleta

jugar al fútbol

andar en patineta

D Hoy hace calor en Miami. **Antes de practicar deportes** me gusta
comprar agua.

comprar

las papas fritas

la fruta

el agua

la pizza

el refresco

el helado

las galletas

Continuará...

Lección 1
treinta y tres

E Me gusta **beber** agua o **jugo** pero no me gusta beber **refrescos.**

preparar la comida

comer

beber

el jugo

Más vocabulario

la actividad *activity*
alquilar un DVD *to rent a DVD*
aprender el español
   to learn Spanish
la escuela *school*
hacer la tarea *to do homework*
Expansión de vocabulario p. R2

F No me gusta **trabajar** los sábados y domingos. Me gusta
escribir correos electrónicos y **descansar.** También me gusta
mirar la televisión. ¿Te gusta pasar un rato con los amigos?

escribir correos
electrónicos

descansar

mirar la televisión

¡A responder!   Escuchar

Listen to the list of activities. As you listen, act out the activities.

@HomeTutor VideoPlus
Interactive Flashcards
ClassZone.com

Práctica de VOCABULARIO

1 | El sábado

Leer
Escribir

Miguel, Teresa, and Alicia are talking about the activities they like to do. Complete the conversation with the appropriate words.

Alicia: Miguel, ¿te gusta escuchar __1.__ los sábados?

Miguel: Sí, pero me gusta más practicar __2.__ . Teresa, ¿te gusta montar en __3.__ ?

Teresa: No, no me gusta. Me gusta más leer __4.__ .

Alicia: Teresa, ¿te gusta hacer __5.__ los sábados?

Teresa: ¿Los sábados? No, sólo me gusta preparar __6.__ , alquilar __7.__ y descansar.

un libro

la tarea

deportes

bicicleta

un DVD

música

la comida

2 | ¿Te gusta?

Hablar
Escribir

Tell whether you like or don't like to eat or drink these foods and beverages.

modelo: beber
(No) Me gusta beber refrescos.

1. comer

2. beber

3. comer

4. comer

5. beber

6. comer

Más práctica   Cuaderno *pp. 1–3* Cuaderno para hispanohablantes *pp. 1–4*

PARA Y PIENSA

Did you get it?
1. Tell someone that you like to listen to music.   Me gusta _____.
2. Ask a friend if he or she likes to do homework.   ¿Te gusta _____?

Get Help Online
ClassZone.com

VOCABULARIO en contexto

¡AVANZA! **Goal:** Listen to the words Alicia and Sandra use to talk about activities. Then practice what you have heard to talk about the activities you and others like to do. ***Actividades 3–5***

¿Recuerdas? Weather expressions p. 20

Telehistoria escena 1

@HomeTutor VideoPlus ClassZone.com

STRATEGIES

Cuando lees

Search for clues Look for clues in the picture before starting to read. Who's in the photos? What are they doing?

Cuando escuchas

Listen for intonation The way people speak, not just what they say, often reflects how they feel. Listen for Alicia's intonation. How does she feel about the activities mentioned?

VIDEO DVD

AUDIO

Alicia: *(on phone, to Sandra, a friend in San Antonio, Texas)* En Miami, hace calor. ¿Te gusta andar en patineta?

Sandra: No, me gusta más pasear o montar en bicicleta. Los sábados me gusta hacer la tarea.

Alicia: ¿Sí? Los sábados me gusta pasar un rato con amigos... ¡y dibujar! Y los domingos, ¡jugar al fútbol! Los viernes me gusta alquilar un DVD y comer pizza.

Sandra: Sí, sí. Mmm. Me gusta comer pizza y hablar por teléfono.

Alicia: ¿Hablar por teléfono? No me gusta hablar por teléfono. *(Father gives a look of disbelief.)*

Continuará... p. 42

También se dice

Miami To talk about riding bicycles, Sandra uses the phrase **montar en bicicleta.** In other Spanish-speaking countries you might hear:
- **muchos países** **andar en bicicleta**

3 | A Alicia y a Sandra les gusta... *Comprensión del episodio*

Escuchar
Leer

Tell if what Alicia and Sandra say is true or false. Correct the false statements.

> **modelo:** **Alicia:** Los viernes no me gusta comer pizza.
>
> Falso. Los viernes me gusta comer pizza.

1. **Alicia:** Llueve en Miami.
2. **Sandra:** Me gusta correr los sábados.
3. **Alicia:** Me gusta pasar un rato con los amigos.
4. **Sandra:** Me gusta hacer la tarea los domingos.
5. **Alicia:** Los sábados me gusta alquilar un DVD.
6. **Sandra:** Me gusta hablar por teléfono.

4 | ¡Hace frío! ♻ *¿Recuerdas?* Weather expressions p. 20

Hablar

Tell a partner what you like to do in each situation.

> beber agua   leer un libro   jugar al fútbol   montar en bicicleta
>
> correr   descansar   pasear   mirar la televisión   ¿ ?

modelo: Hace viento.

A Hace viento. ¿Qué te gusta hacer?

B Me gusta mirar la televisión o descansar.

1. Hace frío y llueve.
2. Hace sol.
3. Hace viento y hace frío.
4. Hace calor.
5. Nieva y hace sol.
6. Llueve y hace calor.

5 | ¡Me gusta!

Escribir
Hablar

Write a list of your after-school activities and then compare them with other students' activities.

— escribir correos electrónicos
— practicar deportes
— dibujar
— andar en patineta

A ¿Te gusta pasear después de las clases?

B Sí, me gusta pasear.

C No, me gusta pasear antes de las clases.

PARA Y PIENSA

Did you get it? Fill in Alicia's sentences with the appropriate vocabulary word.

1. Me gusta _____ al fútbol.
2. ¿Te gusta escuchar _____ ?
3. También me gusta _____ pizza.

Get Help Online
ClassZone.com

Presentación de GRAMÁTICA

Goal: Learn how to use subject pronouns and the verb **ser.** Then practice the verb forms of **ser** with **de** to talk about where you and others are from. *Actividades 6–11*

English Grammar Connection: Pronouns are words that take the place of nouns. **Subject pronouns** indicate who is being described or who does the action in a sentence.

We are friends.   Nosotros somos amigos.

Subject Pronouns and ser

Ser means *to be.* Use **ser** to identify a person or say where he or she is from. How do you use this verb with **subject pronouns**?

Here's how:

	Singular			Plural			
	yo	**soy**	*I am*		nosotros(as)	**somos**	*we are*
familiar	tú	**eres**	*you are*		vosotros(as)	**sois**	*you are*	*familiar*
formal	usted	**es**	*you are*		ustedes	**son**	*you are*
	él, ella	**es**	*he, she is*		ellos(as)	**son**	*they are*

Yo soy de Buenos Aires.   **Ellas son** de Venezuela.
I am from Buenos Aires.   *They are* from Venezuela.

Singular

Use **tú** with
  • a friend
  • a family member
  • someone younger

Use **usted** with
  • a person you don't know
  • someone older
  • someone for whom you want to show respect

Plural

• Use **vosotros(as)** with friends, family, and younger people only in Spain.

• Use **ustedes** with people you don't know, older people, and people for whom you want to show respect in Spain; use it in Latin America with any group of people.

• Use **nosotras, vosotras,** and **ellas** when all the people you are talking about are female.

Más práctica
  Cuaderno *pp. 4–6*
  Cuaderno para hispanohablantes *pp. 5–7*

@HomeTutor
Leveled Grammar Practice
ClassZone.com

Práctica de GRAMÁTICA

6 | ¿Quién?

Escribir

Write the corresponding pronoun.

   modelo: ella

1.

2.

3.

4.

5.

6.

Nota gramatical

Use **de** with the verb **ser** to talk about where someone is from.

Daniela y Sonia **son de** Miami.   Martín **es de** Honduras.

*Daniela and Sonia **are from** Miami.*   *Martín **is from** Honduras.*

---

7 | ¿De dónde son?

Leer
Escribir

Lucía's friends and teachers are from different places. Write the correct form of **ser** to learn where they are from.

Hola, me llamo Lucía. Mi amigo Andrés y yo **1.** de la
República Dominicana. Yo **2.** de Santo Domingo y él **3.**
de San Pedro de Macorís. La señora Muñoz y el señor
Vázquez **4.** de Puerto Rico. Son mis maestros favoritos.
Mis amigas Laura y Ana **5.** de Colombia. Laura **6.** de
Bogotá y Ana **7.** de Cartagena. Y tú, ¿de dónde **8.** ?

8 | Ella es de...

Choose the correct form of **ser** to say where each person is from. Some forms may be used more than once.

> **modelo:** Ella _____ de Uruguay.
> Ella **es** de Uruguay.

1. Nosotros _____ de Bolivia.

2. Ellos _____ de Chile.

3. Usted _____ de Paraguay.

4. Yo _____ de El Salvador.

5. Él _____ de Nicaragua.

6. Tú _____ de Cuba.

7. Nosotras _____ de Venezuela.

8. Ustedes _____ de Panamá.

a. eres

b. es

c. somos

d. son

e. soy

9 | Los amigos de Alicia

Escribir

Alicia has a lot of friends that you are going to meet in the following chapters. Write where they are from.

> **modelo:** Maribel y Enrique / España
> Maribel y Enrique son de España.

1. yo / Miami

2. Claudia y Pablo / México

3. Marisol / Puerto Rico

4. papá y yo / Miami

5. Fernando / Ecuador

6. Mario / la República Dominicana

10 | De muchos países

Hablar

Ask another student where Miguel's friends are from. Your partner should use pronouns to answer.

modelo: Luis

A ¿De dónde es Luis?

B Él es de Colombia.

1. Leticia
2. Álvaro y Linda
3. Isabel y Ángela
4. Andrés y Jorge
5. Ana Sofía y Elena
6. Y tú, ¿ ?

11 | Mis amigos

Escribir

Write five sentences telling where your friends are from.

modelo: Amy es de Minnesota. Mike es de Indiana...

Más práctica   Cuaderno *pp. 4–6*   Cuaderno para hispanohablantes *pp. 5–7*

PARA Y PIENSA

Did you get it? Match the phrases to make a complete sentence.

1. Cristóbal y yo   a. soy de México.
2. Tomás   b. somos de Honduras.
3. Yo   c. es de la República Dominicana.

Get Help Online
ClassZone.com

GRAMÁTICA *en contexto*

Goal: Notice how Alicia and her friends say where they are from. Then use **ser** with **de** to tell where people are from. *Actividades 12–14*

Telehistoria escena 2

@HomeTutor VideoPlus
ClassZone.com

STRATEGIES

Cuando lees

Scan for details Quickly look ahead for certain details before you read the scene. Scan for names and people. What do you think this scene is about?

Cuando escuchas

Listen for guesses Listen as Mr. Costas guesses where Teresa and Miguel are from. What does he guess? What does Miguel guess about where Mr. Costas is from?

VIDEO
DVD

AUDIO

Alicia: ¡Hola! Señor Costas, le presento a dos amigos... Teresa y Miguel. Ellos son de...

Mr. Costas stops her because he wants to guess.

Sr. Costas: Tú eres de... ¿Puerto Rico? ¿Panamá? ¿Costa Rica?

Teresa: No, yo soy de...

Mr. Costas interrupts and gestures toward Miguel.

Sr. Costas: ¿Él es de México? ¿El Salvador? ¿Colombia?

Miguel: No, nosotros somos de *(pointing to himself)* Cuba y *(pointing to Teresa)* de Honduras. Y usted, ¿de dónde es?

Sr. Costas: Soy de...

Miguel: ¿Argentina? ¿Chile? ¿Cuba?

Sr. Costas: Soy de la Florida.

Continuará... p. 48

12 | Los orígenes *Comprensión del episodio*

Escuchar
Leer

Answer the questions about the episode.

1. Teresa y Miguel son los amigos de
   a. Alicia.
   b. el señor Costas.
   c. el señor Díaz.
2. ¿De dónde es Miguel?
   a. Es de Puerto Rico.
   b. Es de Cuba.
   c. Es de la República Dominicana.
3. ¿De dónde es Teresa?
   a. Es de Puerto Rico.
   b. Es de Costa Rica.
   c. Es de Honduras.
4. ¿Quién es de la Florida?
   a. Miguel
   b. el señor Costas
   c. Teresa

13 | Los famosos en Miami

Leer
Hablar

Comparación cultural

Juanes

Los Premios Juventud
*How have Latino performers and athletes affected popular culture in the United States? Los Premios Juventud is an awards show held in **Miami** and broadcast on Spanish-language television. Teens vote for their favorite stars in music, film, and sports. Past nominees include Shakira and Juanes (Colombia), Paulina Rubio and Gael García Bernal (Mexico), Miguel Cabrera (Venezuela), and Jennifer Lopez (New York).*

Compara con tu mundo *Who are your favorite figures in music, film, and sports, and why?*

Paulina Rubio

Talk with a partner about where the nominees are from.

A ¿De dónde es Juanes?

B Juanes es de Colombia.

14 | ¿De dónde somos?

Hablar

Ask other students where they are from.

A Nora, ¿de dónde eres?

B Soy de Miami. ¿Y tú?

También soy de Miami.

PARA Y PIENSA

Did you get it? Create sentences to tell where the people are from.

1. el Sr. Costas / la Florida
2. Alicia / Miami
3. Teresa y Miguel / Honduras y Cuba

Get Help Online
ClassZone.com

Presentación de GRAMÁTICA

Goal: Learn how to express what people like to do using the verb **gustar**. Then use **gustar** to say what you and others like to do. *Actividades 15–19*

English Grammar Connection: An **infinitive** is the basic form of a **verb**, a word that expresses action or a state of being. In English, most infinitives include the word *to*. In Spanish, infinitives are always one word that ends in **-ar, -er,** or **-ir**.

I like to **run**. → infinitive

Me gusta **correr**. → infinitive

Gustar with an Infinitive

Animated Grammar
ClassZone.com

Use **gustar** to talk about what people like to do.

Here's how: Use phrases like **me gusta + infinitive.**

Me gusta dibujar.	*I like to draw.*
Te gusta dibujar.	*You (familiar singular) like to draw.*
Le gusta dibujar.	*You (formal singular) like to draw.* *He/She likes to draw.*
Nos gusta dibujar.	*We like to draw.*
Os gusta dibujar.	*You (familiar plural) like to draw.*
Les gusta dibujar.	*You (plural) like to draw.* *They like to draw.*

When you want to really emphasize or identify the person that you are talking about, add **a + noun/pronoun.**

A Sonia le gusta leer.
Sonia likes to read.

A ella le gusta leer.
She likes to read.

These are the **pronouns** that follow **a**.

A **mí** **me gusta** dibujar.   A **nosotros(as)** **nos gusta** dibujar.

A **ti** **te gusta** dibujar.   A **vosotros(as)** **os gusta** dibujar.

A **usted** **le gusta** dibujar.   A **ustedes** **les gusta** dibujar.

A **él, ella** **le gusta** dibujar.   A **ellos(as)** **les gusta** dibujar.

Más práctica
Cuaderno *pp. 7–9*
Cuaderno para hispanohablantes *pp. 8–11*

@HomeTutor
Leveled Grammar Practice
ClassZone.com

Práctica de GRAMÁTICA

15 | ¿Les gusta o no?

Escribir

Write what these people like and don't like to do.

> modelo: a Luisa / preparar la comida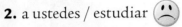
> No le gusta preparar la comida.

1. a nosotras / 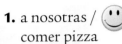 comer pizza

2. a ustedes / estudiar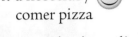

3. a ti / montar en bicicleta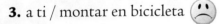

4. a mí / escuchar música

5. a Alicia y a Miguel / 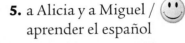 aprender el español

6. a usted / trabajar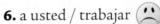

7. a Teresa / tocar la guitarra

8. a ellos / hacer la tarea

Comparación cultural

El arte de Miami

How would being Cuban American influence an artist's work? Growing up in **Miami**, artist Xavier Cortada learned about his Cuban heritage through his family and community around him. Many of his paintings reflect his identity as a Cuban American. His colorful painting *Music* presents a variety of instruments found in traditional Cuban music *(son, rumba, mambo, Afro-Latin jazz)* as well as American music. How many instruments can you identify?

Music *(2005), Xavier Cortada*

Compara con tu mundo *What would you paint to represent your community? Where would you display your painting?*

16 | ¿Qué les gusta hacer?

Hablar

With a partner, use the photos to say what Alicia and others like to do.

Teresa

A ¿Qué le gusta hacer a Teresa?

B Le gusta leer un libro.

1. Alicia

2. ella

3. él

4. Alicia y Miguel

5. Teresa

6. ustedes

17 | En el parque

**Hablar
Escribir**

Look at the drawing and say whether the people like or don't like what they are doing.

modelo: Le gusta jugar al fútbol.

18 | Las actividades

Escuchar
Escribir

Copy this chart on a piece of paper. Listen to Mariana's description of what she and her friends like to do on Saturdays, and complete your chart with **sí** or **no.** Then answer the questions.

¿Le gusta...?	descansar	pasear	mirar la televisión	tocar la guitarra
A Mariana	sí			
A Jorge		no		
A Federico				

1. ¿Qué le gusta hacer a Jorge?
2. ¿Qué le gusta hacer a Mariana?
3. ¿Qué le gusta hacer a Federico?
4. ¿Qué no le gusta hacer a Mariana?
5. ¿Qué no les gusta hacer a Jorge y a Federico?
6. ¿Qué les gusta hacer a los tres amigos?

19 | A mi amigo(a) le gusta

Hablar

Ask a classmate what he or she likes to do on Saturdays and Sundays. Then tell the class.

¿Te gusta montar en bicicleta?

AUDIO

Pronunciación Las letras p y t

When you pronounce the **p** and **t** in English, a puff of air comes out of your mouth. In Spanish, there is no puff of air. Listen and repeat.

pasar   por favor   Puerto Rico
pizza   pero   papas

Pepe prepara las papas fritas.

fruta   televisión   practicar
tocar   estudiar   tarea

Más práctica   Cuaderno *pp. 7–9*   Cuaderno para hispanohablantes *pp. 8–11*

PARA Y PIENSA

Did you get it? Complete each sentence with the correct **gustar** phrase.

1. _____ correr. (a ella)
2. ¿_____ andar en patineta? (a ti)
3. _____ tocar la guitarra. (a nosotros)

Get Help Online
ClassZone.com

Todo junto

Goal: *Show what you know* Pay attention to Alicia and her friends as they describe the activities they like to do. Then use **ser** and **gustar** to say where you are from and what you like to do. *Actividades 20–24*

Telehistoria completa

@HomeTutor VideoPlus
ClassZone.com

STRATEGIES

Cuando lees

Unlock the main idea Find repeated phrases that can unlock the overall meaning. Find all the phrases that contain the verb **gustar**. What is this scene about?

Cuando escuchas

Listen for cognates A cognate is a Spanish word that sounds like an English word and means the same thing. For example, *telephone* and **teléfono**. In the video, listen for at least three cognates.

Escena 1 *Resumen*

A Alicia y a Sandra les gusta hacer muchas actividades. Les gusta dibujar, comer pizza y más.

Escena 2 *Resumen*

Miguel es de Cuba y Teresa es de Honduras. El señor Costas es de la Florida.

VIDEO
DVD

AUDIO

Escena 3

Alicia: ¿Qué les gusta hacer?

Miguel: Me gusta mirar la televisión.

Teresa: No me gusta mirar la televisión. Me gusta más tocar la guitarra o escuchar música.

Miguel: Me gusta comer.

Teresa: Sí, me gusta comer.

Alicia: ¡Nos gusta comer!

They stand to go eat.

Alicia: ¿Qué les gusta comer? ¿Pizza? ¿Les gusta comer helado? ¿Fruta? ¿Beber jugos?

Both say no, and they all sit. Teresa shows them the paper.

Alicia: ¿Trini Salgado? ¿En San Antonio? *(She quickly takes out her cell phone.)* ¡Sandra!

20 | ¿Quiénes son? *Comprensión de los episodios*

Escuchar
Leer

Write the name(s) of the character(s) according to the descriptions.

1. No le gusta andar en patineta.
2. Es de Honduras.
3. Les gusta comer.
4. Es de la Florida.
5. Le gusta tocar la guitarra.
6. Es de San Antonio, Texas.
7. Le gusta hablar por teléfono.
8. Le gusta escuchar música.

21 | Los amigos *Comprensión de los episodios*

Escuchar
Leer

Answer the questions according to the episodes.

1.
   a. ¿Cómo se llama?
   b. ¿Qué le gusta hacer?
   c. ¿Qué no le gusta hacer?

2.
   a. ¿Cómo se llama?
   b. ¿De dónde es?
   c. ¿Qué le gusta hacer?

22 | Nuevos amigos

Hablar

STRATEGY Hablar

Boost your "speaking self-confidence" with positive statements
To increase your speaking self-confidence, say something positive to yourself like:
I learn from my mistakes. I can say things now that I couldn't say last week. Create your own positive statement. Say it to yourself before the speaking activity below.

You are a new student at school. Talk with other students about where you are from and what you like and don't like to do. Make a list of the things you have in common.

A Hola, me llamo Víctor. Soy de Chicago. Me gusta escuchar música y correr.

B Hola, me llamo Carolina y soy de Chicago también. No me gusta escuchar música pero me gusta practicar deportes.

C Hola. Me llamo Alex...

23 | Integración

Read the e-mail from Vanessa, then listen to Carmen and take notes. Say what both of them like and don't like.

Fuente 1 Correo electrónico

¡Hola, Carmen! Soy Vanessa. Soy de Morelos, México. Me gusta mucho practicar deportes. También me gusta andar en patineta. No me gusta escuchar música. Después de las clases me gusta pasar un rato con los amigos y comer pizza. Los sábados y domingos no me gusta hacer la tarea. Me gusta más alquilar un DVD o descansar. ¿Y a ti? ¿Qué te gusta hacer?

Fuente 2 Escucha a Carmen

Listen and take notes
• ¿Qué le gusta hacer a Carmen?
• ¿Qué no le gusta hacer?

modelo: A las chicas les gusta...

24 | Un correo electrónico

Write to your new e-pal in Puebla, Mexico. Introduce yourself and tell him or her where you are from and what you like and don't like to do. Also write three questions for him or her to answer.

modelo: Hola, Eva. Me llamo Ana, y soy de la Florida. Me gusta leer un libro, pero no me gusta mirar la televisión. ¿Te gusta hablar por teléfono?

Writing Criteria	Excellent	Good	Needs Work
Content	Your e-mail includes a lot of information and questions.	Your e-mail includes some information and questions.	Your e-mail includes little information and not enough questions.
Communication	Most of your e-mail is organized and easy to follow.	Parts of your e-mail are organized and easy to follow.	Your e-mail is disorganized and hard to follow.
Accuracy	Your e-mail has few mistakes in grammar and vocabulary.	Your e-mail has some mistakes in grammar and vocabulary.	Your e-mail has many mistakes in grammar and vocabulary.

Más práctica   Cuaderno *pp. 10–11* Cuaderno para hispanohablantes *pp. 12–13*

PARA Y PIENSA

Did you get it? Tell where these people are from and what they like to do, based on the Telehistoria.

1. Teresa / Honduras / tocar la guitarra
2. Alicia / Miami / comer
3. Miguel / Cuba / mirar la televisión

Get Help Online
ClassZone.com

Juegos y diversiones

Review the verb **ser** by playing a game.

The Setup

Your teacher will hand you a card with the name of a country on it. This will be your country of origin for use in the game. Do not show your card to anyone. The object of the game is to find another person in your class with the same country card.

Materials

index cards with names of Spanish-speaking countries (two cards for each country)

Colombia   Perú   Honduras

Playing the Game

You will go around asking your classmates where they are from in order to find the person who has the same country card as you. You must use the correct Spanish phrasing and answer in complete sentences.

The Winners!

The first two students to match country cards and say the word **¡Ganamos!** (we win) are the winners.

¿Eres de Honduras?

No, soy de Perú.

Lectura

¡AVANZA! **Goal:** Read about what students in a dual-language school in Florida like to do in their free time. Then compare the activities they like to do with what you like to do.

AUDIO

¿Qué te gusta hacer?

This is a survey about what students like to do in their free time. It was conducted among students at a dual-language school in Florida.

STRATEGY Leer

Use a judgment line Draw a line like this one with *least popular* on the left and *most popular* on the right. On the line, list all the activities in the survey according to their popularity.

leer estudiar   dibujar

| least popular | most popular |

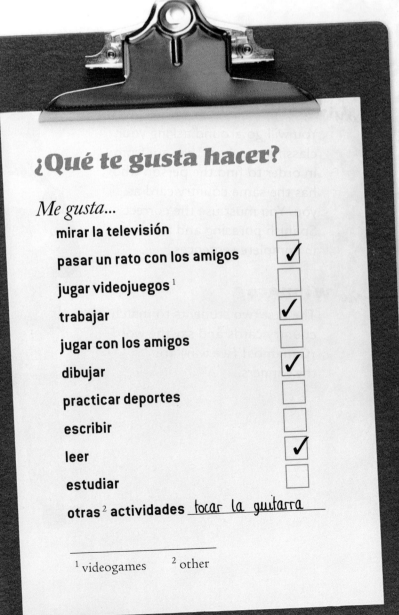

¿Qué te gusta hacer?

Me gusta...

- mirar la televisión ☐
- pasar un rato con los amigos ✓
- jugar videojuegos [1] ☐
- trabajar ✓
- jugar con los amigos ☐
- dibujar ✓
- practicar deportes ☐
- escribir ☐
- leer ✓
- estudiar ☐
- otras [2] actividades tocar la guitarra

[1] videogames   [2] other

Una encuesta en la escuela

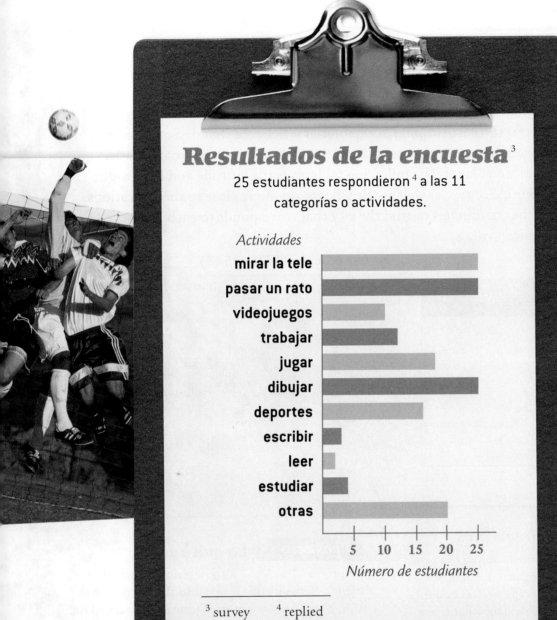

Resultados de la encuesta[3]

25 estudiantes respondieron[4] a las 11 categorías o actividades.

Actividades

- mirar la tele
- pasar un rato
- videojuegos
- trabajar
- jugar
- dibujar
- deportes
- escribir
- leer
- estudiar
- otras

5   10   15   20   25

Número de estudiantes

---

[3] survey   [4] replied

¡Interpreta!

Based on the chart and survey, answer the following questions.

1. How many students took the survey?

2. What are the three most popular activities and the three least popular activities?

3. Would you get the same results if you used the survey with your classmates? Give specific reasons why or why not.

¿Y tú?

Record your answers to the survey on the previous page and compare them to the results of these students.

PARA Y PIENSA

Conexiones   *La geografía*

La expedición de Hernando de Soto

Hernando de Soto

The map below shows one account of the expedition of Hernando de Soto, a sixteenth-century Spanish explorer. It is believed that de Soto's team traveled through ten present-day U.S. states, and through many Native American villages. The following table gives the latitude and longitude of four U.S. cities, as well as the villages that were close to these locations. Use the coordinates to find the city that corresponds to each Native American village.

NATIVE AMERICAN VILLAGE	LOCATION OF CITY	NAME OF CITY
Ucita	27° 56' N 82° 27' O	
Casqui	35° 15' N 90° 34' O	
Mabila	30° 41' N 88° 02' O	
Anhayca	30° 26' N 84° 16' O	

La expedición (1539–1543)

OKLAHOMA · Parkin · TENNESSEE · CAROLINA DEL NORTE · 35°N · ARK. · Río Misisipi · MISISIPÍ · CAROLINA DEL SUR · TEXAS · ALA. · GEORGIA · LUISIANA · Mobile · Tallahassee · 30°N · Golfo de México · Tampa · FLORIDA · 25°N · 95°O · 90°O · 85°O · 80°O

0 100 200 millas
0 100 200 kilómetros

Proyecto 1 *Las matemáticas*

A common form of measurement during the time of de Soto was the league (**legua**). A league was based on the distance an average person could walk in an hour: 3.5 miles. Calculate what these distances would be in leagues.

Ucita to Anhayca:	204 miles
Anhayca to Mabila:	224 miles
Mabila to Casqui:	347 miles

Proyecto 2 *El lenguaje*

Many places in the United States have Spanish names. **Florida,** for instance, means *full of flowers.* Use an atlas or the Internet to find three places in the United States with Spanish names. Then write the meaning of each place.

Proyecto 3 *La música*

The term "Tex–Mex" also describes music that blends elements of Mexico and the southwestern U.S. Most Tex–Mex music features the accordion, brought to Texas in the 1890s by German immigrants. Find an example of Tex–Mex music—such as Selena or Los Tigres del Norte—and listen to it. Then write a paragraph describing the instruments and the music and list the Spanish names of the instruments.

Los Tigres del Norte

En resumen
Vocabulario y gramática

Animated Grammar
Interactive Flashcards
ClassZone.com

Vocabulario

Talk About Activities

alquilar un DVD	to rent a DVD	hacer la tarea	to do homework
andar en patineta	to skateboard	jugar al fútbol	to play soccer
aprender el español	to learn Spanish	leer un libro	to read a book
beber	to drink	mirar la televisión	to watch television
comer	to eat	montar en bicicleta	to ride a bike
comprar	to buy	pasar un rato con los amigos	to spend time with friends
correr	to run		
descansar	to rest	pasear	to go for a walk
dibujar	to draw	practicar deportes	to practice / play sports
escribir correos electrónicos	to write e-mails	preparar la comida	to prepare food / a meal
escuchar música	to listen to music	tocar la guitarra	to play the guitar
estudiar	to study	trabajar	to work
hablar por teléfono	to talk on the phone		

Say What You Like and Don't Like to Do

¿Qué te gusta hacer?	What do you like to do?	Me gusta...	I like . . .
¿Te gusta...?	Do you like . . . ?	No me gusta...	I don't like . . .

Snack Foods and Beverages

el agua (fem.)	water
la fruta	fruit
la galleta	cookie
el helado	ice cream
el jugo	juice
las papas fritas	French fries
la pizza	pizza
el refresco	soft drink

Other Words and Phrases

la actividad	activity
antes de	before
después (de)	afterward, after
la escuela	school
más	more
o	or
pero	but
también	also

Gramática

Nota gramatical: **de** to describe where you are from *p. 39*

Pronouns and ser

Ser means *to be.* Use **ser** to identify a person or say where he or she is from.

Singular		Plural	
yo	soy	nosotros(as)	somos
tú	eres	vosotros(as)	sois
usted	es	ustedes	son
él, ella	es	ellos(as)	son

Gustar with an Infinitive

Use **gustar** to talk about what people like to do.

A mí **me gusta** dibujar.
A ti **te gusta** dibujar.
A usted **le gusta** dibujar.
A él, ella **le gusta** dibujar.
A nosotros(as) **nos gusta** dibujar.
A vosotros(as) **os gusta** dibujar.
A ustedes **les gusta** dibujar.
A ellos(as) **les gusta** dibujar.

Repaso de la lección

¡LLEGADA!

@HomeTutor
ClassZone.com

Now you can
- talk about activities
- tell where you are from
- say what you like and don't like to do

Using
- subject pronouns and **ser**
- **de** to describe where you are from
- **gustar** with an infinitive

To review
- **gustar** with an infinitive p. 44
- **de** to describe where you are from p. 39

AUDIO

1 Listen and understand

Listen to Pablo and Sara talk about their activities. Then match the descriptions with the name or names.

1. Es de Puerto Rico.
2. Es de Miami.
3. Le gusta escuchar música.
4. No le gusta andar en patineta.
5. No le gusta comer frutas.
6. Le gusta comer helado.

a. Pablo
b. Sara
c. Pablo y Sara

To review
- **gustar** with an infinitive p. 44

2 Say what you like and don't like to do

Write sentences describing the activities you like and don't like to do.

modelo: alquilar un DVD
(No) Me gusta alquilar un DVD.

1. beber refrescos
2. preparar la comida
3. hacer la tarea
4. descansar
5. escribir correos electrónicos
6. pasar un rato con los amigos
7. practicar deportes
8. trabajar
9. comprar libros
10. comer pizza

To review
• subject pronouns and **ser** p. 38
• **de** to describe where you are from p. 39

3 | Tell where you are from

Complete the e-mail with the appropriate form of **ser**.

Hola, me llamo Eduardo. Yo __1.__ de Miami. Y tú, ¿de dónde __2.__ ? Mis amigos y yo __3.__ de diferentes países. Roberto __4.__ de Chile y Yolanda __5.__ de Perú. Nosotros __6.__ estudiantes. El señor Santana y la señora Zabala __7.__ maestros. Ellos __8.__ de Cuba.

To review
• **gustar** with an infinitive p. 44

4 | Talk about activities

Tell what activities these people like to do, according to the photos.

modelo: a José
A José le gusta tocar la guitarra.

1. a Sonia

2. a ellos

3. a usted

4. a nosotras

5. a ustedes

6. a ti

To review
• Miami's Freedom Tower p. 29
• Fiesta San Antonio p. 29
• Comparación cultural pp. 43, 45

5 | United States

Comparación cultural

Answer these culture questions.

1. What is inside Miami's Freedom Tower?
2. What occurs during Fiesta San Antonio?
3. Who votes for the winners of **Los Premios Juventud**?
4. What is Xavier Cortada's heritage?

Más práctica Cuaderno *pp. 12–23*   Cuaderno para hispanohablantes *pp. 14–23*

Get Help Online
ClassZone.com

Estados Unidos

Lección

2

Tema:

Mis amigos y yo

¡AVANZA!

In this lesson you will learn to

- describe yourself and others
- identify people and things

using

- **ser** to describe what someone is like
- definite and indefinite articles
- noun-adjective agreement

♻ *¿Recuerdas?*

- snack foods, after-school activities
- **ser, gustar** with an infinitive

Comparación cultural

In this lesson you will learn about

- Latin-American and Tex-Mex food
- the tradition of making **cascarones**
- after-school activities in Miami and San Antonio
- students from Miami, Colombia, and Mexico

Compara con tu mundo

These Texas teens are exploring the Paseo del Río, one of San Antonio's main attractions. In this refreshing city retreat, people eat in restaurants, ride riverboats, or stroll along the river. *Does your city or town have a park or place of interest? What do people do there?*

¿Qué ves?

Mira la foto
¿Son amigos?
¿Llueve o hace sol?
¿Qué les gusta hacer?

Online SPANISH **CLASSZONE.COM**

Featuring...
Cultura INTERACTIVA

Animated Grammar
@HomeTutor

And more...
• **Get Help Online**
• **Interactive Flashcards**
• **Review Games**
• **WebQuest**
• **Self-Check Quiz**

Paseo del Río
San Antonio, Texas

Presentación de VOCABULARIO

Goal: Learn how Sandra describes herself and her friends. Then practice what you have learned to describe yourself and others. *Actividades 1–2*

♻ *¿Recuerdas?* The verb **ser** p. 38

VIDEO
DVD

AUDIO

A ¡Hola! Soy Sandra.
Soy **artística** y **tengo pelo castaño**.
A mi **amigo** Ricardo le gusta practicar
deportes **porque** es **atlético**.

artística

atlético

B Alberto es **trabajador** y **estudioso**. Le gusta estudiar. David es **un poco perezoso**. No es **un estudiante muy bueno**. No le gusta trabajar.

trabajador

perezoso

C Soy **una persona** muy **organizada.** Mi **amiga** Ana es **inteligente** pero un poco **desorganizada.**

organizada

desorganizada

D Rafael es muy **alto,** pero Laura es **baja.** Manuel es **grande,** pero Francisco es **pequeño.** La señora Santa Cruz es un poco **vieja,** pero Rosita es **joven.**

alto

baja

grande

pequeño

vieja

joven

Más vocabulario
bonito(a) *pretty*
guapo(a) *good-looking*
malo(a) *bad*
Expansión de vocabulario p. R2

Continuará...

Presentación de VOCABULARIO
(continuación)

E La señora Guardado es **pelirroja** y el señor Guardado **tiene** pelo castaño.
Marco y Laura son **chicos** muy buenos. Marco tiene **pelo rubio** y Laura
tiene pelo castaño.

pelirroja

la mujer

pelo castaño

el hombre

pelo rubio

el chico   la chica

F Yo soy un poco **seria,** pero mi amigo Alberto es muy **cómico. Todos** mis
amigos son muy **simpáticos.** ¿Y tú? **¿Cómo eres?**

cómico   seria

¡A responder! Escuchar

Listen to these descriptions of Sandra and her friends. Point to the
person in the photo who matches each description you hear.

@HomeTutor VideoPlus
Interactive Flashcards
ClassZone.com

Práctica de VOCABULARIO

1 | Los opuestos

Leer   Sandra describes her friends but Ricardo says the opposite. Match Sandra's description with Ricardo's response.

Sandra
1. Marco es pequeño.
2. Luisa es trabajadora.
3. Pablo es organizado.
4. Joaquín es malo.
5. Anabel es joven.
6. Francisco es cómico.

Ricardo
a. No, es bueno.
b. No, es grande.
c. No, es desorganizado.
d. No, es perezosa.
e. No, es serio.
f. No, es vieja.

Nota gramatical    **¿Recuerdas?** The verb **ser** p. 38

Use **ser** to describe what people are like.

La mujer **es** alta.   Los chicos **son** organizados.
*The woman **is** tall.*   *The boys **are** organized.*

---

2 | Porque...

**Hablar
Escribir**

Explain why Ricardo and Alberto like or don't like the following activities.

serio   atlético   artístico

estudioso   desorganizado   trabajador

modelo: A Ricardo le gusta practicar deportes porque es atlético.

1. A Ricardo le gusta hacer la tarea.
2. A Ricardo le gusta dibujar.
3. A Alberto no le gusta ser cómico.
4. A Alberto le gusta correr.
5. A Alberto no le gusta ser perezoso.
6. A Alberto no le gusta ser organizado.

Más práctica   Cuaderno *pp. 24–26*   Cuaderno para hispanohablantes *pp. 24–27*

PARA Y PIENSA   **Did you get it?**
1. Say that Juan is short.
2. Say that David is artistic.
3. Say that Carlos is serious.

Get Help Online
ClassZone.com

VOCABULARIO *en contexto*

Goal: Notice how Sandra and her friends describe themselves and each other. Then practice these words to describe others. *Actividades 3–4*

Telehistoria escena 1

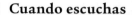

@HomeTutor VideoPlus
ClassZone.com

STRATEGIES

VIDEO DVD

AUDIO

Cuando lees

Skim Find the main idea by skimming (rapidly glancing over) the text before reading it carefully. What is the main idea of the scene below?

Cuando escuchas

Find the humor Humor makes a scene fun and memorable. Listen for exaggeration, teasing, and jokes. What are some examples of humor in the following scene?

Sandra

Alberto

Ricardo

Sandra, speaking to Alicia via webcam, holds up Alicia's T-shirt.

Sandra: Es bonita. Pero te gusta más con el autógrafo de Trini Salgado, ¿no?

Alberto and Ricardo join Sandra.

Sandra: Alicia, te presento a mis amigos: Alberto y Ricardo.

Alberto: Hola, Alicia. Me llamo Alberto. Soy alto... no soy muy alto. Tengo pelo castaño, y soy muy trabajador. Pero me gusta mirar la televisión y escuchar música. *(He pulls CDs from his backpack.)*

Sandra: No, él no es perezoso pero es un poco desorganizado.

Ricardo: Hola, Alicia. ¿Qué tal? Me llamo Ricardo. Soy inteligente, simpático y estudioso. Me gusta practicar deportes porque soy atlético. Y me gusta dibujar porque soy muy artístico.

Sandra shows one of Ricardo's drawings that is not very good.

Sandra: Sí. Él es muy artístico.

Ricardo: Ella es cómica, ¿no?

Alberto: Ella no es muy seria.

Sandra: OK, OK. Adiós, Alicia. Hasta luego.

Continuará... p. 70

3 | Las características *Comprensión del episodio*

Copy the Venn diagram on a piece of paper and use it to compare Ricardo and Alberto. Write their differences below their names. In the center, write what they have in common.

Ricardo   Alberto

Le gusta dibujar.

4 | Una entrevista

Read the interview with Raúl López, a famous young soccer player. Then talk to another student about the article. Use at least three adjectives to ask him or her questions.

A ¿Es Raúl perezoso?

B No, es trabajador porque le gusta estudiar.

ENTREVISTA

¡ESTRELLA DEL FUTURO!

Revista Estrella: Raúl, ¿cómo eres?

Raúl: Soy muy atlético. Me gusta mucho jugar al fútbol y practicar deportes. Pero también me gusta descansar.

Revista Estrella: Y eres un estudiante serio, ¿no?

Raúl: Sí, me gusta leer libros y estudiar.

Revista Estrella: ¿Te gusta escuchar música?

Raúl: Sí, me gusta escuchar música, pero me gusta más tocar la guitarra. También me gusta dibujar.

Comparación cultural

Comida mexicana y Tex-Mex

Unas fajitas

How does local environment affect the food that people eat? Tex-Mex is a regional cuisine that combines styles of cooking from **Mexico** and **Texas.** Did you know that *nachos,* crispy tacos, tortilla chips with salsa, *fajitas,* and *chili con carne* are all Tex-Mex dishes? Common Tex-Mex ingredients include flour tortillas, yellow cheese, refried beans, and beef. In the interior of Mexico, traditional ingredients are corn tortillas, white cheese, black beans, chicken, seafood, and pork.

Compara con tu mundo *What are some restaurants in your community that serve foods from other countries? Have you eaten at any of them?*

PARA Y PIENSA

Did you get it? Fill in the appropriate adjective.
1. Alberto es trabajador. No es _____ .
2. A Ricardo le gusta practicar deportes. Es _____ .
3. A Ricardo le gusta hacer la tarea. Es _____ .

Get Help Online
ClassZone.com

Presentación de GRAMÁTICA

Goal: Learn about definite and indefinite articles. Then practice using these articles to identify people and things. *Actividades 5–11*

 ¿Recuerdas? Snack foods p. 33, **gustar** with an infinitive p. 44

English Grammar Connection: Definite articles (in English, *the*) are used with nouns to indicate *specific* persons, places, or things. **Indefinite articles** (*a, an*) are used with nouns to indicate *nonspecific* persons, places, or things.

The boy is **a** friend.

| definite article | indefinite article |

El chico es **un** amigo.

| definite article | indefinite article |

Definite and Indefinite Articles

Animated Grammar
ClassZone.com

In Spanish, articles match nouns in gender and number.

Here's how: All Spanish nouns, even if they refer to objects, are either **masculine** or **feminine.**

- Nouns ending in **-o** are usually **masculine.**
- Nouns ending in **-a** are usually **feminine.**

		Definite Article	Noun	Indefinite Article	Noun
Masculine	Singular	**el** *the*	chico *boy*	**un** *a*	chico *boy*
	Plural	**los** *the*	chicos *boys*	**unos** *some*	chicos *boys*
Feminine	Singular	**la** *the*	chica *girl*	**una** *a*	chica *girl*
	Plural	**las** *the*	chicas *girls*	**unas** *some*	chicas *girls*

matches   *matches*
Los libros son para **la maestra.**   *The books are for the teacher.*

To form the **plural** of a noun, add **-s** if the noun ends in a vowel. Add **-es** if the noun ends in a consonant.

vowel ↓   *consonant* ↓
estudiante → estudiant**es**   mujer → muj**eres**

Más práctica
Cuaderno *pp. 27–29*
Cuaderno para hispanohablantes *pp. 28–30*

@HomeTutor
Leveled Grammar Practice
ClassZone.com

Práctica de GRAMÁTICA

5 | ¿Cómo son las personas en la oficina?

Leer Miguel is describing various people in the school office. Complete his sentences with **el, la, los, las.**

1. _____ chicas son atléticas.
2. _____ maestra es inteligente.
3. _____ amigos son simpáticos.
4. _____ chico es pelirrojo.
5. _____ mujeres son artísticas.

6. _____ hombre es guapo.
7. _____ personas son organizadas.
8. _____ amigas son jóvenes.
9. _____ estudiantes son bajos.
10. _____ mujer es cómica.

6 | La lista de Sandra

Escuchar Escribir Sandra likes to buy many things. Listen and write a list of what she likes to buy, using **el, la, los, las.**

7 | ¿Qué es? ♻ *¿Recuerdas?* Snack foods p. 33

Hablar Escribir Identify these foods, using **un, una, unos, unas.**

modelo: Son unas galletas.

1.

2.

3.

4.

5.

6.

7.

8.

8 ¿Son estudiosos?

Hablar
Escribir

Describe these people, using **ser** and **un, una, unos, unas.**

modelo: chico cómico
Daniel es un chico cómico.

1. chicas estudiosas
2. chicos serios
3. amigas trabajadoras
4. chico desorganizado

5. chica alta
6. chico alto
7. estudiante pelirroja
8. chico grande

9 Después de las clases

Escribir

Describe what Marta likes to do after school. Combine elements from the three columns to create six different sentences. You may use each article more than once.

modelo: tocar / la / guitarra
Le gusta tocar la guitarra.

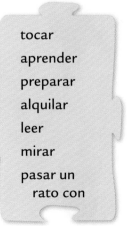

tocar
aprender
preparar
alquilar
leer
mirar
pasar un
    rato con

la
los
un
el

guitarra
DVD
libro
amigos
televisión
español
comida

10 | ¿Qué te gusta más? ♻ *¿Recuerdas?* gustar with an infinitive p. 44

Hablar

Ask a partner what he or she likes more.

modelo: comprar

A ¿Te gusta más comprar una fruta o unas papas fritas?

B Me gusta más comprar una fruta.

1. leer

2. hablar con

3. pasar un rato con

4. comer

5. beber

6. comprar

11 | En una isla desierta

Hablar

Work in a group of five. Take turns naming some of the items you would wish for if you were stranded on a desert island. Repeat the items other group members wished for, and then add one of your own. Include the definite or indefinite article with each item.

A Una pizza.

B Una pizza, unos libros.

C Una pizza, unos libros, un refresco.

Más práctica   Cuaderno *pp. 27–29*   Cuaderno para hispanohablantes *pp. 28–30*

PARA Y PIENSA

Did you get it?
Match the article to its corresponding noun.

1. la
2. unas
3. el
4. unos

a. libro
b. hombres
c. televisión
d. frutas

Get Help Online
ClassZone.com

GRAMÁTICA *en contexto*

¡AVANZA!

Goal: Listen to the conversation between Sandra and her friends. Then use definite and indefinite articles to talk about people. *Actividades 12–13*

¿Recuerdas? After-school activities p. 32

Telehistoria escena 2

@HomeTutor VideoPlus
ClassZone.com

STRATEGIES

Cuando lees
Answer questions related to context Knowing the context helps you understand the meaning. Ask yourself: Where is the action taking place?

Cuando escuchas
Listen for unstated wishes People often reveal their wishes without saying them out loud. How do Alberto and Ricardo make it obvious that they want to meet Ana?

VIDEO DVD

AUDIO

Ricardo: Un helado.

Alberto: Unas papas fritas y un refresco.

Sandra: Un jugo y una pizza. *(Alberto looks over at another table.)*

Alberto: ¿Son las chicas de la clase de la señora García?

Ricardo: Sí, son Marta, Carla y...

Sandra: Ana.

Both boys look interested.

Alberto: ¿Quién es ella?

Sandra: Ella es la amiga de Carla. Es muy inteligente. Le gusta leer y tocar la guitarra.

Alberto: Me gusta escuchar música. Ana, ¿no?

Sandra: Sí. Y le gusta practicar deportes.

Ricardo: Yo soy atlético. Soy muy bueno.

Sandra: ¡Ay, los chicos! *(Leaving, Alberto trips and lands in the seat next to Ana and her friends.)*

Alberto: Uh... hola. Perdón.   **Continuará...** p. 76

También se dice

San Antonio Alberto says **unas papas fritas** to talk about French fries. In other Spanish-speaking countries you might hear:
• **España** **las patatas fritas**
• **Colombia, México** **las papitas**
To talk about juice, Sandra says **un jugo.** In other Spanish-speaking countries you might hear:
• **España** **el zumo**

12 | A corregir *Comprensión del episodio*

Escuchar
Leer

All of these sentences are false. Correct the errors.

1. Las chicas se llaman Marta, Beatriz y Ana.
2. Ana es la amiga de Sandra.
3. A Ricardo le gusta escuchar música.
4. Ana no es inteligente.
5. A Alberto le gusta tocar la guitarra.
6. Ricardo no es atlético.

13 | En el parque ♻ *¿Recuerdas?* After-school activities p. 32

Hablar

Choose a person or a group of people from the drawings. Follow the model to give clues to another student, who will guess the people you describe. Change roles and describe everyone.

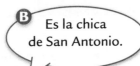

A Es una chica. Le gusta tocar la guitarra.

B Es la chica de San Antonio.

San Antonio

Bogotá

AUDIO

Pronunciación La letra ñ

The **ñ** sounds like the /ny/ of the word *canyon*. The letter **ñ** does not exist in English, but the sound does. Listen and repeat.

señor   España   mañana   pequeño   castaño

La señora es española.   El señor es de España y tiene pelo castaño.

PARA Y PIENSA

Did you get it? Change the article to make the noun more or less specific.

1. Ricardo es el amigo de Alberto.
2. Marta y Carla son las chicas de la clase de Juan.
3. Ana es la chica muy inteligente.

🔎 **Get Help Online**
ClassZone.com

Presentación de GRAMÁTICA

Goal: Learn how to use adjectives with nouns. Then practice using adjectives to describe people. *Actividades 14–19*

English Grammar Connection: Adjectives are words that describe **nouns**. In English, the adjective almost always comes before the noun. In Spanish, the adjective usually comes after the noun.

before the noun
the **serious** students

after the noun
los estudiantes **serios**

Noun-Adjective Agreement

Animated **Grammar**
ClassZone.com

In Spanish, adjectives match the gender and number of the nouns they describe.

Here's how:

	Singular	Plural
Masculine	el chico alto *the tall boy*	los chicos altos *the tall boys*
Feminine	la chica alta *the tall girl*	las chicas altas *the tall girls*

- Adjectives that end in **-e** match both genders.

  el maestro inteligente
  la maestra inteligente

- Many adjectives that end in a **consonant** match both genders.

  el amigo joven
  la amiga joven

- Some adjectives that end in a **consonant** add **-a** to form the feminine singular. These exceptions have to be memorized.

  el chico trabajador
  la chica trabajadora

- To make an adjective plural, add **-s** if it ends in a **vowel**; add **-es** if it ends in a **consonant.**

  las chicas trabajadoras
  los chicos trabajadores

Más práctica
Cuaderno *pp. 30–32*
Cuaderno para hispanohablantes *pp. 31–34*

@HomeTutor
Leveled Grammar Practice
ClassZone.com

Práctica de GRAMÁTICA

14 | Un correo electrónico

Leer | Help Sandra solve the puzzle in Alicia's e-mail by choosing the correct words in parentheses.

A: Sandra

Asunto: ¡Una persona famosa en Miami!

Hola, amiga. Te gusta jugar al fútbol y eres __1.__ (inteligente / inteligentes), ¿no? ¿Quién es la persona famosa en Miami? No es un chico __2.__ (grande / grandes). No es una chica __3.__ (pequeño / pequeña). Tiene pelo __4.__ (castaño / castaña) y es una persona __5.__ (simpático / simpática). Es una mujer __6.__ (serio / seria) pero le gusta pasar un rato con los amigos. Los amigos de ella son __7.__ (atléticos / atlético) también y les gusta practicar deportes. Ella se llama Trini...

Alicia

15 | Descripciones

Escribir | Write descriptions of the people in the drawing.

alto(a)   guapo(a)   cómico(a)   atlético(a)

estudioso(a)   desorganizado(a)   serio(a)   ¿?

la Sra. De Silva

Rafael

Mónica

Mario

16 | ¡No son iguales!

Laura and her brother Luis are almost total opposites. Change each statement about one to say what the other is like. Use an adjective in each answer. Be careful! Laura and Luis do have a few things in common.

modelo: A Luis no le gusta practicar deportes.
Laura es atlética.

1. Laura es alta.
2. Luis es desorganizado.
3. Laura es pelirroja.
4. Luis es serio.
5. Laura es joven.
6. A Luis no le gusta dibujar.
7. A Laura no le gusta estudiar.
8. Luis es guapo.

17 | Un amigo

Write a short description of a friend. Be sure to describe what your friend looks like, his or her personality, and what he or she likes to do.

modelo: Cristina tiene pelo rubio. Es baja. Le gusta leer libros.
Ella es inteligente...

18 | ¿Cómo son los amigos de clase?

Escribir
Hablar

Write descriptions of three people in the class. Read the descriptions to a partner, who will guess the people being described.

A Es un chico. Es alto, inteligente y atlético. Es un poco serio también. Tiene pelo castaño.

B Es Felipe.

19 | La Fiesta San Antonio

Hablar

Comparación cultural

Fiesta San Antonio

Los cascarones

How do cultural traditions influence an artist's work? Cascarones are painted eggs filled with confetti. They are popular at Easter and events such as parties or graduations. They are also a common sight during Fiesta San Antonio, an annual citywide celebration that honors the history and culture of San Antonio, **Texas.** But *cascarones* are not meant for decoration. Children sneak up on their friends and try to crack the eggs over their heads. If a *cascarón* is broken over your head, it is supposed to bring you good luck. Artists are often influenced by traditions like these. Carmen Lomas Garza is a Mexican-American artist who depicts scenes of traditional celebration. In her 1989 painting *Cascarones,* Lomas Garza presents a family making the colorful eggs.

Compara con tu mundo *What are some traditions in your family and why are they important to you? Which is your favorite tradition?*

Point to a person in the photo and ask a partner what he or she is like. Your partner will answer. Change roles. Describe all of the people.

A ¿Cómo es la chica?

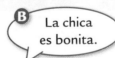
B La chica es bonita.

Más práctica   Cuaderno *pp. 30–32*   Cuaderno para hispanohablantes *pp. 31–34*

PARA
Y
PIENSA

Did you get it? Give the correct ending for each adjective.
1. una estudiante desorganizad_____
2. unos chicos simpátic_____
3. unas mujeres trabajador_____
4. un hombre grand_____

Get Help Online
ClassZone.com

Lección 2
setenta y cinco   **75**

Todo junto

Goal: *Show what you know* Pay attention to how Sandra and her friends describe specific people. Then use definite and indefinite articles and adjectives to tell what someone is like. *Actividades 20–24*

Telehistoria completa

@**HomeTutor** VideoPlus
ClassZone.com

STRATEGIES

Cuando lees

Discover a problem Scenes often reveal problems that the characters must solve. While reading the text below, search for a problem. What is it? Can it be solved?

Cuando escuchas

Listen for the parts Even a short scene can have parts, each with a somewhat different topic or action. These can be keys to meaning. How would you divide this scene?

Escena 1 *Resumen*

Alberto y Ricardo son amigos de Sandra. Alberto es un poco desorganizado. Ricardo es artístico.

Escena 2 *Resumen*

Ana es la amiga de Carla. A Ricardo y a Ana les gusta practicar deportes, y a Alberto y a Ana les gusta escuchar música.

VIDEO DVD

AUDIO

Escena 3

Ricardo: ¿Es Trini Salgado?

Alberto: ¿Quién?

Ricardo: La mujer seria. Tiene pelo castaño.

Sandra: No es ella. Es un poco baja. Trini es alta y más joven.

Ricardo finds the sign announcing Trini Salgado and points to the date.

The group enters a store where Trini Salgado will be signing autographs.

Alberto: Ana es bonita, inteligente, simpática... y nosotros somos inteligentes y simpáticos, ¿no?

Sandra: Sí, sí, ustedes son inteligentes, atléticos, cómicos. Ricardo, tú eres estudioso y Alberto, tú eres trabajador.

Ricardo notices a woman in the store.

Sandra: Pero... es el sábado. Hoy es domingo.

Ricardo: Sí, el sábado en San Antonio y el lunes en México.

Sandra: ¿México? ¿Puebla, México? Pablo, un amigo muy simpático de Alicia, es de México.

Sandra thinks of a plan to send the T-shirt to Pablo.

20 | ¿Cómo son? *Comprensión de los episodios*

Escuchar
Leer

Combine phrases from the two columns to make sentences about the people in the Telehistoria.

1. Alberto y Ricardo son
2. Sandra es
3. Ana es
4. Ricardo es
5. Alberto es
6. Todos los chicos son
7. La mujer seria es
8. Pablo es

a. un poco baja.
b. una amiga de Ricardo y Alberto.
c. un amigo de Alicia.
d. jóvenes.
e. alto y trabajador.
f. cómicos.
g. inteligente y le gusta leer.
h. artístico y atlético.

21 | Los amigos *Comprensión de los episodios*

Escuchar
Leer

Write descriptions of the Telehistoria characters, based on the three episodes.

22 | Las personas famosas

Escribir
Hablar

> **STRATEGY Hablar**
>
> **Practice pronunciation** To speak more fluently and accurately, practice the sounds of words you need to use in your descriptions. Paying attention to pronunciation will help you with cognates.

Write descriptions of three famous people. Include what they like and don't like to do. Read your descriptions to a partner, who will guess the people being described.

A Es un hombre. Tiene pelo rubio. Es muy atlético. Le gusta montar en bicicleta. No es muy joven y no es muy viejo. Es de Estados Unidos. ¿Quién es?

B Es Lance Armstrong.

23 | Integración

Leer
Escuchar
Hablar

Read the Web page and listen to the boys' messages. Describe the two boys.

Fuente 1 Página Web

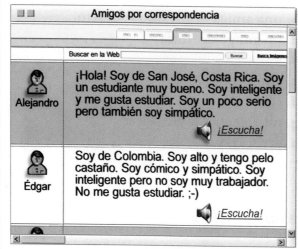

Amigos por correspondencia

Buscar en la Web [_____] Buscar Busca Imágenes

Alejandro: ¡Hola! Soy de San José, Costa Rica. Soy un estudiante muy bueno. Soy inteligente y me gusta estudiar. Soy un poco serio pero también soy simpático.

¡Escucha!

Édgar: Soy de Colombia. Soy alto y tengo pelo castaño. Soy cómico y simpático. Soy inteligente pero no soy muy trabajador. No me gusta estudiar. ;-)

¡Escucha!

Fuente 2 Audio en Internet

Listen and take notes
- ¿Cómo es Alejandro? ¿Qué le gusta hacer?
- ¿Cómo es Édgar? ¿Qué le gusta hacer?

modelo: Alejandro es un poco serio, pero Édgar es cómico...

24 | Un(a) amigo(a) perfecto(a)

Escribir

Describe the perfect friend for a special page in the yearbook. What is this person like? What does he or she like to do? Why?

modelo: Ella se llama Megan. Es bonita, inteligente y artística. Es una chica muy simpática. Le gusta escuchar música y...

Writing Criteria	Excellent	Good	Needs Work
Content	Your description includes a lot of information.	Your description includes some information.	Your description includes little information.
Communication	Most of your description is organized and easy to follow.	Parts of your description are organized and easy to follow.	Your description is disorganized and hard to follow.
Accuracy	Your description has few mistakes in grammar and vocabulary.	Your description has some mistakes in grammar and vocabulary.	Your description has many mistakes in grammar and vocabulary.

Más práctica Cuaderno *pp. 33–34* Cuaderno para hispanohablantes *pp. 35–36*

PARA Y PIENSA

Did you get it? Create sentences with the following information.

1. Alberto / chico(a) / simpático(a)
2. Ricardo / estudiante / trabajador(a)
3. Sandra / persona / organizado(a)

Get Help Online
ClassZone.com

Juegos y diversiones

Review descriptive adjectives, noun-adjective agreement, and indefinite articles by playing a game.

20 preguntas

The Setup

Get a good look at your classmates, as you will need to identify them based on descriptions used in the game. Form two teams.

Palabras útiles

equipo *team*
puntos *points*

Playing the Game

First: One person from each team will go to the board and face the class, with his or her back to the board.

Then: Your teacher will write on the board the name of someone in the class. Each player at the board will alternate asking a yes/no question to his or her teammates about the mystery person. The player at the board who correctly identifies the mystery person first gets a point for his or her team.

Two new players go to the board, and the game continues.

The Winner!

The team with the most points at the end wins.

Lectura cultural

Goal: Read about things to do in San Antonio and Miami. Then compare what teens do in those cities with what you like to do where you live.

Comparación cultural

AUDIO

Saludos desde [1]
San Antonio y Miami

STRATEGY Leer

Make a comparison chart
Create a chart like the one below to compare San Antonio and Miami.

	San Antonio	Miami
sitios de interés		
actividades		
comida		

En San Antonio, Texas, hay [2] parques de diversiones [3], museos [4], el Paseo del Río y el Álamo. Después de las clases, a los chicos y a las chicas les gusta pasar un rato con los amigos en El Mercado, donde es posible escuchar música de los mariachis y comer comida típica mexicana.

---

[1] **Saludos...** Greetings from   [2] there are
[3] amusement parks   [4] museums

San Antonio

El Álamo en San Antonio, Texas

En Miami, Florida, si[5] hace buen tiempo, a los chicos y a las chicas les gusta andar en patineta o montar en bicicleta. Después de las clases, a muchos chicos les gusta pasear con los amigos por la Calle Ocho, en la Pequeña Habana de Miami. ¡Es una pequeña Cuba en la Florida! Allí[6] es posible comer sándwiches cubanos y beber jugo de mango.

---

[5] if   [6] There

Andar en patineta en Miami, Florida

PARA Y PIENSA

¿Comprendiste?
1. ¿Qué hay en San Antonio?
2. ¿Qué les gusta hacer a muchos chicos en Miami?
3. ¿Qué hay en la Pequeña Habana de Miami?

¿Y tú?
¿De dónde eres? ¿Qué te gusta hacer después de las clases?

Proyectos culturales

Platos tradicionales de México y Cuba

Why do traditional dishes change when they are brought from one country to another? In the U.S. we enjoy foods from many different Spanish-speaking countries. In many parts of the U.S. you can easily find dishes from Mexico, the Caribbean, Central America, and South America. Yet you might be surprised that those dishes aren't exactly the same as they are in their countries of origin. Here are two traditional recipes. The original list of ingredients for both has been modified to include foods more readily available in the U.S. They also reflect the widespread cooking practices and tastes that were already in place when the recipes were brought to this country.

Proyecto 2 Sándwich cubano

Cuba This is a traditional Cuban lunch dish found throughout Florida. The sandwich is pressed in a special grill or on a skillet.

Proyecto 1 Salsa fresca

México This is a common sauce in Mexico and all Central America. It is made from scratch and can be eaten as a dip with tortilla chips.

Ingredients for sándwich cubano
1 long sandwich roll
Slices of roast pork, ham, turkey, or bacon
Slice of Swiss or monterey jack cheese
Mustard or mayonnaise
Olive oil

Instructions
First brush the outside of the roll with olive oil. Then split it open and lay meat, cheese, and mustard or mayonnaise as desired. Put the sandwich in a hot skillet, placing a small, heavy skillet on top and pressing lightly. Cook three minutes or until cheese melts and bread is toasted.

Ingredients for salsa fresca
4–5 fresh tomatoes, diced
1 onion, diced
1 green chile, diced
1 clove of garlic, crushed
Juice of 1 fresh lime

Instructions
Combine the ingredients in a bowl. Cover and let stand for an hour in the refrigerator so that the flavors mix. Serve with tortilla chips.

En tu comunidad

Check your phone book for restaurants that serve foods from Mexico, Cuba, or other Spanish-speaking countries. Do any of the restaurants in your area serve **salsa fresca** or **sándwiches cubanos**?

Animated Grammar
Interactive Flashcards
ClassZone.com

Vocabulario

Describe Yourself and Others

¿Cómo eres?	*What are you like?*

Personality

artístico(a)	*artistic*
atlético(a)	*athletic*
bueno(a)	*good*
cómico(a)	*funny*
desorganizado(a)	*disorganized*
estudioso(a)	*studious*
inteligente	*intelligent*
malo(a)	*bad*
organizado(a)	*organized*
perezoso(a)	*lazy*
serio(a)	*serious*
simpático(a)	*nice*
trabajador(a)	*hard-working*

Appearance

alto(a)	*tall*
bajo(a)	*short (height)*
bonito(a)	*pretty*
grande	*big, large; great*
guapo(a)	*good-looking*
joven (pl. jóvenes)	*young*
pelirrojo(a)	*red-haired*
pequeño(a)	*small*
viejo(a)	*old*
Tengo...	*I have . . .*
Tiene...	*He / She has . . .*
pelo rubio	*blond hair*
pelo castaño	*brown hair*

People

el (la) amigo(a)	*friend*
la chica	*girl*
el chico	*boy*
el (la) estudiante	*student*
el hombre	*man*
la mujer	*woman*
la persona	*person*

Other Words and Phrases

muy	*very*
un poco	*a little*
porque	*because*
todos(as)	*all*

Gramática

Nota gramatical: **ser** to describe what someone is like *p. 63*

Definite and Indefinite Articles

In Spanish, articles match nouns in gender and number.

		Definite Article	Noun	Indefinite Article	Noun
Masculine	Singular	el	chico	un	chico
	Plural	los	chicos	unos	chicos
Feminine	Singular	la	chica	una	chica
	Plural	las	chicas	unas	chicas

Noun-Adjective Agreement

In Spanish, adjectives match the gender and number of the nouns they describe.

	Singular	Plural
Masculine	el chico alto	los chicos altos
Feminine	la chica alta	las chicas altas

Repaso de la lección

¡LLEGADA!

@HomeTutor
ClassZone.com

Now you can
- describe yourself and others
- identify people and things

Using
- **ser** to describe what someone is like
- definite and indefinite articles
- noun-adjective agreement

To review
- definite and indefinite articles p. 66
- **ser** to describe what someone is like p. 63
- noun-adjective agreement p. 72

1 | Listen and understand

AUDIO

Listen to Carlos talk about himself and his teacher. Then write a description of Carlos and Mrs. Pérez, according to what Carlos says.

To review
- definite and indefinite articles p. 66

2 | Identify people and things

Identify the people in the drawing.

modelo: señor viejo / hombre
El señor viejo es un hombre de Honduras.

México   Honduras   Uruguay   Panamá   Bolivia   Argentina   Estados Unidos

1. chica pelirroja / estudiante
2. hombre grande / maestro
3. chicos pelirrojos / amigos
4. mujer joven / maestra

5. señora alta / mujer
6. chico atlético / estudiante
7. chico desorganizado / persona
8. hombres simpáticos / amigos

To review
• noun-adjective agreement p. 72

3 | Describe yourself and others

Read this entry in Alejandra's diary. Complete the entry with the correct form of the word in parentheses.

lunes

Todos mis amigos son muy __1.__ (simpático). Miguel es un chico __2.__ (inteligente) y muy __3.__ (guapo). Beatriz es __4.__ (bonito) y __5.__ (estudioso). A Miguel y a Beatriz les gusta practicar deportes porque son __6.__ (atlético). Carmen y yo no somos __7.__ (atlético). Nosotras somos __8.__ (artístico). Todos nosotros somos unos estudiantes __9.__ (serio) y muy __10.__ (bueno).

To review
• **ser** to describe what someone is like p. 63
• noun-adjective agreement p. 72

4 | Describe yourself and others

Ramón and Ramona are complete opposites. Write sentences describing them, based on the descriptions.

modelo: **Ramón es malo.**
Ramona es buena.

1. Ramón es viejo.
2. Ramona es seria.
3. Ramón es organizado.
4. Ramona es pequeña.
5. Ramón es perezoso.
6. Ramona es baja.

To review
• Comparación cultural pp. 58, 65, 75
• Lectura cultural pp. 80–81

5 | United States

Comparación cultural

Answer these culture questions.

1. What can people do at San Antonio's Paseo del Río?
2. Give an example of a Tex-Mex dish and a Mexican dish.
3. When do people generally use **cascarones** and what do they do with them?
4. What can people do in San Antonio's El Mercado and Miami's Calle Ocho?

Más práctica Cuaderno *pp. 35–46* Cuaderno para hispanohablantes *pp. 37–46*

Get Help Online
ClassZone.com

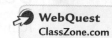

Comparación cultural

AUDIO

Me gusta...

Lectura y escritura

🔎 **WebQuest**
ClassZone.com

① **Leer** Read how José Manuel, Martina, and Mónica describe themselves and state their favorite activities.

② **Escribir** Using the three descriptions as models, write a short paragraph about yourself.

> **STRATEGY Escribir**
> **Use a personal chart**
> Make a chart showing information about yourself. This will help you write your description.

Categoría	Detalles
país de origen	
descripción física	
personalidad	
actividades favoritas	
comidas favoritas	

Step 1 Complete the chart by adding details about where you are from, a physical description, personality, and favorite activities and foods.

Step 2 Write your paragraph, including all the information from your chart. Check your writing by yourself or with help from a friend. Make final corrections.

Compara con tu mundo

Use the paragraph you wrote to compare your personal description to a description by *one* of the three students. What similarities do you find? What differences?

Cuaderno *pp. 47–49*   Cuaderno para hispanohablantes *pp. 47–49*

Colombia
José Manuel

Me llamo José Manuel. Soy de Bogotá. Soy cómico y un poco desorganizado pero también soy estudioso. Después de hacer la tarea me gusta jugar al fútbol con mis amigos en el parque El Tunal. También me gusta mirar el fútbol en la televisión.

Estados Unidos
Martina

¡Hola! Me llamo Martina y soy de Miami. Soy inteligente, alta y atlética. Los domingos, me gusta montar en bicicleta. También me gusta preparar jugo de mango o de melón con mi amiga, María. Nos gusta beber mucho jugo porque en Miami hace calor.

México
Mónica

¿Qué tal? Me llamo Mónica y soy de México, D.F. Tengo pelo castaño y soy seria. Mis amigas Maite y Alejandra también tienen pelo castaño y son muy simpáticas. Maite y yo somos artísticas. Nos gusta tocar la guitarra. También nos gusta dibujar.

Repaso inclusivo
♻ Options for Review

1 | Listen, understand, and compare

Escuchar

Listen to two teen radio reporters talk about typical after-school activities in Miami and San Antonio. Then answer the questions.

1. ¿Cómo son los estudiantes de Miami?
2. ¿Qué les gusta hacer a los estudiantes de Miami?
3. ¿Cómo son los estudiantes de San Antonio?
4. ¿Qué tiempo hace en San Antonio?
5. ¿Qué les gusta hacer a los estudiantes de San Antonio?

Are you and your friends like the students in Miami and/or San Antonio? Do you like to do the same kinds of activities?

2 | Oral presentation

Hablar

Your principal is making a video about your school and you are going to be a featured student. In a segment that lasts at least 30 seconds, introduce yourself, say where you are from, describe yourself, and talk about what you like to do after school.

3 | Role-play conversation

Hablar

Role-play a conversation with a new student at your school. The new student, played by your partner, will introduce himself or herself and ask you what you are like and what you and your friends like to do. Answer the new student's questions and ask questions of your own to get to know him or her. Your conversation should be at least two minutes long.

¿Cómo eres?

Soy inteligente y atlética.

4 | Create a yearbook entry

Bring in a photo of yourself and create a caption that could be used in a yearbook. Give your name, where you are from, what you are like, who you like to spend time with, and what activities you like to do. Copy this chart on a piece of paper and use it to organize your information.

¿Cómo te llamas?	
¿De dónde eres?	
¿Cómo eres?	
¿Qué te gusta hacer?	

5 | Create a collage

Hablar

Work with a partner to create individual collages. Use magazine clippings, photos, or your own drawings. Use the collage to introduce yourself to your partner, say where you are from, and show some of the things you like to do. When you finish, exchange your collages and use them to introduce each other to the class.

6 | Write a profile

Leer
Escribir

You are collecting information for this school's Web site. Read the questionnaire and write a profile of this student. Include his name, where he is from, and what he likes and doesn't like to do.

Escuela Secundaria Cuauhtémoc
Cuestionario estudiantil

Nombre: Esteban Leñeros

País de origen: México

ACTIVIDADES

¿Qué te gusta hacer? practicar deportes, estudiar, comer enchiladas, escuchar música

¿Qué no te gusta hacer? andar en patineta, comer helado, dibujar

Estados Unidos
ochenta y nueve   89

UNIDAD 2

México

¡Vamos a la escuela!

Lección 1
Tema: **Somos estudiantes**

Lección 2
Tema: **En la escuela**

«**¡Hola!**
Somos Pablo y Claudia.
Somos de México.»

Estados Unidos

• Ciudad Juárez

• Chihuahua

BAJA
CALIFORNIA

Golfo de California

México

• Monterrey

Golfo de
México

Bahía de
Campeche

• Chichén Itzá

*Océano
Pacífico*

Zempoala

• San Miguel de Allende

PENÍNSULA
DE YUCATÁN

Guadalajara

México, D.F. ★   • Puebla

Oaxaca •

Guatemala

El Salvador

Población: 104.959.594

Área: 761.606 millas cuadradas

Capital: México, D.F. (Ciudad de México)

Moneda: el peso mexicano

Idiomas: español, maya y otras lenguas
indígenas; el país con más hispanohablantes
del mundo

Comida típica: tortillas, tacos, enchiladas

Gente famosa: Carlos Fuentes (escritor), Salma Hayek
(actriz), Mario Molina (químico), Thalía (cantante)

Chocolate

*Jóvenes en el Jardín Principal
de San Miguel de Allende*

◀ **Un rato con familia y amigos** In San Miguel de Allende, people of all ages go to the **Jardín Principal,** a tree-lined park in the center of town, to stroll, listen to live music, and spend time with family and friends. *When you want to spend time outside, where do you go?*

La estatua de Chac-Mool y la pirámide de Kukulcán

Las ruinas de Chichén Itzá The ruins of the ancient Mayan city of Chichén Itzá include structures built for worship, sports, and studying astronomy. The pyramid of **Kukulcán** was used as a temple. *What are some important buildings in your area used for?* ▶

◀ **Una universidad con mucha historia y arte** La Universidad Nacional Autónoma de México (UNAM) is one of the oldest universities in the Americas, and the largest public university in Mexico, with over 270,000 students. The library's mosaic mural depicts moments in the cultural history of Mexico. *What are some well-known universities in your area?*

*La biblioteca de la UNAM
con el mural mosaico*

México

Lección 1

Tema:

Somos estudiantes

¡AVANZA!

In this lesson you will learn to
- talk about daily schedules
- ask and tell time
- say what you have and have to do
- say what you do and how often you do things

using
- the verb **tener** and **tener que**
- expressions of frequency
- present tense of **-ar** verbs

♻ ¿Recuerdas?
- after-school activities
- days of the week

Comparación cultural

In this lesson you will learn about
- what students wear to school
- Mexican mural painter Diego Rivera
- courses in a bilingual school in Mexico

Compara con tu mundo
These Mexican students are walking to school through a **zócalo,** or a town square. These are very common in Mexico and other Spanish-speaking countries, where they are also called **plazas.** *Does your city or town have a main square? If not, is there a central meeting place?*

¿Qué ves?
Mira la foto
¿Hace sol?
¿Es domingo o lunes?
¿Cómo es él? ¿Y ella?

Online SPANISH **CLASSZONE.COM**

Featuring...
Cultura INTERACTIVA
Animated Grammar
@HomeTutor

And more...
• Get Help Online
• Interactive Flashcards
• Review Games
• WebQuest
• Self-Check Quiz

La fuente de San Miguel en el Zócalo
Puebla, México

Presentación de VOCABULARIO

¡AVANZA! **Goal:** Learn about Pablo's school and class schedule. Then practice what you have learned to talk about daily schedules. *Actividades 1–2*

VIDEO DVD

AUDIO

A ¡Hola! Me llamo Pablo. Mi amiga es Claudia. Somos estudiantes **en** Puebla, México. Me gusta **llegar** a clase **temprano.** Claudia, **¿qué hora es?**

7:00 matemáticas
8:10 ciencias
9:15 usar la computadora
10:15 inglés
11:50 arte
12:30 historia
1:30 español
3:30 jugar al fútbol

el horario

Más vocabulario

de vez en cuando *once in a while*
muchas veces *often, many times*
nunca *never*
todos los días *every day*
casi *almost*
difícil *difficult*
fácil *easy*
hay... *there is, there are . . .*
la hora *hour; time*
el minuto *minute*
¿Cuántos(as)...? *How many . . . ?*
Expansión de vocabulario p. R3

Numbers from 11 to 100

11 once	20 veinte	30 treinta
12 doce	21 veintiuno	31 treinta y uno
13 trece	22 veintidós	
14 catorce	23 veintitrés	40 cuarenta
15 quince	24 veinticuatro	50 cincuenta
16 dieciséis	25 veinticinco	60 sesenta
17 diecisiete	26 veintiséis	70 setenta
18 dieciocho	27 veintisiete	80 ochenta
19 diecinueve	28 veintiocho	90 noventa
	29 veintinueve	100 cien

B ¿A qué hora son mis clases? Tengo muchas clases.

las matemáticas

La clase de **matemáticas** es **a las siete de la mañana.**

las ciencias

La clase de **ciencias** es **a las ocho y diez** de la mañana.

el inglés

La clase de **inglés** es **a las diez y cuarto** de la mañana.

el arte

La clase de **arte** es **a las doce menos diez** de la mañana.

la historia

La clase de **historia** es **a las doce y media de la tarde.**

el español

La clase de **español** es **a la una y media** de la tarde.

Continuará...

C Son las ocho y diez y tengo la clase de ciencias. A Claudia **siempre** le gusta **contestar** las preguntas del maestro. Ella es muy inteligente. Yo **tengo que** estudiar **mucho** y **tomar apuntes** en clase.

enseñar

contestar

tomar apuntes

D Tengo que **sacar una buena nota** en la clase de inglés. A Claudia y a mí nos gusta estudiar a las ocho **de la noche.** Es un poco **tarde** pero **necesito** estudiar. ¡No me gusta **sacar una mala nota**!

sacar una buena nota

el examen

usar la computadora

¡A responder! Escuchar

On separate pieces of paper, write the words **la mañana** and **la tarde.** Listen to Pablo describe his schedule. Hold up the piece of paper that indicates when he has each class.

@HomeTutor VideoPlus
Interactive Flashcards
ClassZone.com

Práctica de VOCABULARIO

1 | Las clases de Claudia

Hablar Escribir

Identify Claudia's classes according to the time.

modelo: a la una y diez
A la una y diez Claudia tiene la clase de español.

1. a las once menos cuarto   **4.** a las nueve menos veinte

2. a las siete y media   **5.** a las nueve y cuarto

3. a las doce   **6.** a las dos y media

Nota gramatical

For the numbers **21, 31,** and so on, use **veintiún, treinta y un,** and so on before a masculine noun and **veintiuna, treinta y una,** and so on before a feminine noun.

Hay **veintiún** maestros en la escuela.   Hay **treinta y una** personas en mi clase.
*There are **twenty-one** teachers in the school.*   *There are **thirty-one** people in my class.*

2 | ¿Cuántas personas?

Hablar

Ask a partner how many people there are in these classes.

modelo: chicos / historia
y arte (29)

A ¿Cuántos chicos hay en las clases de historia y arte?

B Hay veintinueve chicos en las clases de historia y arte.

1. chicas / matemáticas (16)

2. estudiantes / inglés y arte (58)

3. chicos / historia y ciencias (27)   **6.** estudiantes / arte (40)

4. estudiantes / historia y arte (62)   **7.** chicas / todas las clases (71)

5. chicas / música y español (33)   **8.** chicos / todas las clases (74)

Más práctica   Cuaderno *pp. 51–53*   Cuaderno para hispanohablantes *pp. 51–54*

PARA Y PIENSA

Did you get it?   **1.** Tell someone you like to draw in art class.
2. Say that there are 23 boys in math class.

Get Help Online
ClassZone.com

VOCABULARIO *en contexto*

¡AVANZA! **Goal:** Listen to how Pablo and Claudia talk about at what time they will study. Then practice these words to ask and tell time. *Actividades 3–4*

Telehistoria escena 1

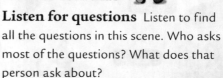
@**HomeTutor** VideoPlus
ClassZone.com

STRATEGIES

Cuando lees

Focus on time Read for expressions of time like **hoy** or **a las ocho.** How many can you find in this scene? What do they mean?

Cuando escuchas

Listen for questions Listen to find all the questions in this scene. Who asks most of the questions? What does that person ask about?

VIDEO DVD

AUDIO

Claudia

Pablo

Claudia: Pablo, hay examen de ciencias mañana, ¿no?

Pablo: Sí... Me gusta la clase de ciencias, pero... sacar una buena nota, un 90 o un 100, ¡es difícil!

Claudia: Necesitas estudiar una o dos horas... ¿Te gusta estudiar con amigos?

Pablo: Sí... pero hoy no. ¡Hay fútbol! ¿Mañana?

Claudia: Sí. ¿En la escuela?

Pablo: Sí. ¿A las ocho de la mañana? ¿O más temprano?

Claudia: A las siete de la mañana. ¿Está bien?

Pablo: ¡Sí!

The bell rings, and they part ways for class.

Pablo: Hmmm... Hay chicas muy inteligentes en la escuela...

Continuará... p. 104

3 | Planes para estudiar *Comprensión del episodio*

Escuchar
Leer

True or false? If the statement is false, say what is true.

1. Hay un examen en la clase de español mañana.
2. A Pablo le gusta estudiar con amigos, pero hoy no.
3. A Pablo le gusta la clase de ciencias.
4. Hay fútbol hoy.
5. La clase de ciencias es fácil.

Nota gramatical

- Use **Es la una** to say that it is one o'clock; use **Son las...** for any other time.
  Son las cinco.   *It is 5:00.*

- Use **y** + **minutes** for the number of minutes after the hour (up to 30).
  Son las dos **y diez.**   *It is 2:10.*

- Use **menos** + **minutes** for the number of minutes before the hour.
  Es la una **menos veinte.**   *It is 12:40.*

- Use **y** or **menos cuarto** for a quarter of an hour and **y media** for half an hour.

- To say at what time something happens, use **a la(s)...**
  La clase de arte es **a la** una y la clase de inglés es **a las** dos.

4 | El horario de clases

Escribir

Write the times of Marisol's classes.

modelo: La clase de historia es a las siete de la mañana.

MARISOL AGUILAR	
HORA	LUNES
7:00	HISTORIA
8:15	MATEMÁTICAS
9:30	INGLÉS
10:45	ARTE
1:05	CIENCIAS
2:10	ESPAÑOL

PARA
Y
PIENSA

Did you get it? Complete each sentence with the appropriate time.
1. El jueves Claudia tiene que llegar a la escuela _____ . (10:15)
2. Son _____ . (8:20)
3. A Pablo le gusta hacer la tarea _____ de la noche. (7:00)

Get Help Online
ClassZone.com

Lección 1
noventa y nueve **99**

Presentación de GRAMÁTICA

Goal: Learn how to form the verb **tener**. Then use this verb to say what people have and have to do and how often. *Actividades 5–9*

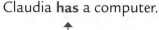 *¿Recuerdas?* After-school activities p. 32

English Grammar Connection: Conjugating is changing the forms of a verb to indicate who is doing the action. For example, the English verb *to have* is conjugated as *I have, you have, he/she/it has, we have, they have.*

Claudia **has** a computer.

Claudia **tiene** una computadora.

> **conjugated verb**

> **conjugated verb**

The Verb tener

Use the verb **tener** to talk about what you have. How do you conjugate this verb?

Here's how:

tener *to have*			
yo	**tengo**	nosotros(as)	**tenemos**
tú	**tienes**	vosotros(as)	**tenéis**
usted, él, ella	**tiene**	ustedes, ellos(as)	**tienen**

Tenemos clase el lunes.
We have class on Monday.

¿**Tienes** una bicicleta?
Do you have a bike?

Tener + **que** + **infinitive** is used to talk about what someone has to do.

Tengo que estudiar.
I have to study.

Miguel **tiene que leer** un libro.
Miguel has to read a book.

Más práctica
Cuaderno *pp. 54–56*
Cuaderno para hispanohablantes *pp. 55–57*

@HomeTutor
Leveled Grammar Practice
ClassZone.com

Práctica de GRAMÁTICA

5 | Los amigos de Raquel

Leer
Escribir

Use the appropriate forms of the verb **tener** to complete Raquel's description of her closest friends.

Yo __1.__ muchos amigos diferentes. Mi mejor amigo, Rafael, es un estudiante muy serio. Él __2.__ seis clases muy difíciles, y __3.__ que estudiar muchas horas todos los días. Mis amigas Clara y Linda son altas y __4.__ pelo castaño. ¡Son muy atléticas! Los lunes, martes y miércoles ellas __5.__ que practicar fútbol. Los viernes, mis amigos y yo __6.__ que trabajar. ¿Qué tipo de amigos __7.__ tú?

6 | Las clases

Escribir

Write what classes these people have, using forms of **tener.**

1. yo

2. nosotros

3. Claudia y Pablo

4. tú

5. Claudia

6. ustedes

AUDIO

Pronunciación   **El sonido ch**

In Spanish, the **ch** sounds like the *ch* of the English word *chip*.

Listen and repeat.

cha	mucha
che	noche
chi	chico
cho	dieciocho
chu	churro

Muchas chicas escuchan música de Pancho Sánchez.

7 | ¿Qué tienes?

Hablar

Find out what items your partner has in his or her room by forming questions with the verb **tener.** Take turns asking and answering.

modelo: una computadora

A ¿Tienes **una computadora**?

B Sí, tengo **una computadora**. (No, no tengo **computadora**.)

1. un DVD
2. una patineta
3. un refresco
4. una bicicleta

5. un teléfono
6. una guitarra
7. un libro de matemáticas
8. una galleta

8 | ¿Qué tienen que hacer?

Escuchar Escribir

Listen to Pablo's description of what he and his friends have to do. Then write sentences indicating what time it is and who has to do these activities.

1. estudiar
2. usar la computadora
3. hacer la tarea

4. tocar la guitarra
5. trabajar
6. leer un libro

Comparación cultural

Estudiantes en México y la República Dominicana

Uniformes escolares

How does the way students dress reflect a culture? In **Mexico,** it is common for students to wear uniforms in both public and private schools. The type and color of the uniforms can vary depending on the individual school. Most students in the **Dominican Republic** also wear uniforms. Public schools have the same uniforms, while private school uniforms may vary.

Compara con tu mundo *Why do some schools require uniforms? Are they common in your community? If you were a principal, would you have uniforms at your school?*

Nota gramatical

The expressions of frequency **siempre** and **nunca** are usually placed before the verb.

Antonio **siempre** toma apuntes.   Antonio **always** takes notes.

Rafael **nunca** llega a clase tarde.   Rafael **never** arrives late to class.

Mucho is usually placed after the verb.

Raquel estudia **mucho**.   Raquel studies **a lot**.

De vez en cuando, muchas veces, and **todos los días** are usually placed at the beginning or the end of the sentence.

Todos los días Jaime trabaja.   Jaime works **every day**.

Jaime trabaja **todos los días**.

---

9 Las obligaciones ♻ *¿Recuerdas?* After-school activities p. 32

Hablar

Ask other students whether they have to do these activities. They will respond using an expression of frequency.

A ¿Tienen que tomar apuntes ustedes?

B Sí, tengo que tomar apuntes muchas veces.

C Sí, tengo que tomar apuntes de vez en cuando.

1.

2.

3.

4.

5.

6.

Más práctica   Cuaderno *pp. 54–56*   Cuaderno para hispanohablantes *pp. 55–57*

PARA Y PIENSA

Did you get it? Answer each question with the word(s) in parentheses.
1. ¿Tiene que preparar la comida Juan? (nunca)
2. ¿Cuándo tenemos la clase de inglés? (todos los días)
3. ¿Tienes que usar la computadora? (siempre)

⟳ **Get Help Online**
ClassZone.com

GRAMÁTICA *en contexto*

Goal: Notice how Pablo and Claudia use the verb phrase **tener que** to talk about what they do at school. Then use **tener** and **tener que** to say what you and others have and have to do. *Actividades 10–12*

♻ *¿Recuerdas?* Days of the week p. 18

Telehistoria escena 2

@HomeTutor VideoPlus
ClassZone.com

STRATEGIES

Cuando lees
Find the "tag questions" This scene contains the "tag question" **¿no?** Where are the tag questions in a sentence? How do they differ from questions like **¿Quién es?**

Cuando escuchas
Weigh the motive Listen for Pablo's reasons for not studying for the test. What are his reasons? Do they sound credible to you? Have you ever used them?

VIDEO
DVD

AUDIO

Pablo's cell phone rings.

Pablo: Hola... ¿Quién es? ¡Claudia! ¿Qué tal?... Sí, sí, a las siete. ¡Tenemos que estudiar mucho!

The next morning, Claudia and Pablo walk to class.

Claudia: Pablo, tienes que estudiar más, ¿no?

Pablo: Sí. Tenemos mucha tarea y los exámenes son muy difíciles.

Claudia: Pero te gusta sacar buenas notas, ¿no?

Pablo: Sí. Tenemos que estudiar más.

Continuará... p. 110

También se dice

México Pablo uses the word **tarea** to talk about homework. In other Spanish-speaking countries you might hear:
• **muchos países** los **deberes**

10 | Un examen importante *Comprensión del episodio*

Escuchar
Leer

Choose the correct answers to the questions.

1. ¿Qué tienen que hacer Pablo y Claudia?
  a. Tienen que descansar mucho.
  b. Tienen que estudiar.
  c. Tienen que enseñar.

2. ¿A qué hora tienen que estudiar?
  a. a las siete
  b. a las siete y media
  c. a las ocho

3. ¿Qué tienen Pablo y Claudia?
  a. muchos libros
  b. un poco de tarea
  c. mucha tarea

4. ¿Qué le gusta hacer a Pablo?
  a. Le gusta estudiar.
  b. Le gusta llegar tarde.
  c. Le gusta sacar buenas notas.

11 | Las responsabilidades ♻ *¿Recuerdas?* Days of the week p. 18

Escribir

You have a lot to do this week. Write an e-mail explaining five things that you have to do this week.

modelo:

```
Hola, Jeff.
Tengo mucho que hacer. El lunes tengo que practicar
la guitarra. El martes tengo que hacer la tarea...
```

12 | ¿Y tú?

Hablar
Escribir

Answer the questions in complete sentences.

1. ¿Qué clases tienes? ¿Son fáciles o difíciles?

2. ¿A qué hora tienes la clase de español?

3. ¿Tienes que tomar apuntes? ¿En qué clases?

4. ¿Qué tienes que hacer todos los días?

5. ¿Qué tienes que hacer todos los sábados y domingos?

6. ¿Qué nunca tienes que hacer?

7. ¿Tienes que trabajar? ¿A qué hora?

8. ¿A qué hora necesitas llegar a la escuela?

PARA Y PIENSA

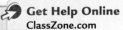
Get Help Online
ClassZone.com

Did you get it? ¿**Tener** or **tener que**? Complete each sentence based on the Telehistoria with the correct form of the verb or expression.
  1. Pablo y Claudia _____ mucha tarea.
  2. Pablo _____ estudiar mucho.
  3. Ellos _____ un examen en la clase de ciencias.

Presentación de GRAMÁTICA

Goal: Learn the forms of **-ar** verbs. Then practice using the verbs to say what people do. *Actividades 13–19*

English Grammar Connection: A **verb tense** is the form of the verb that shows *when* an action is happening. The **present tense** shows that an action is happening *now*. The Spanish present-tense verb form **estudiamos** can be expressed in English in three different ways: *we study, we are studying,* or *we do study.*

We **study** Spanish.   **Estudiamos** español.

↑   ↑

[**present-tense verb**]   [**present-tense verb**]

Many infinitives in Spanish end in **-ar.** How do you form the present tense of these verbs?

Here's how: In Spanish, the present tense is formed by changing the ending of the verb.

To form the present tense of a regular verb that ends in **-ar,** drop the **-ar** and add the appropriate **ending.**

habl~~ar~~ ◀ o, as, a, amos, áis, or an

hablar *to talk, to speak*		
yo	**hablo**	nosotros(as)	**hablamos**
tú	**hablas**	vosotros(as)	**habláis**
usted, él, ella	**habla**	ustedes, ellos(as)	**hablan**

Hablo inglés.   ¿**Hablan** español?

I speak English.   *Do they speak* Spanish?
I am speaking English.   *Are they speaking* Spanish?
I do speak English.

Más práctica

Cuaderno *pp. 57–59*
Cuaderno para hispanohablantes *pp. 58–61*

@HomeTutor
Leveled Grammar Practice
ClassZone.com

Práctica de GRAMÁTICA

13 | ¿Tarde o temprano?

Escribir

Claudia is throwing a surprise party for Pablo and wants all the guests to arrive at seven o'clock sharp. Use the cues to state at what time people arrive at the party. Then tell whether they arrive early or late.

> **modelo:** Luis y Carmen / 8:00
> Luis y Carmen llegan a las ocho. Llegan tarde.

1. nosotros / 5:30
2. Marta / 7:15
3. yo / 6:45
4. Marcos y Benito / 6:00
5. la señora Jiménez / 7:40

6. ellas / 9:25
7. tú / 6:05
8. María y Enrique / 8:10
9. Sara y yo / 6:50
10. Pablo / 7:20

14 | Somos buenos estudiantes

Hablar Escribir

Pablo, Claudia, and their friends are good students. Explain whether they always or never do the following.

> **modelo:** Claudia / llegar a clase temprano
> Claudia **siempre** llega a clase temprano.

1. yo / escuchar en clase
2. Pablo / tomar apuntes
3. nosotros / sacar malas notas
4. Claudia y Pablo / estudiar

5. tú / contestar preguntas
6. Diego y yo / llegar a clase tarde
7. Lorena / mirar la televisión
8. ustedes / sacar buenas notas

15 | El fin de semana

Leer Escribir

Sandra likes to spend time with her friends. Complete the paragraph with the correct form of the appropriate verb.

> escuchar   tocar   alquilar   estudiar
>
> pasar   montar   dibujar   practicar

Nosotros **1.** en bicicleta después de las clases. Amy y Rosa **2.** deportes y yo **3.** la guitarra. A mi amigo Eduardo no le gusta descansar. Él **4.** inglés o **5.** para la clase de arte. Es muy artístico. Si llueve, nosotros **6.** música en un café o **7.** un DVD. ¿Dónde **8.** tú un rato con los amigos?

16 | ¿En la escuela?

Hablar

Ask another student whether he or she does these activities at school. Use expressions of frequency.

modelo: dibujar

A ¿Dibujas en la escuela?

B No, nunca dibujo en la escuela.

1. estudiar
2. escuchar música
3. comprar refrescos
4. practicar deportes
5. tocar la guitarra
6. pasar un rato con los amigos

17 | De septiembre a mayo

Hablar Escribir

Señorita Solar and her students have changed a great deal over the course of the school year. Look at the two drawings below and note the differences between the beginning and the end of the school year.

modelo: En septiembre, Susana escucha música.
En mayo, ella toma apuntes.

18 | ¿Qué estudias?

Hablar

Comparación cultural

Los murales en México

How does society affect public artwork? The Mexican government commissioned Diego Rivera to paint murals about **Mexico's** history. *Alfabetización* reflects the idea of free public education. Between 1920 and 1924, more than 1,000 schools were established in rural areas to teach children to read and study subjects such as history and math.

Compara con tu mundo *What would you paint in a mural representing your community? What objects or people would you include? What would your mural's message be?*

Detalle de Alfabetización *(1926), Diego Rivera*

Talk with a partner about your schedule and what you study.

A ¿Estudias ciencias?

B Sí, tengo la clase de ciencias a las once.

19 | Un sábado típico

Escribir Hablar

Describe what you do on Saturdays and how often you do it. Use verbs from the list. Then compare your activities with other students'.

alquilar   **estudiar**   **descansar**   **comprar**

escuchar   **usar**   **trabajar**   **¿ ?**

modelo: Siempre hablo por teléfono los sábados. Muchas veces paso un rato con las amigas. Nosotras alquilamos un DVD...

Más práctica   Cuaderno *pp. 57–59*   Cuaderno para hispanohablantes *pp. 58–61*

PARA Y PIENSA

Get Help Online
ClassZone.com

Did you get it? Complete each sentence with the correct form of the verb in parentheses.
1. Nosotros _____ la computadora mucho. (usar)
2. Yo _____ la comida de vez en cuando. (preparar)
3. Los chicos _____ en la clase de arte. (dibujar)
4. ¿ _____ tú sacar una buena nota? (necesitar)

Todo junto

Goal: *Show what you know* Pay attention to how Pablo and Claudia use **tener** and **-ar** verbs to talk about their test and what they do after school. Then use these verbs to say what you and others do during and after school. *Actividades 20–24*

Telehistoria completa

@HomeTutor VideoPlus
ClassZone.com

STRATEGIES

Cuando lees

Look for the unexpected As you read, look for two surprises involving Pablo. What are they? Why are they unexpected? What did you expect to happen?

Cuando escuchas

Listen for cognates Listen for cognates like **examen** (exam, test). What cognates do you hear? What English word(s) do they sound like? What do they mean?

Escena 1 *Resumen*

Pablo y Claudia necesitan estudiar porque tienen un examen de ciencias.

Escena 2 *Resumen*

Pablo y Claudia hablan por teléfono. Tienen que estudiar más.

VIDEO DVD

AUDIO

Escena 3

Roberto

Pablo: ¡Claudia! En el examen de ciencias, tengo... ¡un 90!

Claudia: ¡Y yo, un 100!

Pablo: ¿Estudiamos, tú y yo, todos los días?

Claudia: Sí... pero tú necesitas tomar buenos apuntes, ¿no? *(Pablo grins.)* ¿A qué hora practican fútbol?

Pablo: Muchas veces practicamos a las cinco. Mañana practicamos temprano, a las tres y media. ¿Y tú? ¿Qué necesitas hacer mañana?

Claudia: ¿Mañana? Estudiar y hacer la tarea de ciencias.

Claudia says goodbye and leaves. As his friend Roberto walks up, Pablo distractedly pulls Alicia's T-shirt out of his bag and puts it on.

Roberto: ¡Ay, Pablo, qué interesante!

Pablo, embarrassed, takes the shirt off quickly.

20 ¿Quién es? *Comprensión de los episodios*

Escuchar
Leer

Do these sentences refer to Claudia, Pablo, or Claudia and Pablo? Write the name or names and the correct form of the verb in parentheses.

Pablo

Claudia y Pablo

Claudia

1. ____ (tener) que practicar fútbol.
2. ____ (llegar) a la escuela a las siete de la mañana.
3. ____ (hablar) por teléfono.
4. ____ (necesitar) estudiar una o dos horas.

5. ____ (tener) un examen de ciencias.
6. ____ (sacar) una buena nota.
7. ____ (estudiar) para la clase de ciencias mañana.
8. ____ (practicar) a las tres y media mañana.

21 ¿Qué hacen? *Comprensión de los episodios*

Escuchar
Leer

Complete the sentences with information from the episodes.

1. Pablo y Claudia tienen que...
2. A las siete Pablo y Claudia...
3. Mañana Claudia...
4. Pablo necesita tomar...
5. Claudia y Pablo sacan...

22 ¿Qué tienes que hacer?

Hablar

STRATEGY Hablar

Create a dialogue of your own Use the model question and substitute different school subjects. Use the model answer, but change verbs, or use multiple verbs in a single sentence. Bring in humor if you can.

Talk with a partner about what you do and what you have to do in your classes.

A ¿Qué tienes que hacer en la clase de matemáticas?

B Tengo que tomar apuntes. Siempre escucho en clase...

23 | Integración

Leer
Escuchar
Hablar

Tomorrow is a teachers' meeting, so the class schedule is different. Read Manuel's schedule and listen to the principal's message. Tell at what time Manuel needs to arrive at each of his classes.

Fuente 1 Horario de clases

Rojas, Manuel		Colegio Benito Juárez
HORA	CLASE	MAESTRO
7:10	ciencias	Sra. Burgos
8:30	arte	Sr. Rivera
9:50	inglés	Sr. Ortiz
11:10	historia	Sra. Sánchez
1:20	español	Sr. Acevedo
2:40	matemáticas	Sra. Gala

Fuente 2 Mensaje del director

Listen and take notes
• ¿Cuántos minutos después de la hora normal son las clases de la mañana? ¿Las clases de la tarde?

modelo: Manuel necesita llegar a la clase de... a las...

24 | Tu horario

Escribir

Describe your school schedule. What classes do you have? At what times? What do you have to do every day? What do you do once in a while? What activities do you never do in class?

modelo: Tengo muchas clases en mi horario. Tengo la clase de español todos los días a las nueve menos cuarto. Llego a clase temprano...

Writing Criteria	Excellent	Good	Needs Work
Content	Your description includes a lot of information.	Your description includes some information.	Your description includes little information.
Communication	Most of your description is organized and easy to follow.	Parts of your description are organized and easy to follow.	Your description is disorganized and hard to follow.
Accuracy	Your description has few mistakes in grammar and vocabulary.	Your description has some mistakes in grammar and vocabulary.	Your description has many mistakes in grammar and vocabulary.

Más práctica Cuaderno *pp. 60–61* Cuaderno para hispanohablantes *pp. 62–63*

PARA Y PIENSA

Did you get it? Write the correct form of **tomar, estudiar,** or **practicar.**

1. Claudia siempre _____ buenos apuntes.
2. Pablo tiene que _____ fútbol a las cinco.
3. Pablo y Claudia _____ todos los días.

Get Help Online
ClassZone.com

Juegos y diversiones

Review numbers by playing a game.

Silencio

The Setup

The object of this game is to demonstrate understanding without speaking. For each round of play, your teacher will give each player an index card with a number written out in Spanish.

Your teacher will divide the class into several teams with one or two members of each team competing at a given time.

Playing the Game

Each round will have a different number line for highest and lowest. You will be asked to silently line up in order according to what is on your index card and where your card fits in the number line. Your teacher will use a timer, so you need to line up quickly or you will be disqualified and not have a chance to gain points.

The Winner!

Each student who lines up correctly will gain a point. The team with the most points at the end wins.

Materials

• index cards with Spanish words for various numbers
• timer
• cards for number line

Lectura

¡AVANZA! **Goal:** Read about the requirements for graduating from a bilingual school in Mexico. As you read these documents, compare them with the course requirements needed to graduate from your school.

AUDIO

Una escuela bilingüe en México

The following pages are from the student handbook for Colegio Americano, a bilingual school in Guadalajara, Mexico.

STRATEGY Leer

Use what you know As you read the graduation requirements of Colegio Americano, use what you know. Find words that sound and look somewhat similar to those in English — cognates like **ciencias** or **matemáticas.** Then use the context and what you already know to guess what **desarrollo humano** and **optativas** mean.

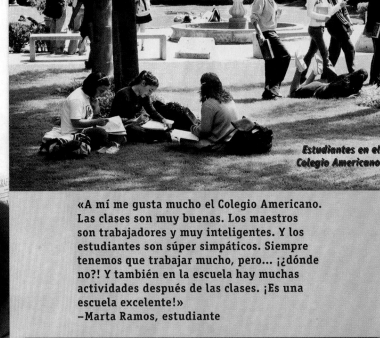

MANUAL DEL ESTUDIANTE

Estudiantes en el Colegio Americano

«A mí me gusta mucho el Colegio Americano. Las clases son muy buenas. Los maestros son trabajadores y muy inteligentes. Y los estudiantes son súper simpáticos. Siempre tenemos que trabajar mucho, pero... ¡¿dónde no?! Y también en la escuela hay muchas actividades después de las clases. ¡Es una escuela excelente!»
—Marta Ramos, estudiante

COLEGIO AMERICANO
Colomos 2100 Colonia Providencia
Guadalajara, Jalisco 44640 México
http://www.asfg.mx

Requisitos para graduarse de bachillerato

A continuación [1], los requisitos para graduarse con los dos certificados: el certificado mexicano y el certificado estadounidense.

Clase	Número de unidades
Inglés	4 unidades
Español	4 unidades
Matemáticas	4 unidades
Ciencias	4 unidades
Ciencias Sociales de México	1 unidad
Historia de México II	1 unidad
Geografía de México	1 unidad
Derecho [2]	1 unidad
Ciencias Sociales	3 unidades
Computación	0,5 unidades
Educación Física	0,5 unidades
Desarrollo Humano [3]	1 unidad
Optativas [4]	2 unidades
Total	**27 unidades**

COLEGIO AMERICANO

[1] **A...** following are [2] Law
[3] Human Development [4] Electives

PARA Y PIENSA

¿Comprendiste?

1. ¿Cuántas clases necesitas para los dos programas?
2. ¿Cuántas unidades de matemáticas tienes que tomar?

¿Y tú?

¿Qué clases del Colegio Americano hay en tu escuela? ¿Cómo son?

Conexiones *La historia*

El pueblo de Zempoala

In 1577, the Spanish crown sent a questionnaire to Mexico to get information about its territories in the New World. The responses that were sent back included local maps drawn by indigenous mapmakers.

The map below depicts the town (**pueblo**) of Zempoala, located in the modern Mexican state of Hidalgo. Research Zempoala to learn more about the town and this map. Then choose three specific map symbols not listed in the legend (**leyenda**) and explain what you think they mean.

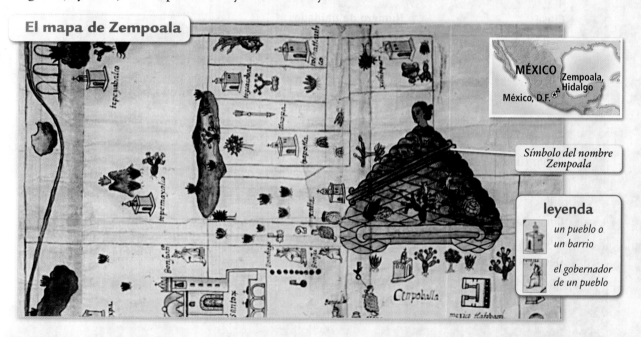

El mapa de Zempoala

MÉXICO
Zempoala, Hidalgo
México, D.F.

Símbolo del nombre Zempoala

leyenda

un pueblo o un barrio

el gobernador de un pueblo

Proyecto 1 *El arte*

Draw a map of your town or city similar to the one of Zempoala. Give information about people, buildings, roads, and vegetation. Use symbols like the ones in the map above and label them in Spanish.

Proyecto 2 *Las ciencias sociales*

In 1968, Mexico established a televised system of secondary schools called **Telesecundaria.** Today, educational video programs are broadcast via satellite to more than 15,000 schools. Write two paragraphs about the use of technology in education. How is it used in your school? Can you think of other ways it can be used in education?

Proyecto 3 *La salud*

The map of Zempoala shows a number of cacti. The cactus has been an important source of food and medicine for people in Mexico for many years. Make a list of different types of cacti found in Mexico and create a chart showing how people have used them for health and beauty purposes.

Un nopal con flores

En resumen
Vocabulario y gramática

Animated Grammar
Interactive Flashcards
ClassZone.com

Vocabulario

Tell Time and Discuss Daily Schedules

¿A qué hora es...?	At what time is...?	la hora	hour; time
¿Qué hora es?	What time is it?	el horario	schedule
A la(s)...	At ... o'clock.	menos	to, before (telling time)
Es la... / Son las...	It is ... o'clock.		
de la mañana	in the morning (with a time)	el minuto	minute
		...y cuarto	quarter past
de la tarde	in the afternoon (with a time)	...y (diez)	(ten) past
		...y media	half past
de la noche	at night (with a time)		

Describe Frequency

de vez en cuando	once in a while
muchas veces	often, many times
mucho	a lot
nunca	never
siempre	always
todos los días	every day

Describe Classes

School Subjects

el arte	art
las ciencias	science
el español	Spanish
la historia	history
el inglés	English
las matemáticas	math

Classroom Activities

contestar	to answer
enseñar	to teach
llegar	to arrive
necesitar	to need
sacar una buena / mala nota	to get a good / bad grade
tomar apuntes	to take notes
usar la computadora	to use the computer

Other Words and Phrases

casi	almost
¿Cuántos(as)...?	How many . . . ?
difícil	difficult
en	in
el examen (pl. los exámenes)	exam, test
fácil	easy
hay...	there is, there are . . .
muchos(as)	many
tarde	late
temprano	early
tener que	to have to

Numbers from 11 to 100 *p. 94*

Gramática

Notas gramaticales: Numbers *p. 97,* Telling time *p. 99,* Expressions of frequency *p. 103*

The Verb tener

Use the verb **tener** to talk about what you have.

tener to have			
yo	**tengo**	nosotros(as)	**tenemos**
tú	**tienes**	vosotros(as)	**tenéis**
usted, él, ella	**tiene**	ustedes, ellos(as)	**tienen**

Tener + que + infinitive is used to talk about what someone has to do.

Present Tense of -ar Verbs

To form the present tense of a regular verb that ends in **-ar,** drop the **-ar** and add the appropriate **ending.**

hablar to talk, to speak			
yo	**hablo**	nosotros(as)	**hablamos**
tú	**hablas**	vosotros(as)	**habláis**
usted, él, ella	**habla**	ustedes, ellos(as)	**hablan**

Repaso de la lección

¡LLEGADA!

@HomeTutor
ClassZone.com

Now you can
- talk about daily schedules
- ask and tell time
- say what you have and have to do
- say what you do and how often you do things

Using
- the verb **tener** and **tener que**
- expressions of frequency
- present tense of **-ar** verbs

To review
- the verb **tener** and **tener que** p. 100
- expressions of frequency p. 103
- present tense of **-ar** verbs p. 106

AUDIO

1 Listen and understand

Listen to Martín and Lupe talk about their classes. Then match the questions and anwers.

1. ¿Qué hora es?
2. ¿A qué hora es la clase de historia?
3. ¿En qué clase tiene que sacar una buena nota Martín?
4. ¿En qué clases contestan muchas preguntas?
5. ¿Cómo es la maestra de ciencias?
6. ¿En qué clase usan la computadora?

a. joven
b. en la clase de ciencias
c. Son las diez y cuarto.
d. Es a las diez y media.
e. en las clases de historia y ciencias
f. en la clase de historia

To review
- the verb **tener** and **tener que** p. 100

2 Say what you have and have to do

Tell what classes Beto and his friends have at these times and what they have to do.

8:00 modelo: Adela: arte / dibujar
Adela tiene la clase de arte a las ocho.
Tiene que dibujar.

1. **9:15** yo: historia / tomar muchos apuntes
2. **10:30** ustedes: matemáticas / trabajar con problemas
3. **11:45** tú: español / hablar español
4. **1:20** David y yo: inglés / contestar muchas preguntas
5. **2:15** Lilia: ciencias / usar la computadora
6. **3:30** Eva y Víctor: música / tocar la guitarra

To review
- present tense of -ar verbs p. 106

3 | Talk about daily schedules

Read the information about Pati León. Then complete the information with the correct form of the verbs in parentheses.

Mi horario es muy bueno. Yo __1.__ (trabajar) mucho los lunes, martes y miércoles. Los jueves Gustavo y yo __2.__ (andar) en patineta. Los viernes Gustavo __3.__ (descansar), pero yo __4.__ (montar) en bicicleta con Eloísa y Héctor. Ellos __5.__ (practicar) deportes casi todos los días. Los viernes nosotros __6.__ (comprar) una pizza y __7.__ (mirar) la televisión. ¿Y los sábados y domingos? Muchas veces mis amigos y yo __8.__ (pasear). ¿Y tú? ¿También __9.__ (pasar) un rato con los amigos los sábados y domingos?

To review
- expressions of frequency p. 103
- present tense of -ar verbs p. 106

4 | Say what you do and how often you do things

Write sentences telling how often these people do the following activities.

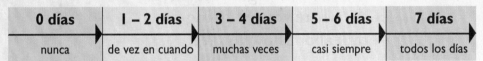

0 días	1 – 2 días	3 – 4 días	5 – 6 días	7 días
nunca	de vez en cuando	muchas veces	casi siempre	todos los días

modelo: nosotros / mirar un DVD (2 días)
Miramos un DVD de vez en cuando.

1. Roberta / contestar preguntas (0 días)
2. tú / hablar español (5 días)
3. Nicolás / practicar deportes (6 días)
4. yo / escuchar música (3 días)
5. Carlos y Pilar / estudiar historia (2 días)
6. nosotros / tocar la guitarra (4 días)
7. los maestros / usar la computadora (7 días)

To review
- Chichén Itzá p. 91
- Comparación cultural pp. 92, 102, 109

5 | Mexico and the Dominican Republic

Comparación cultural

Answer these culture questions.

1. What is Chichén Itzá and what can you find there?
2. What are **zócalos**?
3. What do many students in Mexico and the Dominican Republic wear to school?
4. What does the mural *Alfabetización* represent?

Más práctica Cuaderno *pp. 62–73* Cuaderno para hispanohablantes *pp. 64–73*

Get Help Online
ClassZone.com

México

Lección

2

¡AVANZA!

Tema:

En la escuela
❧❧

In this lesson you will learn to
- describe classes and classroom objects
- say where things are located
- say where you are going
- talk about how you feel

using
- the verb **estar**
- the conjugated verb before the subject to ask a question
- the verb **ir**

♻ *¿Recuerdas?*
- class subjects
- telling time

Comparación cultural

In this lesson you will learn about
- museums of anthropology and artist Frida Kahlo
- schools in Mexico, the Dominican Republic, and Paraguay
- Huichol yarn painting and Taino rock art

Compara con tu mundo
School years vary from country to country. Mexican students go to school from the end of August until June, with short breaks in December and April. *How is this different or similar to your school year?*

¿Qué ves?

Mira la foto

¿Hay una escuela en la foto?

¿Pablo dibuja o escucha música?

¿Qué practican las chicas?

Online SPANISH **CLASSZONE.COM**

Featuring...

Cultura INTERACTIVA

Animated Grammar

@HomeTutor

And more...
- **Get Help Online**
- **Interactive Flashcards**
- **Review Games**
- **WebQuest**
- **Self-Check Quiz**

El patio de una escuela secundaria
México

Presentación de VOCABULARIO

Goal: Learn about Pablo and Claudia's school and how they spend their day. Then practice what you have learned to talk about your school day. *Actividades 1–3*

VIDEO
DVD

AUDIO

A La clase de historia no es **aburrida** porque la maestra es **interesante**. La clase es **divertida** pero es difícil. **Cuando** una clase no es fácil, tengo que trabajar mucho. Necesito sacar buenas notas.

el reloj

el pizarrón

la ventana

el mapa

la tiza

el borrador

la silla

el escritorio

B En la escuela siempre tengo mi **mochila**.

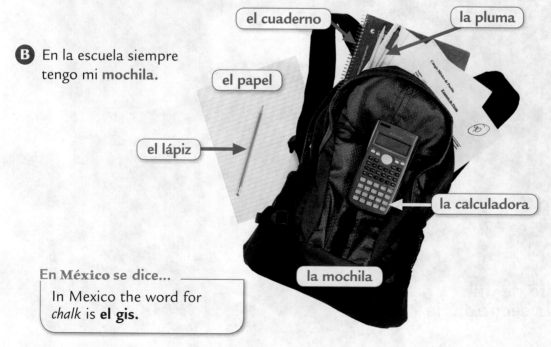

el cuaderno

la pluma

el papel

el lápiz

la calculadora

la mochila

En México se dice...
In Mexico the word for *chalk* is **el gis.**

C Mi escuela es grande. Hay **una cafetería**, **un gimnasio** y **una biblioteca**.

la cafetería

el gimnasio

la biblioteca

los baños

el pasillo

la oficina del director

Más vocabulario

¿(A)dónde? *(To) Where?*	ocupado(a) *busy*
¿Cuándo? *When?*	el problema *problem*
deprimido(a) *depressed*	la puerta *door*
emocionado(a) *excited*	
Expansión de vocabulario p. R3	

Continuará...

Presentación de VOCABULARIO

(continuación)

D Me gusta pasar un rato con Claudia en la biblioteca. Claudia usa la computadora pero yo tengo que estudiar.

cansado(a)

nervioso(a)

contento(a)

enojado(a)

triste

tranquilo(a)

¡A responder! Escuchar

Listen to the list of adjectives and draw a face representing each one.

@HomeTutor VideoPlus
Interactive Flashcards
ClassZone.com

Práctica de VOCABULARIO

1 | Para la escuela

Hablar
Escribir

What do they have at Tienda Martínez? Name the items.

PARA LA ESCUELA...

5 por 30 pesos

250 pesos

3 pesos

2 por 80 pesos

300 pesos

5 por 10 pesos

Tenemos todo para tus clases en

TIENDA MARTÍNEZ

Avenida Hermanos Soriano 80, Puebla, México

2 | ¿Qué lugar es?

Leer
Escribir

Claudia is talking about various places in the school. Complete the sentences with the appropriate place words.

biblioteca   gimnasio   oficina del director

cafetería   baños   clase

En el gimnasio hay dos __1.__ , uno para chicas y uno para chicos. Tenemos que correr y practicar deportes en el __2.__ . Hay muchos libros en la __3.__ . Nos gusta comer pizza y pasar un rato con los amigos en la __4.__ . Hablamos con el director en la __5.__ . Hay escritorios y pizarrones en la __6.__ .

3 | ¿Cuántos hay en la clase?

Hablar

Talk with another student about objects in the classroom.

puerta   ventana   mapa   pizarrón

tiza   escritorio   reloj   ¿ ?

modelo: mapa

A ¿Cuántos mapas hay en la clase?

B Hay tres mapas en la clase.

Más práctica Cuaderno *pp. 74–76* Cuaderno para hispanohablantes *pp. 74–77*

PARA Y PIENSA

Did you get it?
1. Name three rooms in your school.
2. Name three objects you could find in your classroom.

Get Help Online
ClassZone.com

VOCABULARIO *en contexto*

Goal: Identify the words Pablo and Claudia use to talk about what they do after school. Then use the words you have learned to describe classes and classroom objects. *Actividades 4–5*

♻ *¿Recuerdas?* Class subjects p. 95

Telehistoria escena 1

@HomeTutor VideoPlus
ClassZone.com

STRATEGIES

Cuando lees

Look for exclamations Many sentences below are exclamations. Exclamations reveal emphasis, warning, or emotions. How many exclamation-type sentences can you find? Why is each one used?

Cuando escuchas

Listen for emotions What different emotions do Claudia and Pablo show? How do they express them? How would you feel in their place?

VIDEO
DVD

AUDIO

Maestro

Pablo

Claudia

A poster announces Trini Salgado's guest appearance in the school gym.

Maestro: Trini Salgado, ¿eh? ¿Y vas tú al gimnasio?

Pablo: ¡Sí!

Maestro: ¡Muy divertido! *(later on in science class...)* ¿Quién contesta la pregunta? ¿Pablo? Bueno, ¡al pizarrón!

Pablo tries, but gets the problem wrong. Claudia goes to the board and corrects it. The bell rings and they leave class together.

Claudia: Pablo, ¿vamos a la biblioteca? Estudiamos, hacemos la tarea y llegamos bien al gimnasio... ¡Trini Salgado, Pablo!

Pablo: ¡Sí! Necesito estudiar, ¡y tú enseñas muy bien! ¿Y tu mochila? *(He points to her backpack, which she has left in the classroom.)*

Claudia: ¡Gracias, Pablo!

Continuará... p. 132

También se dice

México The teacher uses the word **pizarrón** to call Pablo to the board. In other Spanish-speaking countries you might hear:
· **muchos países**
  la pizarra

4 En clase *Comprensión del episodio*

Escuchar
Leer

Describe what happens in the episode by matching phrases from each column.

1. Pablo no contesta la pregunta   **a.** la pregunta en el pizarrón.

2. Después de Pablo,
     Claudia contesta   **b.** la mochila.

                               c. estudiar con Claudia.

3. Pablo y Claudia necesitan ir   **d.** a la biblioteca y al gimnasio.

4. Pablo necesita   **e.** porque el problema es difícil.

5. Claudia no tiene   **f.** muy bien.

6. Claudia enseña

5 ¿Cómo son las clases?   *¿Recuerdas?* Class subjects p. 95

Hablar

Describe your classes to another student.

A ¿Cómo es la clase de español?

B Es divertida y fácil.

1.

2.

3.

4.

5.

6.

Did you get it? Tell where Pablo and Claudia are going by writing **la biblioteca** or **el gimnasio.**

1. Pablo y Claudia tienen que estudiar.

2. Pablo necesita practicar fútbol.

3. Ellos necesitan un libro.

Get Help Online ClassZone.com

Presentación de GRAMÁTICA

Goal: Learn to use the verb **estar** to talk about location and condition. Then practice using **estar** to say and ask where things are located and how people feel. *Actividades 6–12*

English Grammar Connection: There are two ways to say the English verb *to be* in Spanish: **ser** and **estar.** You already learned **ser** (see p. 38).

The Verb estar

Animated Grammar
ClassZone.com

Use **estar** to indicate location and say how people feel.

Here's how:

estar		to be	
yo	**estoy**	nosotros(as)	**estamos**
tú	**estás**	vosotros(as)	**estáis**
usted, él, ella	**está**	ustedes, ellos(as)	**están**

Pedro **está** en la cafetería.   *Pedro is in the cafeteria.*

Use **estar** with the following words of location.

al lado (de)	**debajo (de)**	**dentro (de)**	**encima (de)**
cerca (de)	**delante (de)**	**detrás (de)**	**lejos (de)**

Use the word **de** after the location word when a specific location is mentioned. When **de** is followed by the word **el**, they combine to form the contraction **del**.

La biblioteca **está al lado** de la cafetería.   La tiza **está encima del** borrador.
The library is next to the cafeteria.   *The chalk is on top of the eraser.*

Estar is also used with **adjectives** to say how someone feels at a given moment.

El maestro **está tranquilo.**   Las chicas **están cansadas.**
The teacher is calm.   *The girls are tired.*

♻ ***¿Recuerdas?*** Adjectives agree in gender and number with the nouns they describe (see p. 72).

Más práctica
Cuaderno *pp. 77–79*
Cuaderno para hispanohablantes *pp. 78–80*

@HomeTutor
Leveled Grammar Practice
ClassZone.com

Práctica de GRAMÁTICA

6 | ¿Dónde están?

Hablar
Escribir

Tell where the people are, according to Pablo.

modelo: el señor Díaz
El señor Díaz está en la oficina.

1. ustedes

2. yo

3. Miguel y Alejo

4. Sergio

5. Claudia y yo

6. Cristina y Sarita

7 | El horario

Hablar
Escribir

Indicate the most logical place at school for each person to be.

modelo: Víctor llega a la escuela.
Está en el pasillo.

1. Carlos y Juan dibujan.

2. Maya habla español.

3. Yo toco la guitarra.

4. Nosotros compramos la comida.

5. Luz practica deportes.

6. Tú necesitas muchos libros.

7. Ustedes usan la calculadora.

8. El maestro habla con el director.

Nota gramatical

You already know that you can use rising intonation to ask a yes/no question.
You can also switch the position of the **verb** and the **subject** to form a question.

María tiene una patineta.   ¿**Tiene María** una patineta?
María has a skateboard.   *Does María have a skateboard?*

8 | Las emociones

Hablar

Talk with another student about how these people are feeling.

modelo: el maestro / nervioso(a)
el maestro 🙂

A ¿Está nervioso el maestro?

B No, está tranquilo.

Estudiante A

1. Pablo / tranquilo(a)
2. Claudia / triste
3. los maestros / cansado(a)
4. los amigos / enojado(a)
5. las amigas / emocionado(a)
6. tú / ocupado(a)

Pablo 😬
Claudia 🙁
los maestros 😣
los amigos 😠
las amigas 🙁
yo ¿ ?

9 | Las salas del museo

Hablar

Comparación cultural

El museo de antropología

What do ancient artifacts teach us about a culture? The National Museum of Anthropology in Mexico City contains artifacts from **Mexico's** many indigenous cultures. A main attraction is the *Piedra del Sol,* or Sun Stone, an Aztec calendar that weighs almost 25 tons. In **Paraguay,** the Andrés Barbero Museum of Ethnography in Asunción contains tools, musical instruments, and artwork from its indigenous cultures.

Piedra del Sol

1. Sala Mexica (Azteca)
2. el patio central
3. la oficina
4. Sala Norte de México
5. Sala Maya
6. Sala Oaxaca
7. Sala Tolteca
8. Sala Teotihuacán
9. Sala Preclásico
10. Sala de Introducción a la Antropología
11. el auditorio

El Museo Nacional de Antropología

Un plano de El Museo Nacional de Antropología en la Ciudad de México

Compara con tu mundo *What items might people find 1,000 years from now that give clues about life in the 21st century? What would you put in a time capsule?*

Use the map to tell a partner where the rooms are located in the museum.

A ¿Dónde está la Sala Tolteca?

B La Sala Tolteca está al lado de la Sala Teotihuacán.

10 | ¿Lejos de la escuela?

Escribir

Rewrite the statements below to say that the opposite is true.

1. Nosotros estamos lejos de la escuela.
2. El cuaderno está detrás de la silla.
3. El libro está debajo del escritorio.
4. Los lápices están delante de la mochila.
5. Yo estoy cerca de la biblioteca.
6. La pluma está encima del papel.

11 | ¿Cómo estás?

Hablar
Escribir

Describe how you feel in the following situations.

modelo: hablar español
Estoy nerviosa cuando hablo español.

1. pasar un rato con los amigos
2. tener que hacer la tarea
3. sacar una mala nota
4. llegar tarde a clase
5. sacar una buena nota
6. escuchar música
7. mirar la televisión
8. tener un examen
9. practicar deportes
10. estudiar mucho

12 | ¿Qué es?

Hablar

Give clues about an object in the drawing to another student. He or she has to guess the object.

A Está encima del cuaderno. Está al lado del libro.

B Es la calculadora.

Más práctica Cuaderno *pp. 77–79* Cuaderno para hispanohablantes *pp. 78–80*

PARA Y PIENSA

Did you get it? 1. Tell someone that you are near the windows.
2. Ask Pablo if he is nervous.

Get Help Online
ClassZone.com

GRAMÁTICA en contexto

¡AVANZA!

Goal: Listen to how Pablo and Claudia use **estar** to talk about how Pablo feels. Then practice using **estar** to talk about emotions and locations.
Actividades 13–15

Telehistoria escena 2

@HomeTutor VideoPlus
ClassZone.com

STRATEGIES

Cuando lees
Read for motives behind actions
This scene contains a physical action related to Pablo's complaints. What is the action, and what are his complaints? Are his complaints justified?

Cuando escuchas
Listen for feelings What feelings are mentioned in this scene? How does Pablo explain how he feels? Have you ever felt this way?

VIDEO
DVD

AUDIO

Claudia: Eh, Pablo, ¿qué pasa? ¿Estás deprimido? ¿Estás enojado?

Pablo: No, no estoy enojado... Estoy nervioso... Tengo que estar en el gimnasio a las cinco pero tengo que hacer la tarea.

Pablo leaves the library. Later Claudia joins him outside.

Pablo: Ay, Claudia, nunca descanso... Me gusta pasar un rato con los amigos... Y ¡esta mochila!

Claudia: ¿Qué pasa?

Pablo starts swinging his backpack back and forth.

Pablo: Aquí tengo libros, cuadernos, plumas, calculadoras... ¡estoy cansado!

Suddenly Pablo lets go of his backpack.

Pablo: ¡Ay! ¿Dónde está mi mochila?

Claudia: ¡Pablo, tu mochila!

She points to his backpack, which is caught in a basketball hoop.

También se dice

México To say he has pens in his backpack, Pablo uses the word **plumas.** In other Spanish-speaking countries you might hear:
• **muchos países** el bolígrafo, el boli

Continuará... p. 138

13 | El problema de Pablo *Comprensión del episodio*

Escuchar
Leer

Read the sentences and decide whether they are true or false. Correct the false statements.

1. Claudia y Pablo están en la oficina.
2. Pablo está nervioso porque tiene que jugar al fútbol.
3. Claudia tiene que estar en el gimnasio a las cinco.
4. Pablo está enojado.
5. A Claudia y a Pablo les gusta pasar un rato con los amigos.
6. Pablo está deprimido porque tiene libros, cuadernos, plumas y calculadoras en la mochila.

14 | ¿Cuándo?

Hablar

Ask another student when he or she feels these emotions.

Ⓐ ¿Cuándo estás triste?

Ⓑ Estoy triste cuando saco una mala nota.

Estudiante Ⓐ

1. 2.
3. 4.
5. 6.

Estudiante Ⓑ

sacar una buena / mala nota
escuchar música
practicar deportes
trabajar
estudiar
¿ ?

15 | ¡A jugar! ¿Dónde estoy?

Hablar

Give clues for other students to guess where you are in the school.

Ⓐ Compro papas fritas y jugo. Paso un rato con los amigos. Estoy tranquilo.

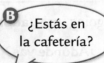

Ⓑ ¿Estás en la cafetería?

PARA
Y
PIENSA

Did you get it? Give three sentences about Pablo and Claudia using the verb **estar**. Use one of the following words in each sentence: **la biblioteca, nervioso(a), el gimnasio.**

Get Help Online
ClassZone.com

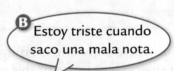

Presentación de GRAMÁTICA

Goal: Learn how to form the verb **ir** in order to say where you and others are going. Then practice using **ir** to say where you go during and after school. *Actividades 16–21*

English Grammar Connection: Remember that **conjugating** is changing the forms of a verb to indicate who is doing the action (see p. 100). In English, *to go* is conjugated as *I go, you go, he/she/it goes, we go, they go.*

Pablo **goes** to the cafeteria at twelve.

Pablo **va** a la cafetería a las doce.

⬆
conjugated verb

⬆
conjugated verb

The Verb ir

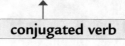
Animated Grammar
ClassZone.com

Use **ir** to talk about where someone is going.
How do you form the present tense of this verb?

Here's how:

ir *to go*			
yo	**voy**	nosotros(as)	**vamos**
tú	**vas**	vosotros(as)	**vais**
usted, él, ella	**va**	ustedes, ellos(as)	**van**

Use **ir** with the word **a** to say that someone is going to a specific place.
When **a** is followed by the word **el**, they combine to form the contraction **al**.

Voy a la biblioteca.
I'm going to the library.

Los estudiantes **van al** gimnasio.
The students are going to the gym.

To ask where someone is going, use ¿**adónde**...?

¿**Adónde** vas?
Where are you going?

Más práctica
Cuaderno *pp. 80–82*
Cuaderno para hispanohablantes *pp. 81–84*

@HomeTutor
Leveled Grammar Practice
ClassZone.com

Práctica de GRAMÁTICA

16 | ¿Un estudiante serio?

**Leer
Escribir**

Claudia and Pablo are talking at school. Complete their conversation with forms of **ir**.

Claudia: ¡Tengo mucha tarea en la clase de inglés! Yo __1.__ a la biblioteca... ¿ __2.__ tú y yo?

Pablo: No, yo no __3.__ a la biblioteca hoy.

Claudia: ¿No __4.__ tú a la biblioteca? ¡Tienes que hacer la tarea!

Pablo: Sí, pero necesito comprar pizza y un refresco. Mis amigos y yo __5.__ a la cafetería. Después yo __6.__ al gimnasio y ellos __7.__ a la clase de matemáticas.

Claudia: ¿ __8.__ Carlos al gimnasio?

Pablo: No, él __9.__ a la biblioteca.

Claudia: ¡Ay, Pablo! Tú también necesitas ir. ¿ __10.__ tú y Carlos mañana?

Pablo: Sí, todos nosotros __11.__ mañana.

17 | ¿Por qué vas allí?

Escribir

Match the statements with the places the people would go. Then write a sentence saying that they are going to these places.

1. Claudia tiene una calculadora.
2. Yo necesito libros.
3. A ti te gusta practicar deportes.
4. Nosotros tenemos lápices para dibujar.
5. A Pablo le gusta comer pizza.
6. Los amigos llegan tarde a la escuela.

a. la clase de arte
b. la oficina del director
c. la clase de matemáticas
d. el gimnasio
e. la biblioteca
f. la cafetería

AUDIO

Pronunciación   La letra d

In Spanish, the letter **d** has two sounds. At the beginning of a sentence, after a pause, or after the letters **l** or **n**, the **d** sounds like the English *d* in *door*. In all other cases, the **d** sounds like the *th* of the word *the*.

Listen and repeat, paying close attention to the two sounds of **d**.

Soy Diego. Dibujo en mi cuaderno.

comida   divertido   ¿Dónde está David?
adiós   falda   Daniel está al lado de la puerta.
lado   grande   ¿Adónde vas con mi cuaderno?

18 | ¿Adónde van?

**Escuchar
Escribir**

Where are Pablo and other people going? Listen to the description and write sentences saying where these people are going.

la oficina de la directora	el gimnasio	la biblioteca
la clase de inglés	la clase de matemáticas	la cafetería

1. Pablo
2. Claudia
3. Martín y Sara
4. la maestra de inglés
5. María y Claudia
6. el señor Treviño

19 | En el pasillo

**Hablar
Escribir**

The bell has just rung to change classes. Tell where the students and the teachers are going, based on the clues in the drawing.

modelo: Las amigas van a la cafetería.

20 | ¿Cuándo vas a...?

Hablar

Ask a partner when he or she goes to these places.

modelo: la oficina

A ¿Cuándo vas a la oficina?

B Voy a la oficina cuando tengo problemas.

Estudiante A

1. el gimnasio
2. la oficina
3. la escuela
4. la biblioteca
5. la cafetería
6. la clase de...

Estudiante B

tengo (que)
necesito
hay
¿ ?

21 | ¿Y tú?

**Hablar
Escribir**

Answer the questions in complete sentences.

1. ¿A qué hora vas a la escuela?
2. ¿Cuándo van tú y tus amigos(as) a la cafetería?
3. ¿Adónde vas después de la clase de español?
4. ¿Vas mucho a la oficina del (de la) director(a)?
5. ¿Adónde vas cuando tienes que estudiar?
6. ¿Qué hay dentro de tu mochila?

Comparación cultural

El autorretrato

What does a self-portrait reveal about an artist?
Mexican artist Frida Kahlo painted many self-portraits,
including *Autorretrato con collar*. She was influenced by the
indigenous cultures of **Mexico** in both her style of painting
and style of clothing. She often wore traditional native
clothing, as depicted in the photograph. What similarities
and differences do you see between the two images?

Compara con tu mundo *What would you include in
a portrait of yourself and why? What would your clothing be like?*

Autorretrato con
collar *(1933),
Frida Kahlo*

*Una fotografía de
Frida Kahlo (1941),
Nickolas Muray*

Más práctica   Cuaderno *pp. 80–82*   Cuaderno para hispanohablantes *pp. 81–84*

PARA
Y
PIENSA

Did you get it? Tell where the following people are going.

1. Teresa / la cafetería
2. los estudiantes / la oficina del director
3. nosotros / el gimnasio
4. yo / la clase de matemáticas

Get Help Online
ClassZone.com

Todo junto

Goal: *Show what you know* Notice how Pablo and Claudia use **ir** to talk about where they are going, and **estar** to say where things are. Then use **ir** and **estar** to talk about your own schedule. *Actividades 22–26*

♻ *¿Recuerdas?* Telling time p. 99

Telehistoria completa

@*HomeTutor* VideoPlus
ClassZone.com

STRATEGIES

Cuando lees
Read for locations This scene mentions specific places people are going. What are those places? Alicia's T-shirt is now located in a specific place. Where is it?

Cuando escuchas
Notice the problems In this scene, Pablo's problems go from bad to worse. What are the problems? How does he react?

Escena 1 *Resumen*
Pablo no contesta la pregunta en la clase de ciencias porque el problema es difícil. Claudia contesta la pregunta.

Escena 2 *Resumen*
Pablo no está contento porque tiene mucho que hacer y no tiene la mochila con la camiseta de Alicia.

VIDEO
DVD

AUDIO

Escena 3

Roberto

Pablo

Claudia

Roberto approaches, holding a poster.

Roberto: ¿Qué pasa?

Claudia: Vamos al gimnasio. Bueno, Pablo va al gimnasio, yo voy a la cafetería...

Pablo: ¡Necesito ir al gimnasio a las cinco, y son las cinco menos cuarto!

Claudia: ¡Y necesita la mochila! Dentro está la camiseta de Alicia.

Pablo: A las cinco Trini Salgado va al gimnasio, y yo...

Roberto: No, no. ¡A las cuatro!

Pablo: No... ¡A las cinco!

Roberto: Mira... a las cuatro.

He shows his autographed poster to Pablo. It says four o'clock.

Pablo: *(dejectedly)* No...

22 | ¡A organizar! *Comprensión de los episodios*

Escuchar
Leer

Put the sentences in order to describe the episodes.

1. La camiseta está en la mochila y Pablo no tiene la mochila.
2. Pablo y Claudia hablan con Roberto.
3. Claudia y Pablo van a la biblioteca y estudian.
4. Pablo está nervioso; tiene que ir al gimnasio a las cinco.
5. Pablo va a la clase de ciencias y no contesta la pregunta.

23 | ¡A describir! *Comprensión de los episodios*

Escuchar
Leer

Describe what is happening in the photos. Include where the people in the photos are and how they feel.

modelo: Pablo está en la clase de ciencias. Va al pizarrón porque tiene que contestar una pregunta. Está nervioso.

1.   **2.**    **3.**

24 | ¿Adónde vamos? ♻ *¿Recuerdas?* Telling time p. 99

Hablar

> **STRATEGY Hablar**
> **Make it lively** Keep the discussion interesting! Add as many details about your classes as possible. Don't just talk about your classes; include other places in your school.

Talk with other students about schedules: where they go and at what times.

A ¿A qué hora van ustedes a la cafetería?

B Voy a la cafetería a las doce y media.

C Voy a la cafetería a la una.

25 | Integración

Leer
Escuchar
Hablar

Raquel and Mario need to study in the library. Read Raquel's daily planner and listen to Mario's message. Then tell when Raquel and Mario will go to the library to study. Explain why they won't go at the other times mentioned.

Fuente 1 Agenda personal

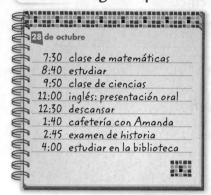

28 de octubre

7:30	clase de matemáticas
8:40	estudiar
9:50	clase de ciencias
11:00	inglés: presentación oral
12:30	descansar
1:40	cafetería con Amanda
2:45	examen de historia
4:00	estudiar en la biblioteca

Fuente 2 Un mensaje por teléfono

Listen and take notes
• Escribe qué hace Mario y a qué hora.

modelo: Ellos van a la biblioteca a las... No estudian a las siete y media porque...

26 | El periódico escolar

Escribir

You have to write an article for the school newspaper about your typical school day. Explain what classes you go to, what they are like, and what you use in each class.

modelo: Yo siempre estoy muy ocupado. A las siete y media voy a la clase de matemáticas. La clase es muy divertida. Usamos calculadoras, pero no es fácil. A las ocho y cuarto...

Writing Criteria	Excellent	Good	Needs Work
Content	Your article includes a lot of information.	Your article includes some information.	Your article includes little information.
Communication	Most of your article is organized and easy to follow.	Parts of your article are organized and easy to follow.	Your article is disorganized and hard to follow.
Accuracy	Your article has few mistakes in grammar and vocabulary.	Your article has some mistakes in grammar and vocabulary.	Your article has many mistakes in grammar and vocabulary.

Más práctica Cuaderno *pp. 83–84* Cuaderno para hispanohablantes *pp. 85–86*

PARA Y PIENSA

Did you get it? Complete each sentence with the correct forms of **estar** and **ir + a.**

1. A la una Pablo _____ en la clase de arte, pero a las dos _____ la cafetería.
2. ¿Dónde _____ Roberto y Claudia? Ellos _____ la cafetería.
3. Claudia _____ nerviosa porque _____ la oficina de la directora.

Get Help Online
ClassZone.com

Juegos y diversiones

Review **estar,** classroom objects, and location words by playing a game.

¿Cierto o falso?

The Setup

Your teacher will divide the class into two teams. Each student will make up a sentence using classroom objects and location words.

Playing the Game

Players from each team go up to the front of the class with their sentences in hand.

The player from Team A reads the sentence to the player from Team B. The player from Team B has to say whether the sentence is true (**cierto**) or false (**falso**). Then they change roles.

El libro está debajo del escritorio.

Falso. El libro está encima del escritorio.

Scoring

Players receive one point for correct answers. Points are taken away for incorrectly formed sentences.

A player can earn an extra point by correcting a false sentence to say something true about the location of the object. A player can also earn an extra point by adding more information to a true sentence.

The Winner!

The team with the most points at the end is the winner.

Lectura cultural

¡AVANZA! **Goal:** Read the excerpts from the essays of two students from Mexico and the Dominican Republic. Then compare the descriptions of their favorite classes and talk about your favorite class.

Comparación cultural

AUDIO

Mi clase favorita

STRATEGY Leer

Use the title The title *Mi clase favorita* helps you anticipate the contents of the reading. Write down the things that you would expect to find, then search for them.

Expected contents	Actual contents
El (La) maestro(a)...	
La clase...	
Más información:	

Below are compositions by two finalists who entered the essay contest called "Mi clase favorita."

Tomás Gutiérrez Moreno
Colegio de la Providencia
Guadalajara, México

Mi nombre es Tomás Gutiérrez Moreno. Soy de Guadalajara, México. Estudio en el Colegio de la Providencia.

La historia es muy interesante; es mi clase favorita. Me gusta mucho estudiar el pasado[1] de México. Soy estudioso y siempre saco buenas notas en la clase.

En la universidad deseo[2] estudiar historia. Deseo ser maestro y enseñar historia mexicana en Guadalajara.

---

[1] past   [2] I wish to

Mural en la Biblioteca Central de la Universidad Nacional Autónoma de México en la Ciudad de México

México

María González
Colegio San Esteban
San Pedro de Macorís, República Dominicana

Me llamo María González. Soy de la República Dominicana. Estudio en el Colegio San Esteban.

Tengo dos clases favoritas: el inglés y el español. Deseo estudiar idiomas[3] en Santo Domingo, la capital, y después, trabajar en mi país.

El turismo es muy importante para[4] la economía de la República Dominicana. Deseo trabajar en un hotel, en las famosas playas[5] de Punta Cana o de Puerto Plata.

---

[3] languages   [4] for   [5] beaches

Mural en la Universidad Nacional en Santo Domingo, República Dominicana

República Dominicana

PARA Y PIENSA

¿Comprendiste?
1. ¿Dónde estudia Tomás?
2. ¿Cómo es Tomás?
3. ¿De dónde es María?
4. ¿Qué le gusta estudiar más a María?

¿Y tú?
¿Cuál es tu clase favorita? ¿Cómo es?

Proyectos culturales

Arte de México y la República Dominicana

How does art reflect a culture's view of the natural world? Many cultures use art to capture the beauty and wonder of their natural surroundings. Two indigenous groups whose art can still be appreciated are the Huichol of **Mexico** and the Taino of the Greater Antilles (including what is now known as the **Dominican Republic**).

Proyecto 1 *Yarn Painting*

México Some Huichol still live in the isolated mountains of western Mexico. They make yarn paintings of birds, flowers, and other natural shapes. Make your own Huichol-style yarn painting.

Materials for yarn painting
Cardboard
2–3 colors yarn
Glue

Instructions
1. On a piece of cardboard, draw a pencil outline of the design you'd like to make.
2. Place one strand of yarn along the outline's length. Glue the yarn to the cardboard.
3. Fill in the design by laying yarn just inside the outline you made, coiling the yarn around until the figure is filled.
4. Section off the background and fill it in the same way.

Proyecto 2 *Rock Drawing*

República Dominicana The Taino lived in the islands of the Caribbean until the 16th century. Their rock art can still be seen in the caverns of the Dominican Republic. Try making your own rock art.

Materials for rock drawing
Rock
Pencil
Optional: Markers, pens, or chalk

Instructions
1. Begin by finding a smooth, oval rock about the size of your hand with an adequate surface for drawing.
2. Use a pencil to sketch the animal or design you'd like to make.
3. Then use a black felt tip pen to make it permanent. Add color by using colored felt tip pens or colored chalk.

En tu comunidad

Visit an arts and crafts store or a museum in your community. Look for any items that have been influenced by Spanish-speaking cultures.

En resumen
Vocabulario y gramática

Animated Grammar
Interactive Flashcards
ClassZone.com

Vocabulario

Describe Classroom Objects

el borrador	eraser	el pizarrón (pl. los pizarrones)	board, chalkboard
la calculadora	calculator	la pluma	pen
el cuaderno	notebook	la puerta	door
el escritorio	desk	el reloj	clock; watch
el lápiz (pl. los lápices)	pencil	la silla	chair
el mapa	map	la tiza	chalk
la mochila	backpack	la ventana	window
el papel	paper		

Say Where Things Are Located

al lado (de)	next to	dentro (de)	inside (of)
cerca (de)	near (to)	detrás (de)	behind
debajo (de)	underneath, under	encima (de)	on top (of)
delante (de)	in front (of)	lejos (de)	far (from)

Talk About How You Feel

cansado(a)	tired	nervioso(a)	nervous
contento(a)	content, happy	ocupado(a)	busy
deprimido(a)	depressed	tranquilo(a)	calm
emocionado(a)	excited	triste	sad
enojado(a)	angry		

Describe Classes

aburrido(a)	boring
divertido(a)	fun
interesante	interesting

Places in School

el baño	bathroom
la biblioteca	library
la cafetería	cafeteria
el gimnasio	gymnasium
la oficina del (de la) director(a)	principal's office
el pasillo	hall

Other Words and Phrases

¿(A)dónde?	(To) Where?
¿Cuándo?	When?
cuando	when
el problema	problem

Gramática

Nota gramatical: Conjugated verb before the subject to ask a question *p. 130*

The Verb estar

Use **estar** to indicate location and say how people feel.

estar *to be*

yo	estoy	nosotros(as)	estamos
tú	estás	vosotros(as)	estáis
usted, él, ella	está	ustedes, ellos(as)	están

The Verb ir

Use **ir** to talk about where someone is going.

ir *to go*

yo	voy	nosotros(as)	vamos
tú	vas	vosotros(as)	vais
usted, él, ella	va	ustedes, ellos(as)	van

Repaso de la lección

¡LLEGADA!

@HomeTutor
ClassZone.com

Now you can
- describe classes and classroom objects
- say where things are located
- say where you are going
- talk about how you feel

Using
- the verb **estar**
- the conjugated verb before the subject to ask a question
- the verb **ir**

To review
- the verb **estar** p. 128
- the conjugated verb before the subject to ask a question p. 130
- the verb **ir** p. 134

1 | Listen and understand

AUDIO

Copy this chart on a piece of paper. Listen to the phone messages and complete the chart. Write sentences using the information.

La hora	¿Dónde está Ana?	¿Adónde va Ana?
modelo: 8:00	delante de la clase de arte	clase de español
10:15		
12:30		
2:45		
4:10		

modelo: A las ocho Ana está delante de la clase de arte.
Ella va de la clase de arte a la clase de español.

To review
- the verb **estar** p. 128
- the conjugated verb before the subject to ask a question p. 130

2 | Talk about how you feel

Write questions to verify how these people are feeling.

 modelo: Bárbara
¿Está emocionada Bárbara?

1. Jorge y Pilar

2. las maestras

3. la directora

4. usted

5. tú

6. ustedes

To review
• the verb **ir** p. 134

3 | Say where you are going

Read Mario's e-mail message and complete it with the correct form of **ir**.

Hola, Luis. Yo __1.__ a la clase de ciencias en quince minutos. Es una clase interesante, pero es difícil. A las doce y media mis amigos y yo __2.__ a la cafetería. Después Inés __3.__ al gimnasio y Jerónimo __4.__ a la oficina del director. A las cinco ellos __5.__ a la biblioteca para estudiar. ¿Adónde __6.__ tú después de las clases?

To review
• the verb **estar** p. 128

4 | Say where things are located

Write sentences telling where Señora Romero's students have put the erasers.

modelo: el pizarrón (cerca / lejos)
Un borrador está cerca del pizarrón.

1. reloj (al lado / debajo)
2. silla (debajo / encima)
3. mochila (dentro / debajo)
4. ventana (delante / detrás)
5. escritorio (encima / delante)
6. maestra (lejos / detrás)

To review
• Comparación cultural pp. 120, 130, 137
• Lectura cultural pp. 142–143

5 | Mexico and the Dominican Republic

Comparación cultural

Answer these culture questions.

1. When do Mexican students attend school?
2. How did indigenous cultures influence Frida Kahlo?
3. What can you find in Mexico City's National Museum of Anthropology?
4. Why is tourism important in the Dominican Republic?

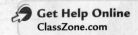
Get Help Online
ClassZone.com

Más práctica Cuaderno *pp. 85–96* Cuaderno para hispanohablantes *pp. 87–96*

México

Paraguay

República Dominicana

AUDIO

Horarios y clases

Lectura y escritura

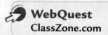
WebQuest
ClassZone.com

1 **Leer** School subjects and daily schedules vary around the world. Read how Rafael, Andrea, and Juan Carlos spend a typical day at school.

2 **Escribir** Using the three descriptions as models, write a short paragraph about your daily schedule.

STRATEGY Escribir

Create a schedule Draw two large clocks, one for a.m. and the other for p.m. Write your school schedule on these clocks.

 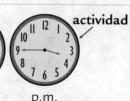

actividad

clase

a.m.   p.m.

Step 1 Complete the two clocks by listing your classes and after-school activities. Use arrows to point to the correct times.

Step 2 Write your paragraph. Make sure to include all the classes, activities, and times. Check your writing by yourself or with help from a friend. Make final corrections.

Compara con tu mundo

Use the paragraph you wrote to compare your school schedule to the schedule of *one* of the three students. What are the similarities in the schedules? What are the differences?

Cuaderno *pp. 97–99*   Cuaderno para hispanohablantes *pp. 97–99*

Paraguay

Andrea

¿Qué tal? Me llamo Andrea y estudio en Asunción, Paraguay. Mis clases son en la tarde, de la una a las cinco. En la escuela los estudiantes tienen muchas clases. Todos los días, tengo clases de español, ciencias, historia y matemáticas. También tengo clase de guaraní[1]. Después de las clases, voy al gimnasio y practico deportes. De vez en cuando uso la computadora en la biblioteca.

[1] an indigenous language spoken in Paraguay

República Dominicana

Rafael

¡Hola a todos! Me llamo Rafael y estudio en una escuela en Santo Domingo. Tengo clases todos los días de las ocho de la mañana a la una de la tarde. A las diez tenemos un descanso de quince minutos. Luego, voy a la clase de historia. Es interesante y yo tomo muchos apuntes. En la tarde muchas veces paso un rato con los amigos.

México

Juan Carlos

¡Hola! Soy Juan Carlos. Soy estudiante en México, D.F. En la escuela necesito trabajar mucho porque tengo nueve clases. Las clases son de las siete de la mañana a las dos de la tarde. ¡Tengo que llegar muy temprano! Mi clase favorita es la clase de matemáticas. Es interesante y divertida. Después de las clases mis amigos y yo estudiamos en la biblioteca.

Repaso inclusivo
♻ Options for Review

1 | Listen, understand, and compare

Escuchar

Javier interviewed teachers and administrators at his school for Teacher Appreciation Day. Listen to his report and answer the questions.

1. ¿Qué enseña el señor Minondo?
2. ¿Qué deporte practica el señor Minondo?
3. ¿Quién es la señora Cruz?
4. ¿Qué le gusta hacer a la señora Cruz?
5. ¿Cómo son los maestros?

Are your teachers and administrators like those at Javier's school? What kind of activities do your teachers like to do after classes?

2 | Give a school orientation

Hablar

You are giving a talk at an orientation meeting for students who are new to your school. Greet the new students, introduce yourself, and give them some background information about yourself: what classes you have, what you like to do after school, etc. Then tell them where the gym, cafeteria, and other locations around the school are. Finish by describing some of the classes that are available and what they have to do in each class. Your talk should be at least two minutes long.

3 | Talk with a school counselor

Hablar

Role-play a conversation with a school counselor. The counselor wants to know what your classes are like and what you like to do after classes. Answer your partner's questions, tell him or her what you do in each class, and ask a few questions of your own about the school. Your conversation should be at least two minutes long.

¿Cómo son tus clases?

Son difíciles. Estudio mucho.

4 | Write a brochure

Escribir

Create a brochure about your school that would be helpful to a new student from a Spanish-speaking country. Include some of the following: places in the school, classes offered, school supplies needed, teachers, and extracurricular activities. Copy this chart on a piece of paper and use it to organize your information. Your brochure should have illustrations and at least six sentences.

Lugares	Clases	Materiales	Maestros	Actividades

5 | Hold a press conference

**Hablar
Escribir**

Hold a mock press conference. You and your classmates are reporters and have to ask your teacher questions about his or her school schedule and favorite activities. Use the answers to write a short profile of your teacher that could appear in a Spanish edition of the school newspaper. The profile should have at least five sentences.

6 | Write a postcard

**Leer
Escribir**

You received the following postcard from your new pen pal in Mexico. Write back, answering all of your pen pal's questions and asking a few of your own. Your letter should have at least eight sentences.

PUEBLA

Hola. Me llamo Manuel Salazar. Soy de Puebla, México. Soy estudioso y atlético. Soy un estudiante organizado. Siempre saco buenas notas. ¿Cómo eres tú? ¿Cómo son tus clases? Tengo clases difíciles pero los maestros son muy simpáticos. Estudio mucho y también paso un rato con los amigos. Me gusta jugar al fútbol y andar en patineta ¿Qué te gusta hacer con los amigos?

Tu amigo,

Manuel

MEXICO
© Tarjetas Postales, S.A.

3

Puerto Rico

Comer en familia

Océano Atlántico

Lección 1
Tema: **Mi comida favorita**

Lección 2
Tema: **En mi familia**

«*¡Hola!*
**Somos Marisol y Rodrigo.
Somos de Puerto Rico.**»

Cuba

Golfo de México

Puerto Rico

República Dominicana

Mar Caribe

México

Honduras

Guatemala

Nicaragua

Costa Rica

El Salvador

Panamá

Venezuela

Colombia

Océano Atlántico

Arecibo   **San Juan**

Mayagüez   **Puerto Rico**   EL YUNQUE   **Culebra**

Humacao   **Vieques**

Ponce   **Guayama**

Mar Caribe

Población: 3.897.960

Área: 3.515 millas cuadradas

Capital: San Juan

Moneda: el dólar estadounidense

Idiomas: español, inglés (los dos son oficiales)

Comida típica: pasteles, arroz con gandules, pernil

Gente famosa: Julia de Burgos (poetisa), Roberto Clemente (beisbolista), Rosario Ferré (escritora), Luis Muñoz Marín (político)

Pasteles

◀ **Comidas al aire libre** Many Puerto Ricans enjoy informal gatherings at a beach or park, where families can spend the day together, barbecue, and listen to music. **Pinchos** (skewers of chicken or pork) are popular at barbecues and snack stands. *Where do people like to eat outdoors where you live?*

Una familia come en la playa

Casas de colores vivos San Juan is famous for its well-preserved colonial quarter, called **Viejo San Juan.** Its narrow streets are lined with brightly-colored houses with balconies. *What are some historic areas close to where you live?* ▶

Casas coloniales en Viejo San Juan

◀ **Un parque nacional** El Yunque is the only tropical rain forest in the care of the U.S. Forest Service. The park has many waterfalls, such as the Cascada de la Coca, and is home to the **coquí,** a tiny tree frog named for its distinctive song. *What are some features of other parks in the United States?*

La Cascada de la Coca en El Yunque

Puerto Rico

Lección 1

Tema:
Mi comida favorita

¡AVANZA!

In this lesson you will learn to
- talk about foods and beverages
- ask questions
- say which foods you like and don't like

using
- interrogative words
- **gustar** with nouns
- present tense of **-er** and **-ir** verbs
- the verb **hacer**

♻ ¿Recuerdas?
- **gustar** with an infinitive
- snack foods
- the verb **estar**
- telling time

Comparación cultural

In this lesson you will learn about
- traditional cooking
- Puerto Rican artist Manuel Hernández Acevedo
- grocery shopping in Puerto Rico

Compara con tu mundo
These teenagers are buying ice cream from a street vendor. Another popular cold treat in Puerto Rico is **la piragua,** a kind of shaved ice with fruit syrup. *What do you like to eat or drink during hot weather?*

¿Qué ves?
Mira la foto
¿Están contentos los chicos?

¿Están delante o detrás del señor?

¿Qué les gusta comer a los chicos?

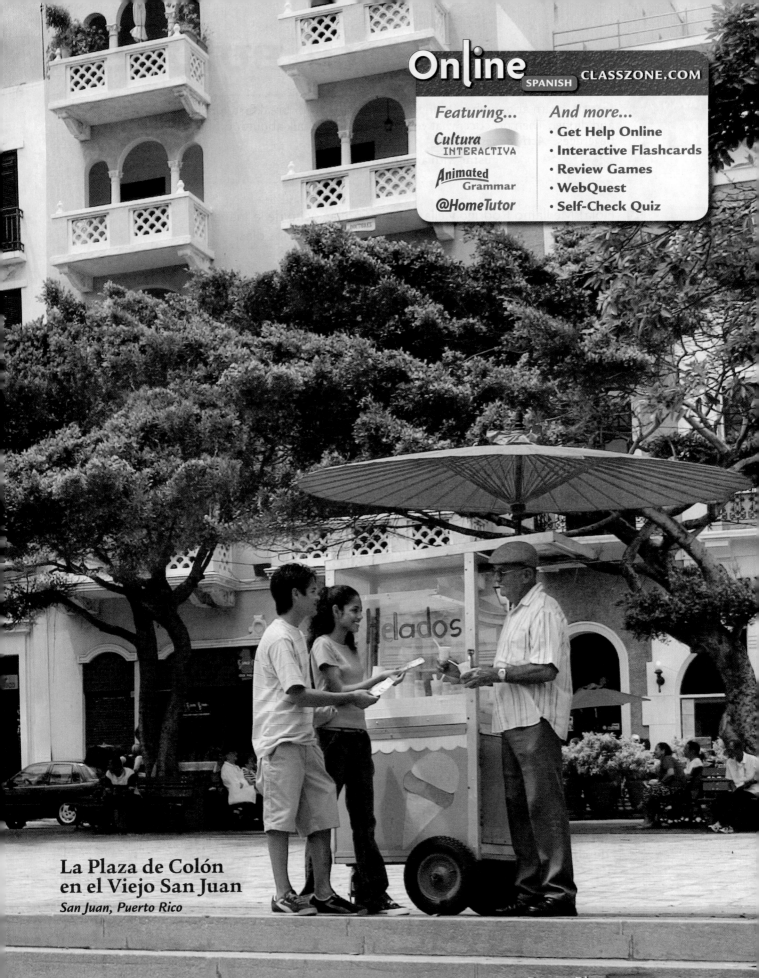

Online SPANISH **CLASSZONE.COM**

Featuring...

Cultura INTERACTIVA

Animated Grammar

@HomeTutor

And more...
• **Get Help Online**
• **Interactive Flashcards**
• **Review Games**
• **WebQuest**
• **Self-Check Quiz**

**La Plaza de Colón
en el Viejo San Juan**
San Juan, Puerto Rico

Presentación de VOCABULARIO

Goal: Learn about what Rodrigo and Marisol eat for breakfast, lunch, and dinner. Then practice what you have learned to talk about foods and beverages. *Actividades 1–2*

♻ *¿Recuerdas?* **gustar** with an infinitive p. 44

VIDEO
DVD

AUDIO

A ¡Hola! Me llamo Rodrigo y ella es Ana. Son las ocho de la mañana. **Es importante** comer **un desayuno nutritivo** todos los días.

el desayuno

los huevos

el pan

B Cuando **tengo hambre**, me gusta comer **huevos** y **pan**. Cuando **tengo sed**, bebo **jugo de naranja**. Me gusta mucho porque es **rico**. Nunca bebo **café** porque es **horrible**.

el cereal

el yogur

de fresa

En **Puerto Rico** se dice...

In Puerto Rico the word for *orange juice* is **el jugo de china.**

las bebidas

el jugo de naranja

el café

la leche

C Es la una y **ahora** Marisol y yo comemos **el almuerzo.** En la cafetería **venden** muchas **comidas:** sándwiches, hamburguesas y sopa. También venden **bebidas: leche,** jugos y refrescos.

el almuerzo

el sándwich de jamón y queso

la hamburguesa

la sopa

Más vocabulario

¿Cómo? *How?*	**¿Quién(es)?** *Who?*
¿Cuál(es)? *Which?*	**compartir** *to share*
¿Por qué? *Why?*	**otro(a)** *other*
¿Qué? *What?*	*Expansión de vocabulario* p. R4

Continuará...

Presentación de VOCABULARIO
(continuación)

D Marisol y yo compramos fruta **para** mi papá: **manzanas, bananas y uvas.**
La cena es a las siete y **tengo ganas de** comer. Siempre como mucho
cuando mi mamá prepara la comida.

la manzana

las uvas

la banana

En Puerto Rico se dice...
The word for *banana* is
el guineo.

la cena

¡A responder! Escuchar

Write **desayuno** and **almuerzo** on separate pieces of paper. Listen to
the list of foods. Hold up the correct piece or pieces of paper to indicate
when you eat each food.

@HomeTutor VideoPlus
Interactive Flashcards
ClassZone.com

Práctica de VOCABULARIO

1 | ¡A jugar! Busca, busca

Escribir

Find and write the names of the eight foods hidden in the cafeteria scene.

2 | ¿Qué te gusta más? ♻ *¿Recuerdas?* gustar with an infinitive p. 44

Hablar

Talk with a partner about which foods and drinks you like more.

(A) ¿Te gusta más comer papas fritas o pizza?

(B) Me gusta más comer pizza.

1.

2.

3.

4.

5.

6.

Más práctica   Cuaderno *pp. 101–103*   Cuaderno para hispanohablantes *pp. 101–104*

PARA Y PIENSA

Did you get it?
1. Name three breakfast foods.   2. Name three lunch foods.

🔎 **Get Help Online**
ClassZone.com

Lección 1
ciento cincuenta y nueve   **159**

VOCABULARIO *en contexto*

Goal: Identify the words Rodrigo and Marisol use to ask questions. Then practice these words to ask questions and give answers. *Actividades 3–4*

♻ *¿Recuerdas?* Snack foods p. 33

Telehistoria escena 1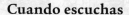

@*HomeTutor* VideoPlus
ClassZone.com

STRATEGIES

Cuando lees

List the question words As you read, list the words that indicate questions, such as **Qué** in **¿Qué amiga?** Save the list so that you can add more question words as you encounter them.

Cuando escuchas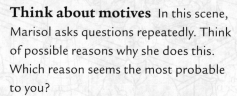

Think about motives In this scene, Marisol asks questions repeatedly. Think of possible reasons why she does this. Which reason seems the most probable to you?

VIDEO
DVD

AUDIO

Rodrigo and Marisol walk to the grocery store. Rodrigo is counting his money.

Marisol: ¿A la escuela? ¿Por qué vas a la escuela hoy? Es sábado.

Rodrigo: Trini Salgado llega hoy y necesito un autógrafo en una camiseta. Es importante.

Marisol: ¿En una camiseta? ¿Qué camiseta?

Rodrigo: Tengo una amiga...

Marisol: *(teasing him)* ¿Una amiga? ¿Qué amiga? ¿Cómo se llama?

Rodrigo: Se llama Alicia.

Marisol: ¿De dónde es?

Rodrigo: Es de Miami. *(He loses count and starts over, sighing.)*

Marisol: ¿Cuándo tienes que estar en la escuela?

Rodrigo: A las cuatro de la tarde. *(Rodrigo loses count.)* ¡Y por favor! ¡No más preguntas! *(He starts to count again.)*

Marisol: Quince, veinte, cuarenta...   **Continuará... p. 166**

También se dice

Puerto Rico Rodrigo uses the word **la camiseta** when he mentions Alicia's T-shirt. In other Spanish-speaking countries you might hear:
• **Argentina** la remera
• **Perú** el polo
• **Venezuela** la franela
• **México** la playera

Nota gramatical

You learned interrogative words on p. 157. Use an **interrogative word** followed by a **conjugated verb** to ask a question. Notice that each interrogative has an accent.

¿Cómo está usted?   **¿Por qué estás** triste?

How are you?   *Why are you sad?*

3 | Muchas preguntas *Comprensión del episodio*

Escuchar
Leer

Complete each question with the appropriate interrogative word and choose the correct answer according to the episode.

cómo   dónde   quién

por qué   qué

1. ¿ _____ necesita Rodrigo?
2. ¿ _____ se llama la amiga de Rodrigo?
3. ¿De _____ es Alicia?
4. ¿ _____ va a la escuela Rodrigo?
5. ¿ _____ es Trini Salgado?

a. Es de Miami.
b. porque Trini Salgado está allí
c. un autógrafo
d. Alicia
e. una atleta famosa

4 | ¿Cómo es? ♲ *¿Recuerdas?* Snack foods p. 33

Hablar

Work with a partner to describe the following foods and drinks in your school's cafeteria.

A ¿Cómo es la leche?

B La leche es buena.

Estudiante A

1. 2. 3. 4.
5. 6. 7. 8.

Estudiante B

nutritivo(a)
bueno(a)
malo(a)
horrible
rico(a)

PARA Y PIENSA

Did you get it? Choose the correct interrogative word.
1. ¿(Qué / Quiénes) son las amigas de Rodrigo?
2. ¿(Cuándo / Cuál) llega Trini Salgado?
3. ¿(Quién / Por qué) necesita Rodrigo el autógrafo?

Get Help Online
ClassZone.com

Presentación de GRAMÁTICA

Goal: Learn how to use **gustar** with nouns. Then practice using this verb to express what foods you like and don't like. *Actividades 5–11*

English Grammar Connection: In English, the phrase *I like* doesn't change. In Spanish, there are two ways to say it, depending on whether what you like is singular or plural. This is because the Spanish phrase **me gusta** literally means that something *is pleasing to me*.

Gustar with Nouns

 ¿Recuerdas? You have already learned to use **gustar** with infinitives to say what people like to do (see p. 44).

To talk about the things that people like, use **gustar + noun**.

Here's how:

If what is liked is singular, use the **singular** form **gusta**.	If what is liked is plural, use the **plural** form **gustan**.
Singular	**Plural**
me gusta **la sopa**	me gustan **los jugos**
te gusta **la sopa**	te gustan **los jugos**
le gusta **la sopa**	le gustan **los jugos**
nos gusta **la sopa**	nos gustan **los jugos**
os gusta **la sopa**	os gustan **los jugos**
les gusta **la sopa**	les gustan **los jugos**

matches singular noun
Me gusta el cereal.
I like cereal.

matches plural noun
Me gustan las uvas.
I like grapes.

Notice that the singular and plural forms of **gustar** match what is liked, not the person who likes it.

Más práctica
　Cuaderno *pp. 104–106*
　Cuaderno para hispanohablantes *pp. 105–107*

@HomeTutor
Leveled Grammar Practice
ClassZone.com

Práctica de GRAMÁTICA

5 | ¿Qué les gusta?

Hablar
Escribir

Tell whether the following people like or don't like the following foods and drinks.

modelo: a Luis / el yogur
A Luis **le gusta** el yogur.

1. a los maestros / el café

6. a ti / las uvas

2. a nosotros / las papas fritas

7. a Jaime y a Rafael / la leche

3. a Adela / las manzanas

8. a usted / el cereal

4. a mí / las hamburguesas

9. a ellos / las bananas

5. a mis amigos / los sándwiches

10. a ustedes / el jugo

6 | En el supermercado

Leer
Escribir

Indicate what these people like and don't like at the supermarket, according to the description.

modelo: El yogur es horrible. (a Rodrigo)
A Rodrigo no le gusta el yogur.

1. Las uvas son ricas. (a ti)

4. Los huevos son horribles. (a mí)

2. La sopa es buena. (a Marisol)

5. El café es muy bueno. (a usted)

3. El cereal es malo. (a nosotros)

6. Los jugos son nutritivos. (a ellos)

AUDIO

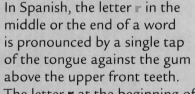

Pronunciación Las letras r y rr

In Spanish, the letter r in the middle or the end of a word is pronounced by a single tap of the tongue against the gum above the upper front teeth. The letter r at the beginning of a word or rr within a word is pronounced by several rapid taps called a trill.

Listen and repeat.

para   cereal   beber   yogur
rico   rubio   horrible   pizarrón

El cereal y el yogur son ricos; no son horribles.

Comparación cultural

La cocina criolla

How do historical influences affect the food that people eat? Traditional cooking in **Puerto Rico,** known as *la cocina criolla,* combines Spanish, African, and indigenous influences. *Tostones* (fried plantains) are a common side dish. Popular snack foods are *alcapurrias* (fried plantains stuffed with meat) and *bacalaítos* (codfish fritters). In **El Salvador,** traditional cuisine blends indigenous and Spanish influences. A typical food is the *pupusa,* a corn tortilla filled with beans, pork, and cheese. *Pupusas* are often served with *curtido,* a spicy coleslaw. *Semita,* a sweet bread layered with pineapple marmalade, is also popular.

Compara con tu mundo *Which of these dishes would you most like to try and why? What is the most interesting dish that you have ever tried?*

Tostones

Pupusas

Use the information to talk with a partner about food preferences in Puerto Rico and El Salvador.

> **A** ¿A quiénes les gustan los tostones?

> **B** A los chicos de Puerto Rico les gustan.

8 | Opiniones

Work in a group of three to talk about the foods and drinks you like and don't like.

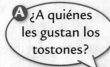

la pizza   las uvas   la leche

las manzanas   el jugo de naranja   ¿ ?

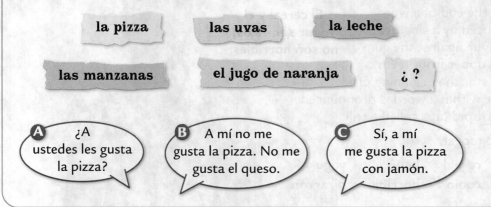

> **A** ¿A ustedes les gusta la pizza?

> **B** A mí no me gusta la pizza. No me gusta el queso.

> **C** Sí, a mí me gusta la pizza con jamón.

9 | El menú

Leer
Hablar

Ask a partner questions about which foods on the menu he or she likes more and why.

A ¿Te gusta más el desayuno uno o el desayuno dos?

B Me gusta más el desayuno dos porque me gusta el cereal y no me gustan los huevos.

Restaurante Borinquen

Desayunos (de 8:00 a 11:00)
1. Huevos fritos o revoltillo con jamón $4.00
2. Cereal frío y fruta $4.00
3. Frutas frescas
   (uvas, guineos, manzanas), yogur $3.50

Bebidas incluidas: jugo de china, café o leche

Almuerzos (de 12:00 a 3:00)
1. Hamburguesa americana, papas fritas $5.50
2. Sándwich de jamón y queso, con fruta $6.50
3. Pizza con jamón y queso $5.50
4. Asopao de vegetales
   (sopa tradicional de Puerto Rico) $4.00

Bebidas incluidas: jugos, refrescos o café
Postres incluidos: helado, flan o pastel del día

10 | ¿Y tú?

Hablar
Escribir

Answer the questions in complete sentences.

1. ¿Qué comida te gusta cuando tienes mucha hambre?
2. ¿Qué bebida te gusta cuando tienes mucha sed?
3. ¿Cuál es una comida nutritiva?
4. ¿Qué comidas nutritivas te gustan y no te gustan?
5. ¿Qué comidas en la cafetería de la escuela te gustan?
6. ¿Qué comidas en la cafetería de la escuela no te gustan?

11 | Le gusta...

Escribir

Think of someone you know who leads an especially healthy lifestyle. Write a short description of that person's favorite activities and the foods he or she likes and doesn't like.

modelo: Mi amigo Javier es muy atlético. Le gusta practicar deportes. Le gustan las frutas, pero no le gusta la pizza porque no es nutritiva...

Más práctica   Cuaderno *pp. 104–106*   Cuaderno para hispanohablantes *pp. 105–107*

PARA Y PIENSA

Did you get it?
1. Tell a friend you like eggs for breakfast.
2. Say that José likes pizza with ham.
3. Ask a friend why he or she doesn't like fruit.

Get Help Online ClassZone.com

GRAMÁTICA en contexto

¡AVANZA!

Goal: Listen to how Marisol and Rodrigo use **gustar** to talk about what they like to eat. Then use **gustar** to talk about likes and dislikes. *Actividades 12–14*

Telehistoria escena 2

@HomeTutor VideoPlus
ClassZone.com

STRATEGIES

Cuando lees

Organize with a chart To keep thoughts organized, make a chart listing Rodrigo's and Marisol's likes and dislikes about breakfast foods. Are your preferences more like Rodrigo's or more like Marisol's?

Cuando escuchas

Use mental pictures to remember words Listen for names of foods. For each name you hear, picture the food mentally. Remember these words by repeatedly linking them to the mental pictures.

VIDEO DVD

AUDIO

Marisol: ¿Qué te gusta comer en el desayuno?

Rodrigo: Me gustan el cereal, el yogur, las frutas... Y a ti, Marisol, ¿qué te gusta comer en el desayuno?

Marisol: No me gusta el yogur y no me gustan los huevos.

Rodrigo: ¿Te gustan las frutas? ¿Las uvas, las manzanas?

Marisol: No me gusta comer mucho en el desayuno.

Rodrigo: ¡Tienes que comer bien en el desayuno! ¿Te gusta el pan? ¿O la leche?

Marisol: Me gustan las galletas. Tengo hambre.

Rodrigo: Sí. ¡Porque no te gusta comer mucho en el desayuno!

Continuará... p. 172

Unidad 3 Puerto Rico
166 ciento sesenta y seis

12 | ¿Un desayuno grande? *Comprensión del episodio*

Escuchar Leer

Answer the questions about the episode.

1. ¿Qué le gusta comer a Rodrigo en el desayuno?
2. ¿A quién no le gustan los desayunos grandes?
3. ¿Qué le gusta comer a Marisol?
4. ¿Por qué tiene hambre Marisol?

13 | En el desayuno y el almuerzo

Escribir

Write a description of what foods and drinks you like and don't like for breakfast and lunch.

modelo: En el desayuno me gusta el pan. Para beber, me gusta el jugo de naranja. También me gustan las bananas. Es importante comer fruta. No me gustan los huevos. Son horribles. En el almuerzo...

14 | Una entrevista

Hablar Escribir

Ask another student what he or she likes and doesn't like for lunch. Write the responses. Then compare your likes and dislikes, using a Venn diagram.

modelo: A Nicolás le gustan los sándwiches de queso en el almuerzo. También le gusta la fruta. No le gusta la pizza...

A mí   A Nicolás

Me gustan las hamburguesas. | Nos gusta la fruta. | No le gusta la pizza.

PARA Y PIENSA

Did you get it? Complete each sentence based on the Telehistoria with the correct form of **gustar**.

1. A Marisol no le _____ la comida nutritiva.
2. A Rodrigo le _____ el cereal.
3. A Marisol le _____ las galletas.

Get Help Online
ClassZone.com

Presentación de GRAMÁTICA

Goal: Learn how to form **-er** and **-ir** verbs. Then use these verbs and **hacer** to talk about school activities and what you and others eat and drink. *Actividades 15–20*

 ¿Recuerdas? The verb **estar** p. 128

English Grammar Connection: Remember that the **present tense** shows an action happening now (see p. 106).

Present Tense of -er and -ir Verbs

> **Animated** Grammar
> ClassZone.com

Regular verbs that end in **-er** or **-ir** work a little differently than regular **-ar** verbs. How do you form the present tense of regular **-er** and **-ir** verbs?

Here's how:

The endings for **-er** and **-ir** verbs are the same except in the **nosotros(as)** and **vosotros(as)** forms. The letter change in these two forms matches the ending of the infinitive.

vender *to sell*		
yo	**vendo**	nosotros(as)	**vendemos**
tú	**vendes**	vosotros(as)	**vendéis**
usted, él, ella	**vende**	ustedes, ellos(as)	**venden**

-er verbs = -**emos**, -**éis**

Mario **vende** comida en la cafetería.
*Mario **sells** food in the cafeteria.*

compartir *to share*		
yo	**comparto**	nosotros(as)	**compartimos**
tú	**compartes**	vosotros(as)	**compartís**
usted, él, ella	**comparte**	ustedes, ellos(as)	**comparten**

-ir verbs = -**imos**, -**ís**

Compartimos las uvas.
*We **are sharing** the grapes.*

Más práctica
Cuaderno *pp. 107–109*
Cuaderno para hispanohablantes *pp. 108–111*

@HomeTutor
Leveled Grammar Practice
ClassZone.com

Práctica de GRAMÁTICA

15 | ¿Comer o beber?

Hablar Escribir

Tell what these people eat or drink.

modelo: Rodrigo (cereal)
Rodrigo come cereal.

1. Rodrigo y Marisol (uvas)
2. tú (refrescos)
3. ustedes (pan)
4. Marisol y yo (sopa)
5. Ana (hamburguesas)
6. usted (sándwiches)
7. yo (jugo de naranja)
8. los maestros (café)

16 | ¿En la cafetería o en clase? ♻ *¿Recuerdas?* The verb **estar** p. 128

Hablar Escribir

Tell what these people are doing and where they are right now.

modelo: Marisol / vender fruta
Marisol vende fruta. Ahora está en la cafetería.

1. yo / beber leche
2. ellas / leer un libro
3. tú / comer yogur
4. Rodrigo / aprender el español
5. ustedes / escribir en el pizarrón
6. tú y yo / compartir una pizza

17 | Actividades en el almuerzo

Escuchar Escribir

Listen to the descriptions of Marisol and her friends, and take notes. Then write sentences saying who does what, using elements from each puzzle piece.

1. Marisol
2. la cafetería
3. Rodrigo y Mateo
4. Carmen
5. Raúl y David
6. Laura y Diana

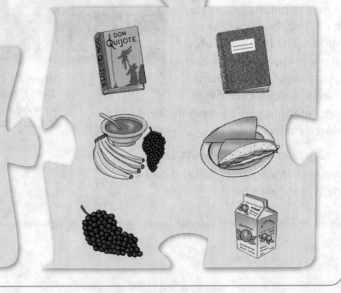

Nota gramatical

The verb **hacer** is irregular in the present tense only in the **yo** form: **hago.**
In the other forms, it follows the pattern for **-er** verbs. (See p. R12 for the complete conjugation.)

Hago un sándwich.   Carmen **hace** la tarea.

I am making a *sandwich.*   *Carmen is doing her homework.*

18 | ¿Con quién?

Hablar

Ask a partner with whom he or she does the following activities.

modelo: comer pizza

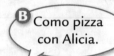

A ¿Con quién comes pizza?

B Como pizza con Alicia.

1. correr

2. compartir el almuerzo

3. hacer la tarea

4. comer ¿ ?

5. escribir correos electrónicos

6. beber ¿ ?

Comparación cultural

La Plaza de Colón

How does an artist's work represent historic landmarks of a country? Many of Manuel Hernández Acevedo's paintings depict scenes of Old San Juan, **Puerto Rico.** In Old San Juan you will find cobblestone streets, Spanish colonial buildings, and many plazas. The Plaza de Colón is popular with both tourists and locals. A statue of Christopher Columbus in the center of the square includes plaques commemorating the explorer's achievements.

Compara con tu mundo *What is a well-known landmark in your area? What does it represent? Why is it important?*

Above: La Plaza de Colón *(1986), Manuel Hernández Acevedo; right:* La estatua de Cristóbal Colón

19 | En el café Buenavida

Hablar
Escribir

Look at the picture below and tell what the people are doing.

20 | Una encuesta

Hablar

Survey your classmates about the following activities.

modelo: leer: en la biblioteca, en la cafetería, en la clase de inglés

A ¿Lees en la biblioteca, en la cafetería o en la clase de inglés?

B Leo en la clase de inglés.

C Leo en la biblioteca y en la cafetería.

1. beber: leche, refrescos, jugo
2. hacer la tarea: en la clase, en la biblioteca, en la cafetería
3. escribir: en un cuaderno, en el pizarrón, en la computadora
4. comer: sándwiches, pizza, hamburguesas
5. aprender: historia, matemáticas, ciencias
6. compartir: pizza, uvas, papas fritas

Más práctica   Cuaderno *pp. 107–109*   Cuaderno para hispanohablantes *pp. 108–111*

PARA Y PIENSA

Did you get it? Complete each sentence with the correct form of the verb in parentheses.
1. ¿Qué _____ ellas? (hacer) Ellas _____ el desayuno. (comer)
2. ¿Qué _____ tú? (hacer) Yo _____ un libro. (leer)
3. ¿Qué _____ Rafael? (hacer) Rafael _____ un refresco. (beber)

Get Help Online
ClassZone.com

Todo junto

 ¡AVANZA!

Goal: Show what you know Pay attention to the **-er** and **-ir** verbs Rodrigo and Marisol use to talk about eating healthy food. Then practice these verbs and **gustar** to talk about lunchtime in the cafeteria. *Actividades 21–25*

♻️ *¿Recuerdas?* Telling time p. 99

Telehistoria completa

@**HomeTutor** VideoPlus
ClassZone.com

STRATEGIES

Cuando lees

Find the twist There is sometimes a "twist," or something unexpected, toward the end of a story or scene. Find the twist in this scene. What is it? Why is it unexpected?

Cuando escuchas 🎧

Listen for attitude changes To understand the scene fully, notice people's attitudes. At the beginning of the scene, what are Marisol's and Rodrigo's contrasting attitudes? Whose attitude changes during the scene? Why?

Escena 1 *Resumen*
Rodrigo necesita el autógrafo de Trini Salgado para Alicia. Tiene que estar en la escuela a las cuatro de la tarde.

Escena 2 *Resumen*
Rodrigo compra comida. Le gusta la comida nutritiva. Marisol tiene hambre porque no le gusta comer mucho en el desayuno.

Escena 3

 VIDEO DVD

 AUDIO

Marisol stops to order an ice cream.

Rodrigo: ¿Helado? ¿En el almuerzo?

Marisol: Sí, tengo ganas de comer helado. ¿Compartimos?

Rodrigo: El helado no es nutritivo.

Marisol: ¡Pero es muy rico!

Rodrigo: ¿Qué comes en la cena? ¿Una hamburguesa con papas fritas?

Marisol: ¿Venden papas fritas?

Rodrigo: Tienes que comer comidas buenas.

Marisol: Sí, sí. Yo como comida nutritiva de vez en cuando.

Rodrigo: ¿Sí? ¿Qué comes?

Marisol: Me gusta la sopa.

Rodrigo: La sopa es muy buena.

Marisol: Necesito una bebida.

Marisol walks away. Rodrigo sneaks a taste of her ice cream.

Rodrigo: El helado es muy rico.

21 | ¡A completar! *Comprensión de los episodios*

Escuchar
Leer

Complete the following sentences, based on the episodes.

1. Rodrigo necesita...
2. La amiga de Miami se llama...
3. En el desayuno Rodrigo come...
4. Marisol tiene hambre porque...
5. Marisol tiene ganas de...
6. Cuando Marisol compra una bebida, Rodrigo...

22 | Organiza la información *Comprensión de los episodios*

Escuchar
Leer

Write an article about Marisol or Rodrigo. Copy this map on a piece of paper and use it to organize the information.

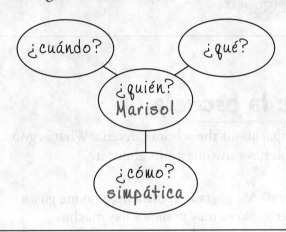

¿cuándo? ¿qué?
¿quién?
Marisol
¿cómo?
simpática

23 | ¿Qué hacen en la cafetería? ♻ *¿Recuerdas?* Telling time p. 99

Hablar

STRATEGY Hablar

Think and practice in advance First write down words or phrases you want to say. Then practice pronouncing them aloud. Say them in sentences several times and you will be ready for your conversation!

Work in a group of three to talk about what you do in the cafeteria. Include what time you go and what they sell there. Also explain what you eat and drink and why.

A ¿A qué hora van ustedes a la cafetería? ¿Qué hacen?

B Como en la cafetería a la una. Los lunes como pizza y bebo jugo porque no me gusta la leche.

C Yo compro una manzana y leo un libro...

24 | Integración

Leer
Escuchar
Hablar

Read the newspaper ad for Supermercado Grande. Then listen to the radio ad for Supermercado Econo. Say what foods you like and where they sell them.

Fuente 1 Anuncio

Supermercado Grande

Uvas
$1.49 lb.
Reg. $1.95 lb.

Galletas
dos por $1.00
Reg. $1.50

Manzanas
75¢ lb.
Reg. 99¢ lb.

$4.99
Reg. $6.99

Pizza de queso

Fuente 2 Anuncio de radio

Listen and take notes
- ¿Qué comidas venden en el Supermercado Econo?
- ¿Qué venden en la cafetería?

modelo: A mí me gustan las uvas. Venden uvas en el Supermercado Grande...

25 | La cafetería de la escuela

Escribir

Write a letter to your principal about the school cafeteria. What is good and bad there? Why? Do you have any questions about it?

modelo: Sr. Hogan:
¿Cómo está usted? Me gusta la escuela pero no me gusta mucho la cafetería. No es muy grande y hay muchos estudiantes. ¿Por qué no venden...

Writing Criteria	Excellent	Good	Needs Work
Content	Your letter includes a lot of information.	Your letter includes some information.	Your letter includes little information.
Communication	Most of your letter is organized and easy to follow.	Parts of your letter are organized and easy to follow.	Your letter is disorganized and hard to follow.
Accuracy	Your letter has few mistakes in grammar and vocabulary.	Your letter has some mistakes in grammar and vocabulary.	Your letter has many mistakes in grammar and vocabulary.

Más práctica Cuaderno *pp. 110–111* Cuaderno para hispanohablantes *pp. 112–113*

PARA Y PIENSA

Did you get it? Complete the first sentence with a form of **gustar,** and the second sentence with the correct form of **compartir** or **beber.**
1. A Rodrigo le _____ la fruta. Él _____ jugo de naranja.
2. A Rodrigo y a Ana les _____ los sándwiches. Siempre _____ un sándwich.

Get Help Online
ClassZone.com

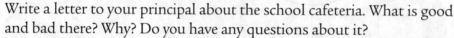

Juegos y diversiones

Review food vocabulary by playing a game of Fly Swatter.

MATAMOSCAS

The Setup

Your teacher will tape a number of picture cards on the board and divide the class into two teams.

Playing the Game

The first player from each team will go up to the board. Your teacher will give each player a fly swatter and then say a vocabulary word represented by one of the pictures. The player who "swats" the correct picture first gets a point.

Play continues with new players from each team.

The Winner!

The team with the most points at the end wins.

Materials
- picture cards representing vocabulary words
- two fly swatters
- tape

Lectura

Goal: Read a fragment from a supermarket circular and then a shopping list. Compare this information with the foods and beverages you eat and drink.

AUDIO

¡A comprar y a comer!

The following is a supermarket circular from Supermercados La Famosa and a shopping list.

STRATEGY Leer
Don't translate; use pictures!
Sketch and label pictures of the foods and beverages on the shopping list. Below each picture, write the brand or type of item you can buy at Supermercados La Famosa.

SUPERMERCADOS LA FAMOSA

TENEMOS BUENOS PRECIOS Y PRODUCTOS SUPERIORES

Hamburguesas El bohío, 1.5 lbs.
$1.29

$1.79
Queso americano de sándwich Vitarroz 12 oz.[1]

Jamón de sándwich Astor
$1.79/LB.[2]

Uvas de California
$1.59/LB.

Yogur de mango La Yogurt
.59¢

$1.29
Queso crema La Cremosa 8 oz.

Leche condensada La Fe 14 oz.
.99¢

[1] onzas   [2] libra

Unidad 3 Puerto Rico
176 ciento setenta y seis

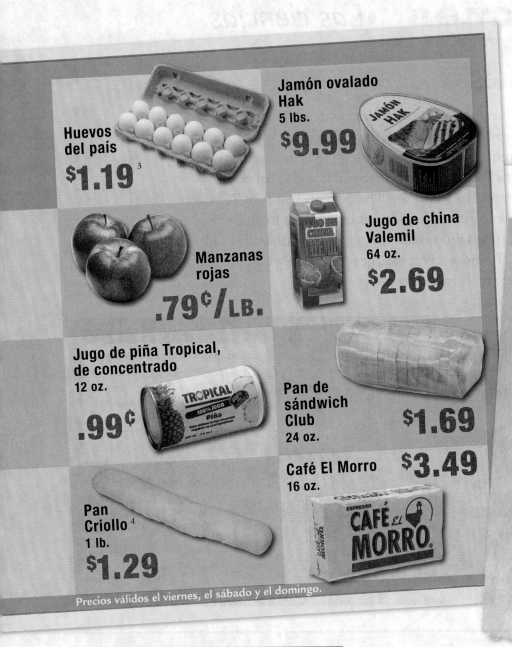

Huevos
del país
$1.19 [3]

Jamón ovalado
Hak
5 lbs.
$9.99

Manzanas
rojas
.79¢/LB.

Jugo de china
Valemil
64 oz.
$2.69

Jugo de piña Tropical,
de concentrado
12 oz.
.99¢

Pan de
sándwich
Club
24 oz.
$1.69

Pan
Criollo [4]
1 lb.
$1.29

Café El Morro
16 oz.
$3.49

Precios válidos el viernes, el sábado y el domingo.

Lista de compras

café
huevos
leche condensada
jugo de china
pan
yogur
cereal
jamón de sándwich
queso de sándwich
uvas
manzanas

---

[3] En Puerto Rico usan dólares estadounidenses

[4] bread similar to French bread

PARA Y PIENSA

¿Comprendiste?

1. ¿Qué hay en la lista que no está en la circular?
2. ¿Qué venden en Supermercados La Famosa que no está en la lista?
3. ¿Qué frutas hay en la lista?

¿Y tú?

¿Qué comida en Supermercados La Famosa comes tú? ¿Qué bebes?

Conexiones *Las ciencias*

Los huracanes

The Caribbean island of Puerto Rico is located in an area prone to hurricanes (**huracanes**). The word *hurricane* comes from the Taino word *hurákan*, which was used by the pre-Columbian inhabitants of the island to describe these storms (**tormentas**). Hurricanes draw energy from the surface of warm tropical waters and from moisture in the air. The extreme winds of 74 miles per hour or more can create storm surges—domes of water up to 20 feet high and 100 miles wide—and can spawn tornadoes, torrential rain, and floods. Research and write about the most severe weather condition where you live. Create a diagram or drawing to illustrate your report.

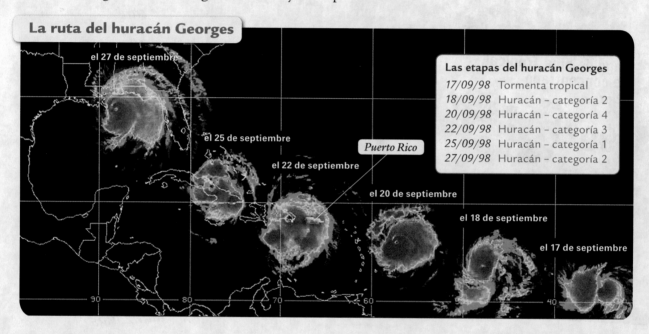

La ruta del huracán Georges

el 27 de septiembre
el 25 de septiembre
Puerto Rico
el 22 de septiembre
el 20 de septiembre
el 18 de septiembre
el 17 de septiembre

Las etapas del huracán Georges

17/09/98	Tormenta tropical
18/09/98	Huracán – categoría 2
20/09/98	Huracán – categoría 4
22/09/98	Huracán – categoría 3
25/09/98	Huracán – categoría 1
27/09/98	Huracán – categoría 2

Proyecto 1 *Las matemáticas*

Hurricane Georges passed over Puerto Rico at a speed of about 24 kilometers per hour (**kilómetros por hora**). Find the distance from Humacao to Mayagüez in kilometers and calculate the time it took for the storm to move from one city to the other.

Proyecto 2 *La historia*

Research another major hurricane that has hit Puerto Rico in the past century. Draw a map showing the trajectory of the hurricane. Then write a paragraph describing the storm.

Proyecto 3 *La geografía*

Compare this map to the one on page xxxiii to name three other countries that were hit by Hurricane Georges. Make a chart in Spanish showing the three countries, the dates of the storm, and the category of the hurricane at the time it hit.

La playa Ocean Park, Puerto Rico, durante el huracán Georges

En resumen
Vocabulario y gramática

Animated Grammar
Interactive Flashcards
ClassZone.com

Vocabulario

Talk About Foods and Beverages					
Meals		**For Breakfast**		**For Lunch**	
el almuerzo	lunch	el café	coffee	la hamburguesa	hamburger
la bebida	beverage, drink	el cereal	cereal	el sándwich de	ham and cheese
la cena	dinner	el huevo	egg	jamón y queso	sandwich
compartir	to share	el jugo de naranja	orange juice	la sopa	soup
la comida	food; meal	la leche	milk		
el desayuno	breakfast	el pan	bread	**Fruit**	
vender	to sell	el yogur	yogurt	la banana	banana
				la manzana	apple
				las uvas	grapes

Describe Feelings		Ask Questions		Other Words and Phrases	
tener ganas de...	to feel like . . .	¿Cómo?	How?	ahora	now
tener hambre	to be hungry	¿Cuál(es)?	Which?; What?	Es importante.	It's important.
tener sed	to be thirsty	¿Por qué?	Why?	horrible	horrible
		¿Qué?	What?	nutritivo(a)	nutritious
		¿Quién(es)?	Who?	otro(a)	other
				para	for; in order to
				rico(a)	tasty, delicious

Gramática

Notas gramaticales: Interrogative words *p. 161,* The verb **hacer** *p. 170*

Gustar with Nouns

To talk about the things that people like, use
gustar + **noun.**

Singular
me gusta **la sopa**
te gusta **la sopa**
le gusta **la sopa**
nos gusta **la sopa**
os gusta **la sopa**
les gusta **la sopa**

Plural
me gustan **los jugos**
te gustan **los jugos**
le gustan **los jugos**
nos gustan **los jugos**
os gustan **los jugos**
les gustan **los jugos**

Present Tense of -er and -ir Verbs

vender to sell	
vendo	vendemos
vendes	vendéis
vende	venden

compartir to share	
comparto	compartimos
compartes	compartís
comparte	comparten

Repaso de la lección

¡LLEGADA!

Now you can
- talk about foods and beverages
- ask questions
- say which foods you like and don't like

Using
- interrogative words
- **gustar** with nouns
- present tense of **-er** and **-ir** verbs
- the verb **hacer**

@HomeTutor
ClassZone.com

To review
- **gustar** with nouns p. 162
- present tense of **-er** and **-ir** verbs p. 168

1 | Listen and understand

AUDIO

Lola never eats traditional meals. Listen to the radio interview. Write **el desayuno, el almuerzo,** or **la cena,** according to when she eats or drinks each item.

1. huevos
2. café
3. leche
4. hamburguesas
5. banana
6. refresco
7. pan
8. cereal

To review
- present tense of **-er** and **-ir** verbs p. 168
- the verb **hacer** p. 170

2 | Talk about foods and beverages

Write what these people are doing in the cafeteria.

modelo: Daniel / comer
Daniel come pan.

1. Irene / beber

2. ustedes / compartir

3. yo / hacer

4. nosotros / vender

5. yo / comer

6. tú / hacer

7. los estudiantes / beber

8. Trinidad y yo / compartir

To review
· interrogative
  words p. 161

3 | Ask questions

Gilberto is a new student. It's lunchtime, and he is in the cafeteria with Julia.
Complete the conversation with interrogative words.

modelo: ¿<u>Cuál</u> es el sándwich del día?
Es el sándwich de jamón y queso.

Gilberto: ¿ __1.__ está el yogur?

Julia: Está al lado de las frutas.

Gilberto: ¿ __2.__ no venden pizza?

Julia: Porque hoy no es viernes.

Gilberto: ¿ __3.__ venden los martes?

Julia: Venden hamburguesas.

Gilberto: ¿ __4.__ es la sopa?

Julia: Es muy rica.

Gilberto: ¿ __5.__ prepara la comida?

Julia: La señora Aguirre.

Gilberto: ¿ __6.__ personas trabajan en la cafetería?

Julia: Nueve o diez.

Gilberto: ¿ __7.__ compramos la bebida?

Julia: Ahora, con la comida.

Gilberto: ¿ __8.__ vamos después del almuerzo?

Julia: A la clase de inglés.

To review
· **gustar** with
  nouns p. 162

4 | Say which foods you like and don't like

These people are in the supermarket and are talking about foods and
drinks. Write sentences about what they like and don't like, according to
what they say.

modelo: la señora Medina: «El yogur es bueno.»
A la señora Medina le gusta el yogur.

1. ustedes: «No, el yogur es horrible.»

2. Adán y Susana: «Necesitamos manzanas. Son nutritivas.»

3. el señor Chávez: «El café es bueno.»

4. nosotros: «No, el café es malo.»

5. yo: «Tengo ganas de comer uvas.»

6. tú: «Las hamburguesas son ricas.»

To review
· El Yunque p. 153
· Comparación
  cultural pp. 154,
  164, 170

5 | Puerto Rico and El Salvador

Comparación cultural

Answer these culture questions.

1. What is El Yunque and what can you find there?

2. What is a popular cold treat in Puerto Rico?

3. What can you find in Plaza de Colón?

4. Describe some popular foods from Puerto Rico and El Salvador.

Más práctica Cuaderno *pp. 112–123* Cuaderno para hispanohablantes *pp. 114–123*

Get Help Online
ClassZone.com

Puerto Rico

¡AVANZA!

Tema:
En mi familia

In this lesson you will learn to
• talk about family
• ask and tell ages
• express possession
• give dates
• make comparisons

using
• **de** to show possession
• possessive adjectives
• comparatives

♻ *¿Recuerdas?*
• the verb **tener,** describing others
• numbers from 11 to 100
• after-school activities

Comparación cultural

In this lesson you will learn about
• government elections
• portraits and instruments from Puerto Rico and Peru
• **quinceañeras** in Puerto Rico and Peru
• meals in Puerto Rico, El Salvador, and Peru

Compara con tu mundo
In many Spanish-speaking countries, families share time together at the table long after a meal is over. This custom is called **la sobremesa.** *Does your family have any traditions involving mealtimes? What are they?*

¿Qué ves?
Mira la foto
¿Tiene sed Rodrigo?

¿Qué beben los señores, café o refrescos?

¿Cómo es la chica?

Online

SPANISH CLASSZONE.COM

Featuring...

Cultura INTERACTIVA

Animated Grammar

@HomeTutor

And more...
- Get Help Online
- Interactive Flashcards
- Review Games
- WebQuest
- Self-Check Quiz

Una familia come en casa
San Juan, Puerto Rico

Presentación de VOCABULARIO

Goal: Learn about Rodrigo's family. Then practice what you have learned to talk about families and express possession. *Actividades 1–2*

VIDEO DVD

AUDIO

A Soy Rodrigo. **Vivo** en Puerto Rico con **mis padres.** Ellos tienen dos **hijos.** Yo soy **su hijo** y **mi hermana** Ana es su **hija.** Te presento a las otras personas en **nuestra familia.**

los abuelos

la abuela   el abuelo

María y Cristóbal

los padres

la madre   el padre

Celia y José

los tíos

la tía   el tío

Camila y Pablo

los hermanos

el hermano   la hermana

Rodrigo y Ana

el perro

Capitán

el gato

Príncipe

los primos

el primo   la prima

Tito y Ester

B ¿Cuántos años tienes tú?
Yo **tengo** quince **años**. Ana, mi hermana **menor**, tiene nueve años. Soy su **hermano mayor**.

C ¿Cuál es la fecha? Hoy **es el primero de abril.** Es mi **cumpleaños**. ¿Cuándo es **tu** cumpleaños?

los meses

L	M	M	J	V	S	D
	1	2	3	4	5
6	7	8	9	10	11	12
13	14	15	16	17	18	19
20	21	22	23	24	25	26
27	28	29	30			

enero

febrero

marzo

abril

mayo

junio

julio

agosto

septiembre

octubre

noviembre

diciembre

abril

L	M	M	J	V	S	D
1	2	3	4	5	6
7	8	9	10	11	12	13
14	15	16	17	18	19	20
21	22	23	24	25	26	27
28	29	30				

¡Feliz cumpleaños!

Continuará...

| Los números de 200 a 1.000.000 |

doscientos(as)

trescientos(as)

cuatrocientos(as)

quinientos(as)

seiscientos(as)

setecientos(as)

ochocientos(as)

novecientos(as)

mil

1,000,000

un millón (de)

Más vocabulario

la madrastra *stepmother*
el padrastro *stepfather*

la fecha de nacimiento *birth date*
ya *already*

Expansión de vocabulario p. R4

¡A responder! Escuchar

Listen to the sentences about Rodrigo's family. If the sentence is true,
raise your left hand. If it is false, raise your right hand.

@**HomeTutor** VideoPlus
Interactive Flashcards
ClassZone.com

Práctica de VOCABULARIO

1 | La familia de Rodrigo

Hablar
Escribir

Tell how each person is related to Rodrigo. Use the family tree on page 184 to help you.

modelo: José es el padre.

1.
2.
3.
4.
5.
6.
7.

Nota gramatical

In Spanish, **'s** is never used. To show possession, use **de** and the **noun** that refers to the owner/possessor.

el gato **de Marisa**   *Marisa's cat*   los primos **de Juan**   *Juan's cousins*

2 | La familia de Marisol

Leer

Match the columns to describe the relationship between various members of Marisol's family.

1. El padre de mi madre es...   a. mi hermana.
2. Las hermanas de mi padre son...   b. mi madre.
3. La hija de mi padre es...   c. mis tías.
4. Los hijos de mis padres son...   d. mi abuelo.
5. Las hijas de mi tía son...   e. mis primas.
6. La hermana de mi tía es...   f. mis hermanos.

Más práctica   Cuaderno *pp. 124–126*   Cuaderno para hispanohablantes *pp. 124–127*

PARA Y PIENSA

Did you get it? Fill in the blank with the correct vocabulary word.

1. El ____ de tus tíos es tu primo.
2. Los ____ de tus padres son tus abuelos.
3. Las ____ de tu madre son tus tías.

Get Help Online
ClassZone.com

VOCABULARIO en contexto

Goal: Identify the words Marisol and Rodrigo use to talk about birthdays and other family members. Then practice the words you have learned to ask and tell a person's age. *Actividades 3–4*

 ¿Recuerdas? The verb **tener** p. 100, numbers from 11 to 100 p. 94

Telehistoria escena 1

@HomeTutor VideoPlus
ClassZone.com

STRATEGIES

Cuando lees
Analyze the scene This scene starts out calmly and ends with a problem. What do the characters talk about at the beginning? What is the problem, and whose problem is it?

Cuando escuchas
Remember, listen, and predict
Before listening, remember why Rodrigo wanted Alicia's T-shirt. What happens to the T-shirt in this scene? After listening, predict what will happen next.

VIDEO DVD
AUDIO

Rodrigo — Marisol — Sra. Vélez — Ana

Rodrigo and Marisol arrive in Rodrigo's kitchen.

Marisol: Señora Vélez, ¿es su cumpleaños?

Sra. Vélez: No, es el cumpleaños de Ana.

Marisol: ¡Feliz cumpleaños! ¿Cuántos años tienes?

Ana: Hoy tengo nueve años. Mañana, ¡diez!

Marisol: ¿Mañana? ¿El veintiocho de febrero?

Rodrigo: No. El primero de marzo.

Marisol: El cumpleaños de mi abuela es el primero de marzo.

Ana: Ah, ¿sí? ¿Cuántos años tiene?

Marisol: Tiene sesenta y ocho años.

Rodrigo: Mamá, ¿dónde está la camiseta? Trini Salgado está en la escuela a las cuatro.

Continuará... p. 194

También se dice

Puerto Rico Marisol uses the word **abuela** to talk about her grandmother. In other Spanish-speaking countries you might hear:
• **Perú, Argentina** **la mamama**

3 | Un cumpleaños *Comprensión del episodio*

**Escuchar
Leer**

Tell if the sentences are true or false. Correct the false statements to make them true.

1. Es el cumpleaños de la señora Vélez.

2. Mañana es el veintiocho de febrero.

3. El cumpleaños de Ana es en el mes de febrero.

4. El cumpleaños de la abuela de Marisol es el primero de marzo.

Nota gramatical ♻ *¿Recuerdas?* The verb **tener** p. 100

Use the verb **tener** to talk about how old a person is.

¿Cuántos años **tiene** tu amiga?
How old is your friend?

¿Violeta? **Tiene** quince años.
Violeta? She's fifteen years old.

---

4 | ¿Cuántos años tienen? ♻ *¿Recuerdas?* Numbers from 11 to 100 p. 94

Hablar

Talk with a partner about how old the members of Rodrigo's family are. If you need help, look at the family tree on page 184.

45 años

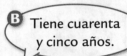

A ¿Cuántos años tiene la madre de Rodrigo?

B Tiene cuarenta y cinco años.

1.

10 años

2.

3 años

3.

66 años

4.

14 años

5.

38 años

6.

47 años

7.

39 años

8.

64 años

PARA Y PIENSA

Did you get it? Give each age, using **tener** and the word for each number in parentheses.

1. Marisol _____ _____ años. (14)

2. El gato de la familia Vélez _____ _____ años. (8)

3. Los padres de Marisol _____ _____ años. (52)

Get Help Online
ClassZone.com

Presentación de GRAMÁTICA

¡AVANZA!

Goal: Learn to express possession. Then practice using possessive adjectives to talk about your family members and to give dates. **Actividades 5–9**

♻ *¿Recuerdas?* After-school activities p. 32, describing others p. 60

English Grammar Connection: **Possessive adjectives** tell you who owns something or describe a relationship between people or things. The forms of possessive adjectives do not change in English, but they do change in Spanish.

They are my cousins.   Ellos son mis primos.

Possessive Adjectives

Animated Grammar
ClassZone.com

In Spanish, **possessive adjectives** agree in number with the nouns they describe.

Here's how:

Singular Possessive Adjectives	
mi *my*	**nuestro(a)** *our*
tu *your (familiar)*	**vuestro(a)** *your (familiar)*
su *your (formal)*	**su** *your*
su *his, her, its*	**su** *their*

Plural Possessive Adjectives	
mis *my*	**nuestros(as)** *our*
tus *your (familiar)*	**vuestros(as)** *your (familiar)*
sus *your (formal)*	**sus** *your*
sus *his, her, its*	**sus** *their*

Es mi tía.
 She is my aunt.

Son mis tías.
 They are my aunts.

Nuestro(a) and **vuestro(a)** must also agree in gender with the nouns they describe.

agrees

Nuestra abuela tiene 70 años.
***Our** grandmother is 70 years old.*

agrees

Nuestros abuelos viven en San Francisco.
***Our** grandparents live in San Francisco.*

Más práctica
Cuaderno *pp. 127–129*
Cuaderno para hispanohablantes *pp. 128–130*

@HomeTutor
Leveled Grammar Practice
ClassZone.com

Práctica de GRAMÁTICA

5 | Las familias

Leer Marisol is talking about families and their pets. Choose the correct possessive adjective to express what she says.

1. Nosotros tenemos tres primas. (Nuestros / **Nuestras**) primas son altas.
2. Ustedes tienen un abuelo. (**Su** / Nuestro) cumpleaños es el dos de abril.
3. Mi familia y yo tenemos una gata vieja. (**Nuestra** / Su) gata es Rubí.
4. Yo tengo dos hermanos mayores. (Mi / **Mis**) hermanos son estudiosos.
5. Mis abuelos tienen un perro. (**Su** / Mi) perro es perezoso.
6. ¡Feliz cumpleaños! Hoy tienes quince años. Es (**tu** / su) cumpleaños.

6 | ¿Qué hacen? 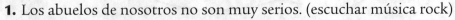 ¿**Recuerdas?** After-school activities p. 32

Leer
Escribir

Use a possessive adjective and tell what activities these people do.

modelo: La hermana de Alicia es inteligente. (sacar buenas notas)
Su hermana saca buenas notas.

1. Los abuelos de nosotros no son muy serios. (escuchar música rock)
2. Los tíos de ustedes son trabajadores. (trabajar mucho)
3. La prima de Marisol no es perezosa. (hacer la tarea)
4. La madre de Rodrigo es atlética. (practicar deportes)
5. La hermana de nosotros es muy estudiosa. (leer muchos libros)
6. El padrastro de Luz es simpático. (pasar un rato con la familia)

Pronunciación | La letra j

AUDIO

The **j** in Spanish sounds similar to the English *h* in the word *hello*.

Listen and repeat.

jamón	mujer
dibujar	joven
junio	hija

La mujer pelirroja es joven.
El cumpleaños del hijo es en julio.

Soy Javier, el hijo de la mujer pelirroja. Mi cumpleaños es en julio.

Nota gramatical

To give the date, use the following phrase: **Es el** + **number** + **de** + **month.**

Hoy **es el diez** de **diciembre.**   *Today is the **tenth of December.***

Only the first of the month does not follow this pattern.

Es el primero de **diciembre.**   *It is **December first.***

The year is expressed in **thousands** and **hundreds.**

mil cuatrocientos noventa y dos   *1492*

In Spanish-speaking countries, the date is written with the number of the day first, then the number of the month: el dos de mayo = 2/5.

7 | Unos puertorriqueños famosos

Hablar

Work with a partner. Use the timeline to give the birth dates of these famous Puerto Ricans.

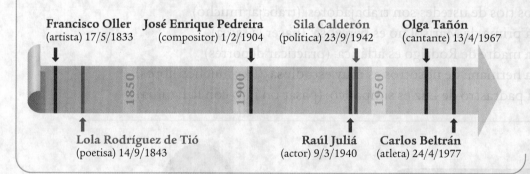

A ¿Cuál es la fecha de nacimiento de Carlos Beltrán?

B Su fecha de nacimiento es el veinticuatro de abril de mil novecientos setenta y siete.

Francisco Oller (artista) 17/5/1833

José Enrique Pedreira (compositor) 1/2/1904

Sila Calderón (política) 23/9/1942

Olga Tañón (cantante) 13/4/1967

1850   1900   1950

Lola Rodríguez de Tió (poetisa) 14/9/1843

Raúl Juliá (actor) 9/3/1940

Carlos Beltrán (atleta) 24/4/1977

8 | ¿Cómo son? ¿*Recuerdas?* Describing others p. 60

Hablar

Talk with another student about the people and pets in your family.

modelo: serio(a)

A ¿Hay una persona seria en tu familia?

B Sí, mi tío David es muy serio.

1. atlético(a)
2. cómico(a)
3. desorganizado(a)
4. inteligente
5. perezoso(a)
6. artístico(a)
7. simpático(a)
8. trabajador(a)
9. ¿ ?

9 | Las fechas de nacimiento

Escribir

Write sentences with the names and birth dates of five of your family members and friends.

madre/madrastra   abuelo(a)   hermano(a)

padre/padrastro   amigo(a)   ¿ ?

modelo: Mi madre se llama Julia. Su fecha de nacimiento es el veintitrés de marzo de mil novecientos sesenta y dos...

Comparación cultural

Las elecciones en Puerto Rico

What do elections reveal about a culture?
Puerto Rico is a commonwealth of the United States. Puerto Ricans have U.S. citizenship and those living on the mainland can vote in presidential elections. On the island, Puerto Ricans vote for their governor and local legislature. Voter turnout is high, often over 80 percent. Puerto Rico has three main political parties: the *Partido Popular Democrático* favors the current political status, the *Partido Nuevo Progresista* wants Puerto Rico to become the 51st state, and the *Partido Independentista Puertorriqueño* supports independence from the U.S.

Compara con tu mundo *What issues would motivate you to vote when you are 18? Have you ever voted in any school elections?*

Residencia y oficina del gobernador, Viejo San Juan

Más práctica   Cuaderno *pp. 127–129*   Cuaderno para hispanohablantes *pp. 128–130*

PARA Y PIENSA

Did you get it? Fill in the correct possessive adjective and dates.
1. El cumpleaños de _____ *(my)* madrastra es _____ . (6/9)
2. El cumpleaños de _____ *(our)* hermanos es _____ . (25/1)
3. El cumpleaños de _____ *(his)* amigo es _____ . (17/4)

Get Help Online
ClassZone.com

GRAMÁTICA en contexto

¡AVANZA!

Goal: Listen to the possessive adjectives Marisol and Rodrigo use to talk about the members of his family. Then use possessive adjectives to talk about your family and the birthdays of people you know. *Actividades 10–12*

Telehistoria escena 2

@HomeTutor VideoPlus
ClassZone.com

STRATEGIES

Cuando lees
List and practice words While reading, list the words for family members, such as **madre.** Then practice! Say these words aloud several times. Say them in sentences and create questions with them.

Cuando escuchas
Track the people and actions While listening, identify the people involved and the actions. What does each one say? Who helps solve the key problem? What new problem arises?

VIDEO
DVD

AUDIO

Rodrigo: ¿Dónde está la camiseta?

Sra. Vélez: ¡Ah, tus primos! *(She picks up the phone and dials.)*

Rodrigo: *(explaining to Marisol)* Ellos comen con nosotros todos los viernes. A nuestros primos les gusta jugar al fútbol.

Sra. Vélez: *(on the phone)* ¿Camila? Es Celia. Tengo una pregunta...

Rodrigo: Es mi tía Camila. La tía Camila es la madre de Ester y Tito. Mis primos tienen catorce y diez años.

Marisol: *(pointing to a family portrait)* ¿Es tu familia?

Rodrigo: Mi madre tiene dos hermanas: Inés y Mónica. Mi padre tiene un hermano, Sergio, y una hermana, Camila.

Sra. Vélez: Rodrigo, tu primo Tito tiene la camiseta de tu amiga Alicia.

Rodrigo: *(to Marisol)* Mi primo tiene perros muy grandes. ¡No me gustan los perros de Tito!

Continuará... p. 200

10 | Una familia grande *Comprensión del episodio*

Escuchar
Leer

Complete the sentences to describe the episode.

1. La madre de Rodrigo
   a. no tiene la camiseta.
   b. no tiene hermanas.

2. Los primos de Rodrigo
   a. comen en su casa todos los días.
   b. comen en su casa todos los viernes.

3. A los primos de Rodrigo
   a. les gusta jugar al fútbol.
   b. les gusta hablar por teléfono.

4. La tía Camila
   a. es la madre de Tito y Ester.
   b. es la hermana de Inés y Mónica.

5. El padre de Rodrigo
   a. tiene dos hermanas.
   b. tiene una hermana.

6. A Rodrigo
   a. no le gusta la camiseta.
   b. no le gustan los perros.

11 | ¿Cuál es tu fecha de nacimiento?

Hablar

Find out the birth dates of eight classmates and make a chart. Share the results with the class.

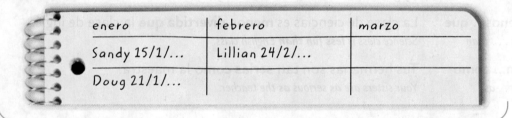

A ¿Cuál es tu fecha de nacimiento?

B Mi fecha de nacimiento es el quince de enero de...

enero	febrero	marzo
Sandy 15/1/...	Lillian 24/2/...	
Doug 21/1/...		

12 | Tu familia

Escribir

Write a paragraph about your family. Include the answers to the following questions.

· ¿Es grande o pequeña tu familia?
· ¿Cuántos hermanos y hermanas tienes?
· ¿Cómo son las personas de tu familia?
· ¿Cuántos años tienen las personas de tu familia?

modelo: Mi familia es grande. Tengo tres hermanos y una hermana.
Mi madre tiene treinta y siete años. Es...

PARA
Y
PIENSA

Did you get it? Using complete sentences, tell the birthdays of the following people.

1. Camila (12/6)   2. Ester (1/10)   3. Tito (28/3)   4. Celia (17/1)

Get Help Online
ClassZone.com

Presentación de GRAMÁTICA

Goal: Learn to make comparisons. Then use them to describe your family, your friends, and yourself. *Actividades 13–18*

English Grammar Connection: **Comparatives** are expressions used to compare two people or things. In English, comparative adjectives are formed by adding *-er* to the end of a word or by using *more, less,* and *as.*

Rodrigo is **taller** than his sister. Rodrigo es **más alto** que su hermana.

Comparatives

Animated Grammar
ClassZone.com

There are several phrases in Spanish used to make comparisons.

Here's how: Use the following phrases with an **adjective** to compare two things. The adjectives agree with the first noun.

agrees

más... que *more . . . than*	Mi abuel**a** es **más artística** que mi padre. *My grandmother is **more** artistic **than** my father.*
menos... que *less . . . than*	La clase de ciencias es **menos divertida** que la clase de inglés. *Science class is **less** fun **than** English class.*
tan... como *as . . . as*	Tus hermanas son **tan serias** como la maestra. *Your sisters are **as** serious **as** the teacher.*

When a comparison does not involve an adjective, use these phrases.

más que... *more than . . .*	Me gusta ir a la biblioteca **más que** al gimnasio. *I like to go to the library **more than** to the gym.*
menos que... *less than . . .*	Me gustan las hamburguesas **menos que** los tacos. *I like hamburgers **less than** tacos.*
tanto como... *as much as . . .*	¿Te gusta hablar **tanto como** escuchar? *Do you like to talk **as much as** listen?*

There are a few irregular comparative words. They agree in number with the first noun.

mayor	**menor**	**mejor**	**peor**
older	*younger*	*better*	*worse*

agrees

Mis tío**s** son **mayores** que mi tía.
*My uncles are **older** than my aunt.*

Más práctica
Cuaderno *pp. 130–132*
Cuaderno para hispanohablantes *pp. 131–134*

@HomeTutor
Leveled Grammar Practice
ClassZone.com

Práctica de GRAMÁTICA

13 | Sus familias

Escribir

Complete the sentences with **que** or **como** to describe the families of Rodrigo and Marisol.

1. Marisol es tan simpática _____ su madrastra.
2. Ana es menor _____ Rodrigo.
3. Marisol corre tanto _____ sus padres.
4. Rodrigo tiene menos hermanos _____ José.
5. El tío Pablo toca la guitarra mejor _____ la tía Camila.
6. Ester es mayor _____ Tito.

14 | Comparaciones

Hablar
Escribir

Look at the drawings and make comparisons using **más... que, menos... que, tan... como,** or **tanto como.**

modelo: Nicolás / grande / Sara
Nicolás es más grande que Sara.

1. Nora / alto(a) / Patricia

2. Marcos / serio(a) / José

3. Ana / perezoso(a) / Alí

4. Pablo / desorganizado(a) / Pedro

5. María / atlético(a) / David

6. a Elena / gustar / correr / escuchar música

15 | ¿Son diferentes?

Escribir

Marta and her friend Clara have some things in common and some differences. Make comparisons between the two girls.

> **modelo:** Marta estudia todos los días. Clara estudia de vez en cuando.
> Marta es más estudiosa que Clara.

1. Marta tiene doce años. Clara tiene trece años.
2. Marta es baja. Clara es alta.
3. Marta trabaja mucho. Clara trabaja mucho también.
4. Marta es muy desorganizada. Clara es un poco desorganizada.
5. Marta tiene dos hermanos. Clara tiene tres hermanos.
6. Marta es cómica. Clara es cómica también.

16 | Las diferencias

Escribir

Look at the drawing and write sentences with as many differences and similarities as you can find between the members of each pair.

> **modelo:** La señora Suárez es más baja que Raquel Suárez.

Carlitos · Ramón · Raquel Suárez · la Sra. Suárez · Betina · Daniel

17 | Capitán y Príncipe

Escuchar
Escribir

Ana is talking about her pets, Capitán and Príncipe. Listen to her description and indicate whether the following sentences are true or false.

1. La familia de Ana tiene más perros que gatos.
2. Príncipe es tan simpático como Capitán.
3. Capitán es más grande que Príncipe.
4. A Príncipe le gusta comer más que descansar.
5. Príncipe es menor que Capitán.
6. Capitán es más perezoso que Príncipe.

18 | Compara a las personas

Escribir

Comparación cultural

Los retratos

How do portraits represent the people in a country? Rafael Tufiño was born in New York and moved to **Puerto Rico,** his parents' homeland, as a child. Much of his work reflects the people and culture of Puerto Rico. He painted many portraits of his mother, giving them the title *Goyita*. These portraits came to represent not just his mother, but Puerto Rican women overall. Fernando Sayán Polo, an artist from **Peru,** also reflects the people of his country through his artwork. His painting *Niña campesina sonriente* depicts a young girl wearing traditional Andean dress.

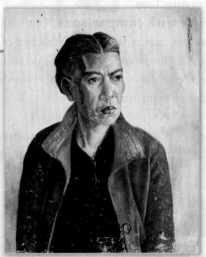

Goyita *(1949),*
Rafael Tufiño

Niña campesina
sonriente *(2005),*
Fernando Sayán Polo

Compara con tu mundo *If you had to paint a portrait of someone famous, which person would you choose and why? How would you portray him or her? What colors or objects would you include?*

Write five sentences comparing the people in the paintings.

> **modelo:** La mujer es mayor que la chica.
> La chica es más...

Más práctica Cuaderno *pp. 130–132* Cuaderno para hispanohablantes *pp. 131–134*

PARA Y PIENSA

Did you get it? 1. Say that your brother is taller than your father.
2. Say that you like apples as much as bananas.
3. Say that math class is better than art class.

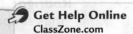

Get Help Online
ClassZone.com

Todo junto

Goal: *Show what you know* Notice the comparative words Marisol and Rodrigo use to talk about why Rodrigo doesn't like Tito's dogs. Then use comparative words and possessive adjectives to describe your family and friends. *Actividades 19–23*

Telehistoria completa

@**HomeTutor** VideoPlus
ClassZone.com

STRATEGIES

Cuando lees
Work with comparisons This scene contains comparisons of animals and of people. How many comparisons do you see? Write down the "comparison words." Practice them in sentences.

Cuando escuchas
Remember, listen, and predict At the beginning of this scene, Marisol is calm. How does she change and why? Does this happen suddenly or slowly? How do you know?

Escena 1 *Resumen*
Mañana es el cumpleaños de Ana, la hermana de Rodrigo. Rodrigo está nervioso porque no tiene la camiseta de Alicia.

Escena 2 *Resumen*
Tito, el primo de Rodrigo, tiene la camiseta. A Rodrigo no le gustan los perros de Tito.

VIDEO
DVD

AUDIO

Escena 3

Tito

Rodrigo and Marisol are walking to Tito's house.

Marisol: ¿No te gustan los perros? Son simpáticos.

Rodrigo: Me gustan más los gatos. Son más simpáticos que los perros.

Marisol: Los perros son menos perezosos que los gatos.

Rodrigo: Los perros de Tito son perezosos y muy grandes. ¡Son tan grandes como tú!

They stop outside the gate and look around. Tito appears, wearing Alicia's T-shirt, which is filthy.

Tito: ¡Hola, Rodrigo! Tu camiseta.

Suddenly the dogs begin growling. Rodrigo and Marisol run away frightened.

19 ¿Rodrigo, Marisol o Tito? *Comprensión de los episodios*

Escuchar
Leer

Tell whether each sentence refers to Rodrigo, Marisol, or Tito.

1. Pasa un rato con su tía Celia.
2. Tiene perros muy grandes.
3. El cumpleaños de su abuela es el primero de marzo.
4. Necesita la camiseta de su amiga Alicia.
5. Come con la familia de Rodrigo todos los viernes.
6. Es menor que Rodrigo.
7. No le gustan los perros.
8. Tiene la camiseta de Alicia.

Rodrigo

Tito

Marisol

20 ¿Comprendiste? *Comprensión de los episodios*

Escuchar
Leer

Answer the questions according to the episodes.

1. ¿Cuándo es el cumpleaños de Ana?
2. ¿A qué hora está Trini Salgado en la escuela?
3. ¿A quién le gustan más los gatos, a Rodrigo o a Marisol?
4. ¿Cuántos años tienen los primos de Rodrigo?
5. ¿Cuántas hermanas tiene la madre de Rodrigo?
6. ¿Quién tiene la camiseta de Alicia?

21 La familia ideal

Hablar

> **STRATEGY Hablar**
>
> **Consider your beliefs** Before the conversation, consider your beliefs about families. What is an ideal family? Describe it on paper and then aloud. Do you know such a family?

Work in a group of three to express opinions about the ideal family. Include your answers to the following questions.

Para organizarte

- ¿Es grande o pequeña la familia? ¿Dónde vive?
- ¿Cuántas personas hay en la familia?
- ¿Cómo son las personas de la familia? ¿Qué hacen?
- ¿Cuántos años tienen las personas de la familia?

A Una familia pequeña es buena.

B Una familia grande es mejor que una familia pequeña porque es más interesante.

C No, una familia cómica es mejor...

22 | Integración

Leer
Escuchar
Hablar

Read the flyer from a family looking for a new home for their dog. Then listen to the radio ad by an animal shelter. Match each dog to someone in your family and explain your choices.

Fuente 1 Cartel

Es tan inteligente como su madre y... ¡más activo!

Le gusta correr, nadar y jugar al fútbol. ¡Es más atlético que yo! ☺

Vamos a Nueva York en enero y Rayo no va con nosotros. ☹

Si necesitas un amigo, Rayo necesita una familia.

Llámanos: 555-8231

Rayo
Labrador marrón.
Tiene un año.

Fuente 2 Anuncio de radio

Listen and take notes
• ¿Cómo es Dino?
• ¿Qué le gusta hacer a Dino?

modelo: Rayo es un buen perro para mi primo Alberto. Rayo es menos tranquilo que Dino y a mi primo le gusta correr...

23 | Un amigo nuevo

Escribir

Write a letter to an exchange student from Puerto Rico who is going to stay with your family. Use comparatives to describe the members of your family.

modelo: ¡Hola! Te presento a mi familia. Tengo dos hermanos. Yo soy mayor que mis hermanos. Mi hermano Lance es menor que...

Writing Criteria	Excellent	Good	Needs Work
Content	Your letter includes a lot of information.	Your letter includes some information.	Your letter includes little information.
Communication	Most of your letter is organized and easy to follow.	Parts of your letter are organized and easy to follow.	Your letter is disorganized and hard to follow.
Accuracy	Your letter has few mistakes in grammar and vocabulary.	Your letter has some mistakes in grammar and vocabulary.	Your letter has many mistakes in grammar and vocabulary.

Más práctica Cuaderno *pp. 133–134* Cuaderno para hispanohablantes *pp. 135–136*

PARA
Y
PIENSA

Did you get it? Create sentences based on the Telehistoria using possessive adjectives and comparatives.
1. los perros (de Tito) / tan grande / Marisol
2. el primo (de Rodrigo) / menor / él
3. los perros (de Tito) / más perezoso(a) / los gatos

Get Help Online
ClassZone.com

Juegos y diversiones

Review possessive adjectives and possession using **de** by playing a game.

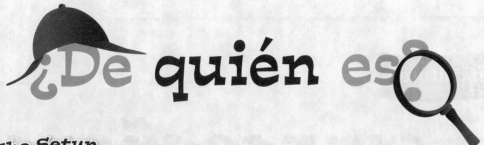

¿De quién es?

The Setup

Your teacher will ask you to bring in two items that represent vocabulary words that you have learned. All the items will be put in a box.

Playing the Game

You and your classmates will take turns picking an item out of the box and trying to guess who owns it by asking questions using possessive adjectives.

The Winner!

The winner is the student who has guessed the owner of the most items.

Materials

- items collected from students
- box

Juan, ¿es tu pluma?

No, no es mi pluma. Es la pluma de Lorena.

Lección 2
doscientos tres **203**

Lectura cultural

Goal: Read about the **quinceañera** celebrations in Peru and Puerto Rico. Then compare the parties and talk about the activities at the birthday parties you go to.

Comparación cultural

AUDIO

La quinceañera

STRATEGY Leer

Compare and contrast Draw a Venn diagram like this one. Use it to compare the **quinceañera** celebrations of Peru and Puerto Rico.

Perú   Puerto Rico

La fiesta[1] de quinceañera es muy popular en muchos países de Latinoamérica. Es similar al *Sweet Sixteen* de Estados Unidos. Muchas veces hay una ceremonia religiosa y una fiesta con banquete. En la fiesta hacen un brindis[2] en honor a la quinceañera y después todos bailan un vals[3].

La chica que celebra su cumpleaños también se llama la quinceañera. En Perú (y otros países) la quinceañera tiene catorce o quince damas de honor[4]: una por cada[5] año que tiene. No hay un menú especial de banquete, pero en Perú es común comer comida típica del país, bailar y escuchar música tradicional.

---

[1] party   [2] toast   [3] **bailan...** dance a waltz
[4] **damas...** maids of honor   [5] **por...** for each

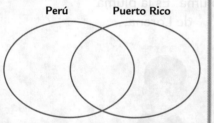

Perú

Comidas tradicionales: lomo saltado, chupe, mondongo y guiso

*Una quinceañera en Puerto Rico
con familia y amigos*

Puerto Rico

En Puerto Rico, la celebración se llama el quinceañero. Muchas veces las chicas tienen la gran fiesta en su cumpleaños número dieciséis (por influencia del *Sweet Sixteen*) y no en el cumpleaños de los quince años.

En el banquete de una quinceañera de Puerto Rico es normal comer comida típica del país, como arroz con pollo[6]. Todos bailan y escuchan música del Caribe: salsa, merengue, reggaetón y el hip-hop cubano.

---

[6] chicken and rice dish

PARA
Y
PIENSA

¿Comprendiste?

1. ¿Qué fiesta en Estados Unidos es similar a la fiesta de quinceañera?
2. ¿Cuántas damas de honor tiene una quinceañera en Perú?
3. ¿Cuándo tienen la fiesta las chicas de Puerto Rico?

¿Y tú?

¿Te gustan las fiestas de cumpleaños? ¿Qué haces en las fiestas?

Proyectos culturales

Instrumentos de Puerto Rico y Perú

How do certain instruments and music become associated with a particular region? Percussion instruments that produce strong beats and rhythms are the base of much of the music of **Puerto Rico.** In **Peru,** the **zampoña** is a wind instrument that adds a deep and distinctive sound to traditional Andean music.

Proyecto 1 *Percussion*

Puerto Rico Make your own rhythm on a homemade percussion instrument.

Materials for your own percussion instrument
An object that can be used as a "found" percussion instrument, such as:
- coffee or juice can
- yogurt cup with pebbles, sand or seeds, secured inside with a lid on top
- wooden, plastic, or metal spoons
- pan lid and long-handled brush
- upside-down basket

Instructions
Practice making a rhythm pattern you can repeat on your "found" percussion instrument. Try creating different tones by striking the instrument in different places or with different objects.

Proyecto 2 *Zampoña*

Perú Use these simple materials to create your own **zampoña.**

Materials for zampoña
4 or more plastic or glass bottles, all the same size
Water

Instructions
1. Bring to class four or more bottles (all the same size) and add water so that they all have different amounts, ranging from empty to two thirds full.
2. Put your mouth to the top of each bottle and blow as if playing the flute. Because each bottle contains a different amount of air and water, you should hear various pitches.
3. Add tape so that the bottles are connected in a row. Arrange the bottles according to their pitch, from low to high.

En tu comunidad

You can find Andean music in most large music stores. If there is one in your community, find out what Andean music is sold there and if music from other countries is also available.

En resumen
Vocabulario y gramática

Animated Grammar
Interactive Flashcards
ClassZone.com

Vocabulario

Talk About Family

la abuela	grandmother	la madrastra	stepmother
el abuelo	grandfather	la madre	mother
los abuelos	grandparents	el padrastro	stepfather
la familia	family	el padre	father
la hermana	sister	los padres	parents
el hermano	brother	el (la) primo(a)	cousin
los hermanos	brothers, brother(s) and sister(s)	los primos	cousins
		la tía	aunt
la hija	daughter	el tío	uncle
el hijo	son	los tíos	uncles, uncle(s) and aunt(s)
los hijos	son(s) and daughter(s), children		

Ask, Tell, and Compare Ages

¿Cuántos años tienes?	How old are you?	mayor	older
		menor	younger
Tengo... años.	I am . . . years old.		

Give Dates

¿Cuál es la fecha?	What is the date?
Es el... de...	It's the . . . of . . .
el primero de...	the first of . . .
el cumpleaños	birthday
¡Feliz cumpleaños!	Happy birthday!
la fecha de nacimiento	birth date

Pets

el (la) gato(a)	cat
el (la) perro(a)	dog

Other Words and Phrases

vivir	to live
ya	already

Numbers from 200 to 1,000,000 *p. 186*

Months *p. 185*

Gramática

Notas gramaticales: **de** to express possession *p. 187*, **tener... años** *p. 189*, Giving dates *p. 192*

Possessive Adjectives

In Spanish, **possessive adjectives** agree in number with the nouns they describe. **Nuestro(a)** and **vuestro(a)** must also agree in gender with the nouns they describe.

Singular Possessive Adjectives

mi	**nuestro(a)**
my	our
tu	**vuestro(a)**
your (familiar)	your (familiar)
su	**su**
your (formal)	your
su	**su**
his, her, its	their

Plural Possessive Adjectives

mis	**nuestros(as)**
my	our
tus	**vuestros(as)**
your (familiar)	your (familiar)
sus	**sus**
your (formal)	your
sus	**sus**
his, her, its	their

Comparatives

Use the following phrases with an adjective to compare two things.
más... que
menos... que
tan... como

When a comparison does not involve an adjective, use these phrases.
más que...
menos que...
tanto como...

There are a few irregular comparative words.

mayor	menor	mejor	peor
older	younger	better	worse

Repaso de la lección

@HomeTutor
ClassZone.com

¡LLEGADA!

Now you can
- talk about family
- ask and tell ages
- express possession
- give dates
- make comparisons

Using
- **de** to express possession
- possessive adjectives
- comparatives

To review
- **de** to express possession p. 187
- possessive adjectives p. 190

1 Listen and understand

AUDIO

Marcos has a family photo and is explaining who everyone is. Listen to Marcos and then indicate each person's relationship to him.

modelo: Pedro
Pedro es el hermano de Marcos.

1. Elena y Rosa
2. Julio
3. Norma
4. Alberto
5. Diego y Felipe
6. Carmen

To review
- possessive adjectives p. 190

2 Talk about family

Write sentences describing what family members these people have, and what their ages are. Use possessive adjectives.

modelo: yo / hermano menor (5 años)
Yo tengo un hermano menor. Mi hermano tiene cinco años.

1. Bárbara / hermana mayor (19 años)
2. tú / dos primos (7 y 11 años)
3. nosotros / abuelo (67 años)
4. Manuel y Óscar / padre (34 años)
5. yo / perro (5 años)
6. ustedes / madre (36 años)
7. tú y yo / dos tíos (48 y 44 años)
8. usted / abuela (81 años)
9. ellas / dos gatos (2 años)
10. yo / tía (30 años)

To review
• comparatives
  p. 196

3 | Make comparisons

Josefina is describing her cat, Memo, and her dog, Sancho. Read the description and choose the appropriate words.

Memo, mi gato, y Sancho, mi perro, viven con mi familia. Memo tiene diez años y Sancho tiene cinco. Memo es __1.__ (menor / mayor) que Sancho. Pero Sancho es __2.__ (tan / más) grande que Memo y come más __3.__ (como / que) él. Memo come __4.__ (mejor / menor) comida que Sancho porque come buena comida para gatos. Sancho come comida __5.__ (mayor / menos) nutritiva porque muchas veces come pizza y papas fritas. Memo y Sancho son muy perezosos. Memo es __6.__ (tanto / tan) perezoso como Sancho. Descansan mucho. A Memo le gusta descansar __7.__ (tanto / más) como a Sancho. Pero Memo y Sancho no son aburridos. También les gusta jugar un poco todos los días. Jugar con ellos es más divertido __8.__ (como / que) mirar la televisión.

To review
• **de** to express
  possession p. 187

4 | Give dates

Write sentences giving these people's birthdays.

> **modelo:** el señor Gómez: 13/4
> El cumpleaños del señor Gómez es el trece de abril.

1. Berta: 23/12
2. Emilio y Emilia: 1/2
3. la señora Serrano: 14/1
4. Olga: 5/8
5. Germán: 15/10
6. el director: 11/6
7. la maestra: 30/9
8. Luis: 27/3
9. Víctor: 12/11

To review
• Comparación
  cultural pp. 182,
  193, 199
• Lectura cultural
  pp. 204–205

5 | Puerto Rico and Peru

Comparación cultural

Answer these culture questions.

1. What do people do during **la sobremesa**?
2. Which political positions do people vote for in Puerto Rico?
3. Who does Rafael Tufiño portray in *Goyita*?
4. What are some **quinceañera** traditions? Describe at least three.

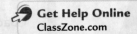

Más práctica Cuaderno *pp. 135–146* Cuaderno para hispanohablantes *pp. 137–146*

Get Help Online
ClassZone.com

Perú

Puerto
Rico

El Salvador

Comparación cultural

AUDIO

¿Qué comemos?

Lectura y escritura

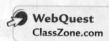

WebQuest
ClassZone.com

1 Leer Meals vary for people around the world. Read how María Luisa, Silvia, and José enjoy a meal on Sundays.

2 Escribir Using the three descriptions as models, write a short paragraph about a typical Sunday meal.

> **STRATEGY Escribir**
> **Make a mind map** To write about a real or imaginary Sunday meal, make a mind map like the one shown.

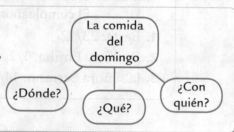

La comida del domingo

¿Dónde? ¿Qué? ¿Con quién?

Step 1 Complete the mind map of your Sunday meal by adding details to the categories of place (where you eat), foods (what you eat), and people (with whom you eat).

Step 2 Write your paragraph. Make sure to include all the information from your mind map. Check your writing by yourself or with help from a friend. Make final corrections.

Compara con tu mundo

Use the paragraph you wrote to compare your Sunday meal to a meal described by *one* of the three students. In what ways is your meal similar? In what ways is it different?

Cuaderno *pp. 147–149*   Cuaderno para hispanohablantes *pp. 147–149*

El Salvador

María Luisa

Hola, soy María Luisa. Yo soy de El Salvador. Los domingos, voy con mi hermana mayor y mi prima a Metrocentro[1]. Después de pasear unas horas, vamos a un café porque estamos cansadas y tenemos sed y hambre. En el café venden sándwiches, refrescos y jugos de papaya, mango, melón y otras frutas. A mí me gusta más la horchata[2]. Es una bebida muy rica.

[1] popular mall in San Salvador

[2] beverage made of rice, water, and milk

Perú

Silvia

Yo soy Silvia y vivo en Lima, Perú. Todos los domingos comemos la cena con mis tíos. Mi tío Ricardo siempre prepara su comida favorita, el ceviche[3]. A mí me gusta más el ají de gallina[4] que hace mi abuela. ¡Es mejor que el ceviche de mi tío! Después de la cena, mis padres y mis tíos beben café y hablan. Mis primos y yo comemos helado y escuchamos música.

[3] fish marinated in lime juice   [4] spicy chicken and potato dish

Puerto Rico

José

¿Qué tal? Me llamo José. Vivo en San Juan, Puerto Rico. Todos los domingos, mi familia y yo comemos el almuerzo en un restaurante. Nos gusta comer carne asada[5]. Es muy, muy buena. También me gustan los tostones[6]. ¡Pero los tostones de mi madre son más ricos que los tostones en un restaurante!

[5] barbecued   [6] fried plantains

Repaso inclusivo
♻ Options for Review

1 | Listen, understand, and compare

Escuchar

Listen to this episode from a call-in radio show giving advice to teens. Then answer the questions.

1. ¿Cómo es Diana? ¿Qué problema tiene?
2. ¿Por qué tiene que estudiar Diana?
3. ¿Qué le gusta hacer a Diana? ¿Y a Óscar?
4. ¿Óscar es mayor o menor que Diana? ¿Cuántos años tienen?
5. ¿Qué va a hacer Diana?

Do you have siblings or cousins? Do you have a lot in common or are you very different? Explain.

2 | Present a friend

Hablar

Bring in a photo or drawing of your best friend or a person you admire. Introduce the person to the class and talk about what personality traits, favorite activities, and favorite foods you have in common. Then mention your differences. Prepare to talk for at least two minutes.

3 | Get to know a new student

Hablar

Role-play a conversation in which you are an exchange student from Puerto Rico, and your partner is your host brother or sister. Introduce yourself and ask about his or her classes, likes and dislikes, and what his or her family is like. Then answer his or her questions for you. Your conversation should be at least three minutes long.

¿Cómo es tu familia?

Mi familia es grande.

4 | Plan a family reunion

Escribir

Your family is hosting a reunion with all of your extended family members. You are in charge of organizing a breakfast for everyone. Create a seating chart, and label each seat with the person's name, age, and relation to you. Write what breakfast foods and drinks each person likes and doesn't like.

5 | Display your family tree

**Hablar
Escribir**

Work with a partner to create a poster of your family tree or that of a TV family. Use photos or make drawings of each family member. Copy this chart on a piece of paper and use it to organize your information. Label each person's name, age, birthday, favorite activity, and favorite food. Use the family tree to describe your family to your partner, making comparisons between family members. Then present your partner's family to the class.

Nombre	Edad	Cumpleaños	Actividad favorita	Comida favorita

6 | Compare twins

**Leer
Escribir**

Read this chart from a magazine article about Manolo and Martín Santos, twins that were recently reunited after being separated at birth. Then write a paragraph comparing the two men. Include at least six comparisons.

MUCHAS COINCIDENCIAS

Manolo
Nacimiento: 30/7, a las 2:20 de la tarde
Personalidad: serio, muy artístico
Profesión: Maestro de español. Enseña cuatro clases. Trabaja 45 horas en la semana.
Familia: dos hijos (Enrique y Arturo) y una hija (Rebeca)
Actividades: Le gusta practicar deportes: correr, montar en bicicleta, jugar al fútbol.

Martín
Nacimiento: 30/7, a las 2:22 de la tarde
Personalidad: cómico, muy artístico
Profesión: Maestro de español. Enseña seis clases. Trabaja 52 horas en la semana.
Familia: dos hijos (Eduardo y Ángel) y dos hijas (Rebeca y Rosa)
Actividades: Le gusta practicar deportes: andar en patineta, jugar al fútbol, jugar al golf.

La historia increíble de los hermanos Santos

España

En el centro

Lección 1

Tema: **¡Vamos de compras!**

Lección 2

Tema: **¿Qué hacemos esta noche?**

Islas Canarias

«¡Hola!

**Somos Maribel y Enrique.
Vivimos en Madrid, la capital.»**

Francia

España

León

Salamanca

Madrid ★

Portugal

Andorra

Barcelona

Valencia

Islas Baleares

Océano
Atlántico

Sevilla

Granada

Mar Mediterráneo

Ceuta

Melilla

Argelia

Marruecos

Población: 40.280.780

Área: 194.897 millas
cuadradas

Capital: Madrid

Moneda: el euro (comparte
con otros 11 países)

Idiomas: castellano
(español), catalán, gallego, vasco

Paella

Comida típica: tortilla española, paella, gazpacho

Gente famosa: Carmen Amaya (bailaora), Francisco
de Goya (artista), Ana María Matute (escritora),
Severo Ochoa (bioquímico)

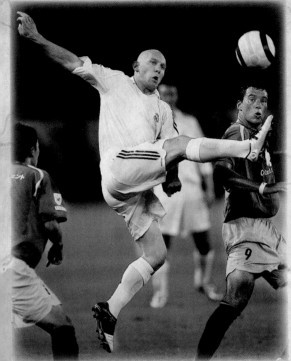

Un jugador de fútbol del Real Madrid

◄ **Aficionados del fútbol** Official songs, or **himnos oficiales,** are an important part of the Spanish soccer experience. Fans of the Real Madrid team sing **¡Hala Madrid!** *(Let's go, Madrid!)*, especially during games against rival team FC Barcelona, known as **El Barça.** *What teams have sports rivalries where you live?*

Don Quijote *(1955), Pablo Picasso*

El arte y la literatura Pablo Picasso, one of the 20th century's greatest artists, portrayed traditional Spanish themes in his work. He made this print of fictional characters Don Quijote and Sancho Panza exactly 350 years after Cervantes wrote his famous novel, *El ingenioso hidalgo Don Quijote de la Mancha. What other works of Picasso are you familiar with?* ▶

Bailarinas de flamenco en Sevilla

◄ **Las costumbres regionales** During the **Feria de Abril** celebration, girls wear Seville's traditional costume, **el traje de sevillana. Sevillanas** are similar to **flamenco,** which involves singing, dance, and guitar as well as rhythmic clapping or foot taps. *What type of music and dress would be considered typically American?*

España

Lección 1

Tema:

¡Vamos de compras!

In this lesson you will learn to
- talk about what clothes you want to buy
- say what you wear in different seasons

using
- **tener** expressions
- stem-changing verbs: **e → ie**
- direct object pronouns

♻ ¿Recuerdas?
- numbers from 11 to 100
- the verb **tener**
- after-school activities

Comparación cultural

In this lesson you will learn about
- surrealism and Salvador Dalí
- climates around the world
- Spanish poet and novelist Antonio Colinas

Compara con tu mundo
These teenagers are shopping for clothes in Madrid, Spain. While there are department stores (**almacenes**) and some shopping centers (**centros comerciales**) in Madrid, most people shop at small stores like the one pictured here. *Where do you like to shop for clothes?*

¿Qué ves?

Mira la foto

¿La chica está al lado del chico?

¿Quién es más alto, el chico o la chica?

¿Cómo están ellos?

Online
SPANISH CLASSZONE.COM

Featuring...

Cultura INTERACTIVA

Animated Grammar

@HomeTutor

And more...
- **Get Help Online**
- **Interactive Flashcards**
- **Review Games**
- **WebQuest**
- **Self-Check Quiz**

Una tienda de ropa
Madrid, España

Presentación de VOCABULARIO

¡AVANZA!

Goal: Learn about the clothes Enrique and Maribel like to wear. Then practice what you have learned to talk about clothes and how much they cost. *Actividades 1–2*

♻ *¿Recuerdas?* Numbers from 11 to 100 p. 94

VIDEO
DVD

AUDIO

A ¡Hola! Me llamo Enrique. **Voy de compras** al **centro comercial** con mi amiga, Maribel. **Queremos** comprar **ropa nueva.** A Maribel le gusta ir a todas **las tiendas.**

la tienda

ir de compras

el centro comercial

B Voy a comprar **una camisa** y **unos jeans. Cuestan** treinta **euros.** El **vestido** de Maribel **cuesta** veinte euros. Es un buen **precio.**

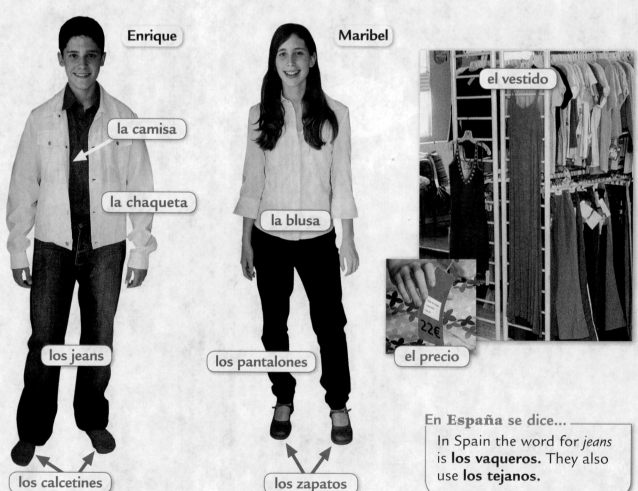

Enrique

la camisa

la chaqueta

los jeans

los calcetines

Maribel

la blusa

los pantalones

los zapatos

el vestido

el precio

22€

En España se dice...

In Spain the word for *jeans* is **los vaqueros.** They also use **los tejanos.**

C Me gusta **llevar** ropa **blanca, roja** y **marrón**. A Maribel le gusta llevar **una camiseta verde** y **unos pantalones cortos azules**.

roja

verde

amarilla

anaranjada

la camiseta

marrones

azules

blancos

negros

los pantalones cortos

D Maribel **piensa** que **el vestido** es un poco **feo**. Ella **tiene razón**; no es muy bonito. Ella compra otro vestido que le gusta más.

pensar

pagar

los euros

el dinero

Continuará...

Presentación de VOCABULARIO
(continuación)

E En España hay cuatro **estaciones**. Maribel siempre **tiene calor durante el verano**. Me gusta **el invierno**, pero siempre **tengo frío**.

las estaciones

la primavera

el verano

el otoño

el invierno

Más vocabulario

cerrar *to close*
¿Cuánto cuesta(n)?
  How much does it (do they) cost?
el dólar *dollar*
empezar *to begin*
entender *to understand*
preferir *to prefer*
tener suerte *to be lucky*
Expansión de vocabulario
  p. R5

tener calor
el sombrero

tener frío
el gorro

¡A responder! Escuchar

Listen to the following descriptions of clothes. Raise your hand if you are wearing that item.

@HomeTutor VideoPlus
Interactive Flashcards
ClassZone.com

Práctica de VOCABULARIO

1 | Los precios de la ropa ♲ ¿Recuerdas? Numbers from 11 to 100 p. 94

Hablar
Escribir

Tell how much the clothing items cost.

> modelo: la camisa
> La camisa cuesta veintiocho euros.

1. el vestido
2. los jeans
3. los zapatos
4. la chaqueta
5. la camiseta
6. los pantalones cortos
7. la blusa

2 | Ropa de muchos colores

Hablar

Ask a partner what color the clothing items are.

A ¿De qué color son los zapatos?

B Los zapatos son rojos.

1.
2.
3.
4.
5.
6.
7.
8.

Más práctica   Cuaderno *pp. 151–153*   Cuaderno para hispanohablantes *pp. 151–154*

PARA Y PIENSA

Did you get it? Ask how much the following items cost.
1. the white socks
2. the blue dress
3. the orange jacket
4. the red shorts

Get Help Online
ClassZone.com

VOCABULARIO *en contexto*

Goal: Pay attention to the different articles of clothing Enrique and Maribel talk about. Then practice these words and **tener** expressions to say what you wear in different seasons. *Actividades 3–4*

 ¿Recuerdas? The verb **tener** p. 100, after-school activities p. 32

Telehistoria escena 1

@HomeTutor VideoPlus
ClassZone.com

STRATEGIES

Cuando lees

Scan for details Before reading, quickly scan the scene to discover basic details: Who's in the scene? What are they doing? Where are they? What time is it? What's the season?

Cuando escuchas

Listen for wishes Listen to Maribel and Enrique express where they want to go. Who gets his or her way in this scene? How does this happen?

VIDEO DVD

AUDIO

Maribel — Enrique

Maribel is opening a package from Alicia.

Enrique: ¿Es una camiseta?

Maribel: *(reading a flyer from the package)* Sí. Y Trini está en el centro comercial del Parque de las Avenidas de las doce a la una de la tarde.

Enrique: ¿Dónde está el Parque de las Avenidas?

Maribel: Necesito un mapa. ¿Vamos?

They start walking. Enrique stops and points at a store.

Enrique: ¡Una tienda de ropa! ¡Y yo necesito comprar una chaqueta! ¡Tengo frío!

Maribel: ¡Eres muy cómico! En el verano, cuando hace calor, ¿necesitas una chaqueta?

Enrique: ¿Hace calor? Yo no tengo calor.

Maribel: En el invierno, cuando hace frío, llevas pantalones cortos. Y durante la primavera, ¡nunca llevas calcetines!

Enrique: ¡Me gusta ser diferente! ¿No necesitas unos zapatos nuevos?

Maribel: *(reluctantly)* ¡Vale! Diez minutos. **Continuará...** p. 228

También se dice

España Maribel uses the word **vale** to say *OK*. In other Spanish-speaking countries you might hear:
- **México** órale, sale, ándale
- **Cuba** dale

3 | La ropa apropiada *Comprensión del episodio*

Escuchar
Leer

Complete the sentences by choosing the correct word or phrase, according to the episode.

1. Maribel tiene _____ .
2. Trini está en _____ .
3. Enrique necesita comprar _____ .
4. Enrique lleva _____ en el invierno.
5. Enrique nunca lleva _____ en la primavera.
6. A Enrique le gusta ser _____ .

a. pantalones cortos
b. diferente
c. calcetines
d. una camiseta
e. el centro comercial
f. una chaqueta

Nota gramatical **¿Recuerdas?** The verb **tener** p. 100

Tener is used to form many expressions that in English would use the verb *to be*.

tener **calor**	*to be hot*	tener **razón**	*to be right*
tener **frío**	*to be cold*	tener **suerte**	*to be lucky*

En el invierno **tengo frío,** y en el verano **tengo calor.**
In winter, I'm cold, and in summer, I'm hot.

---

4 | ¿Qué ropa llevas? **¿Recuerdas?** After-school activities p. 32

Hablar

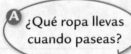

Ask a partner what he or she wears in these situations.

A ¿Qué ropa llevas cuando paseas?

B Llevo pantalones, una camiseta y un sombrero.

Estudiante Ⓐ
1. montar en bicicleta
2. tener calor
3. practicar deportes
4. tener frío
5. ir a la escuela
6. ¿ ?

Estudiante Ⓑ
gorro
pantalones cortos
chaqueta
camiseta
vestido
¿ ?

PARA Y PIENSA

Did you get it? Enrique likes to be different. Complete each sentence with the correct form of **tener calor** or **tener frío**.

1. En el verano, Enrique _____ y lleva una chaqueta.
2. En el invierno, él lleva pantalones cortos porque _____ .
3. Cuando Maribel tiene calor, Enrique _____ .

Get Help Online
ClassZone.com

Lección 1
doscientos veintitrés **223**

Presentación de GRAMÁTICA

Goal: Learn how to form **e → ie** stem-changing verbs. Then use these verbs to talk about clothes you and others want to buy. *Actividades 5–10*

English Grammar Connection: There are no stem-changing verbs in the present tense of English.

Stem-Changing Verbs: e → ie

Animated Grammar
ClassZone.com

In Spanish, some verbs have a stem change in the present tense. How do you form the present tense of **e → ie** stem-changing verbs?

Here's how:

Stem-changing verbs have regular **-ar, -er,** and **-ir** present-tense endings. For **e → ie** stem-changing verbs, the **e** of the stem changes to **ie** in all forms except **nosotros(as)** and **vosotros(as).**

stem changes to

que**r**er → qu**ie**ro

querer	*to want*
quiero	queremos
quieres	queréis
quiere	quieren

Other **e → ie** stem-changing verbs you have learned are **cerrar, empezar, entender, pensar,** and **preferir.** In stem-changing verbs, it is the next-to-last syllable that changes.

Paula **prefiere** el vestido azul.
*Paula **prefers** the blue dress.*

Notice that when one verb follows another, the **first verb** is conjugated and the second is in its **infinitive** form.

¿**Quieres** mirar la televisión o leer un libro?
*Do you **want** to watch television or read a book?*

Más práctica
Cuaderno *pp. 154–156*
Cuaderno para hispanohablantes *pp. 155–157*

@HomeTutor
Leveled Grammar Practice
ClassZone.com

Práctica de GRAMÁTICA

5 | Después de las clases

Leer Enrique is talking to his parents after school. Match the sentences that he would logically say together.

1. La clase de matemáticas es difícil.
2. Tengo hambre.
3. No me gusta andar en patineta.
4. Tenemos sed.
5. Hace calor.
6. Queremos unos zapatos nuevos.

a. Prefiero montar en bicicleta.
b. Preferimos llevar pantalones cortos.
c. Quiero un sándwich.
d. No cuestan mucho dinero.
e. Queremos un refresco.
f. No entiendo la tarea.

6 | Todos quieren ropa

Escribir Enrique and Maribel are looking at a clothes catalog. Use the pictures to write sentences about what clothing items they and other people want.

modelo: la madre de Enrique
La madre de Enrique quiere la blusa anaranjada.

1. Maribel
2. tú
3. vosotros
4. usted
5. yo
6. los amigos de Maribel
7. mis amigos y yo
8. ustedes

7 | El regalo de cumpleaños

Leer
Escribir

Maribel wants to buy a present for her sister. Complete what she says with the correct form of the appropriate verb.

| querer | cerrar | preferir |
| entender | pensar | empezar |

Mañana celebramos el cumpleaños de mi hermana mayor. Voy a la tienda de ropa porque ella **1.** una chaqueta nueva. Ya tiene dos chaquetas, pero ella **2.** que las otras chaquetas son feas. Mis padres no **3.** por qué necesita tres chaquetas. Pero ahora el otoño **4.** y a ella no le gusta tener frío. Mis hermanos y yo vamos a la tienda Moda 16. Yo **5.** otra tienda pero ellos tienen el dinero. Tenemos que llegar antes de las ocho porque la tienda **6.** a las ocho.

8 | ¿Tiene suerte en la tienda?

Escuchar
Escribir

Enrique is at the mall. Listen to what he says, and answer the questions.

1. ¿Qué estación empieza?
2. ¿Qué quiere comprar Enrique?
3. ¿Prefiere tener frío o calor él?

4. ¿Qué quiere comprar Micaela?
5. ¿Qué no entiende Enrique?
6. ¿Quién tiene suerte?

AUDIO

Pronunciación ⟩ La letra c con a, o, u

Before **a**, **o**, or **u**, the Spanish **c** is pronounced like the /k/ sound in the English word *call*. Listen and repeat.

ca	→	camisa	calor
		tocar	nunca
co	→	comprar	corto
		poco	blanco
cu	→	cumpleaños	cuando
		cuaderno	escuela

Carmen compra pantalones cortos.
Carlos tiene calor; quiere una camiseta.

Before a consonant other than **h**, it has the same sound: **clase, octubre.**

Soy Carlos. Compro una camiseta.

9 | ¿Qué piensas de la ropa?

Hablar

Talk with a classmate about your opinions on clothes.

A ¿Quieres comprar un sombrero marrón?

B No, pienso que los sombreros marrones son feos. Prefiero los sombreros negros. (Sí, quiero comprar un sombrero marrón.)

1. Compra
2. Compra
3. Compra
4. Compra
5. Compra
6. Compra
7. Compra
8. Compra

10 | ¿Y tú?

Hablar
Escribir

Answer the following questions in complete sentences.

modelo: ¿Qué piensas hacer este fin de semana?
Pienso montar en bicicleta y leer un libro.

1. ¿A qué hora empieza tu clase de español?
2. ¿Qué entiendes mejor, las matemáticas o las ciencias?
3. ¿Qué quieres hacer después de las clases hoy?
4. ¿Qué colores prefieren tú y tus amigos?
5. ¿Piensas que ir de compras es divertido o aburrido?
6. ¿Qué estación prefieres? ¿Por qué?

Más práctica   Cuaderno *pp. 154–156*   Cuaderno para hispanohablantes *pp. 155–157*

PARA Y PIENSA

Did you get it? Complete each sentence with the correct form of the appropriate verb: **empezar, cerrar,** or **pensar.**
1. Yo _____ que la blusa amarilla es bonita.
2. Ya hace frío cuando _____ el invierno.
3. El centro comercial _____ a las nueve de la noche.

Get Help Online
ClassZone.com

GRAMÁTICA en contexto

Goal: Listen to the **e → ie** stem-changing verbs that Enrique and Maribel use while they are shopping for clothes. Then use the stem-changing verbs to talk about your clothing preferences. **Actividades 11–12**

Telehistoria escena 2

@**HomeTutor** VideoPlus
ClassZone.com

STRATEGIES

Cuando lees
Look for color words In this scene, Enrique and Maribel discuss colors and types of clothing. Which color words do you find?

Cuando escuchas
Disregard stereotypes Who wants to keep looking at clothes and who is worried about being late? Is this expected? Why or why not?

VIDEO
DVD

AUDIO

Maribel: Tenemos que estar en el centro comercial a las doce, ¿entiendes?

Enrique: Sí, entiendo. Dos minutos más. ¿Prefieres los vaqueros negros o los pantalones verdes?

Maribel: Prefiero ir al centro comercial, ¡ahora!

Enrique: Quiero la camisa blanca.

Vendedora: Tenemos camisas en color azul y en verde. ¿Queréis ver?

Maribel: *(to the clerk)* No, gracias. *(to Enrique, frustrated)* Pero Enrique, ¿una tienda de ropa? ¿No prefieres ir de compras al centro comercial?

Enrique: No. No quiero comprar la ropa en el centro comercial. Los precios no son buenos. *(still shopping)* ¿Te gustan los pantalones cortos azules?

Maribel: *(rushing him)* Sí, sí. Y me gustan los calcetines rojos, la camisa amarilla y los zapatos marrones...

Enrique: No, no, no. ¿Rojo, amarillo y marrón? No, no me gustan.

Continuará... p. 234

11 | En la tienda de ropa *Comprensión del episodio*

Escuchar
Leer

Who prefers the following things: Maribel or Enrique?

1. ir de compras en una tienda de ropa
2. la camisa amarilla
3. la camisa blanca
4. los calcetines rojos
5. los zapatos marrones
6. ir al centro comercial temprano

 **Maribel**    **Enrique**

12 | La ropa y las estaciones

Hablar

Talk with a partner about what you prefer to wear and not wear during each season.

A ¿Qué prefieres llevar durante el verano?

B Prefiero llevar pantalones cortos. Nunca llevo chaqueta durante el verano.

Comparación cultural

El arte surrealista de España

How might dreams influence an artist's work? Artist Salvador Dalí from **Spain** is well known for his surrealist paintings. In surrealist art, the imagery reflects an artist's imagination and is often inspired by dreams. *La persistencia de la memoria,* considered one of Dalí's masterpieces, shows pocket watches that appear to be melting. Many interpret this painting as a commentary about the nature of time. What do you think Dalí's message is?

Compara con tu mundo *Can you think of a dream you had that would make an interesting painting? What would your painting look like?*

La persistencia de la memoria *(1931),* Salvador Dalí

PARA Y PIENSA

Did you get it? Complete each sentence based on the Telehistoria with the correct form of the verb in parentheses.

1. Enrique _____ que van al centro comercial. (entender)
2. Maribel _____ ir al centro comercial. (preferir)
3. Enrique _____ comprar la camisa blanca. (querer)

Get Help Online ClassZone.com

Lección 1
doscientos ventinueve **229**

Presentación de GRAMÁTICA

¡AVANZA!

Goal: Learn how to use direct object pronouns. Then practice using them to talk about the clothes you wear and those you want to buy. *Actividades 13–18*

English Grammar Connection: Direct objects receive the action of the verb in a sentence. They answer the question *whom?* or *what?* about the verb. The direct object can be a **noun** or a **pronoun**.

Luisa is buying the **blouse.** Luisa is buying **it.**   Luisa compra la **blusa.** Luisa **la** compra.

noun   **pronoun**   **noun**   **pronoun**

Direct Object Pronouns

Animated Grammar
ClassZone.com

Direct object pronouns can be used to replace **direct object nouns.**

Here's how:

	Singular		Plural	
	me	me	**nos**	us
	te	you (familiar)	**os**	you (familiar)
masculine	**lo**	you (formal), him, it	**los**	you, them	masculine
feminine	**la**	you (formal), her, it	**las**	you, them	feminine

The **direct object noun** is placed *after* the **conjugated verb.**

The **direct object pronoun** is placed directly *before* the **conjugated verb.**

replaced by

Quiero la **camisa** azul.

I want the blue shirt.

La quiero.

I want it.

When an **infinitive** follows the **conjugated verb,** the **direct object pronoun** can be placed *before* the **conjugated verb** or be *attached* to the **infinitive.**

replaced by

Quiero comprar **zapatos** negros.

I want to buy black shoes.

Y **los** quiero comprar hoy.

or Y quiero comprar**los** hoy.

*And I want to buy **them** today.*

Más práctica

Cuaderno *pp. 157–159*

Cuaderno para hispanohablantes *pp. 158–161*

@HomeTutor
Leveled Grammar Practice
ClassZone.com

Práctica de GRAMÁTICA

13 | Ropa para una fiesta

Leer Maribel and her friend are talking about the clothes they want to buy for a party on Saturday. Complete their instant messages with the correct direct object pronouns.

---

mensajero instantáneo

pelirroja16: Quiero comprar un vestido azul pero no tengo mucho dinero. ¿ __1.__ (Lo/La) compro?

busco_rebaja: Mmm... __2.__ (me/te) entiendo. Bueno, ¿cuánto cuesta el vestido?

pelirroja16: Veintinueve euros. Y tú, ¿qué necesitas comprar? ¿Una blusa blanca?

busco_rebaja: Ya __3.__ (la/los) tengo. Necesito unos zapatos. Los zapatos negros son más elegantes. ¿ __4.__ (Me/Os) entiendes?

pelirroja16: Sí, tienes razón. Si quieres zapatos negros, __5.__ (nos/los) venden en la Tienda Betún.

busco_rebaja: ¡Vale! También venden vestidos azules. __6.__ (Nos/Los) tienen por veinte euros.

---

14 | Lo que Enrique quiere

Escribir Use direct object pronouns to tell what Enrique wants or doesn't want to buy.

> **modelo:** No le gustan **los zapatos anaranjados.**
> No **los** quiere comprar. (No quiere comprar**los.**)

1. Los pantalones son feos.
2. No le gusta la camiseta.
3. Le gustan mucho las camisas.
4. Prefiere los calcetines verdes.
5. El sombrero es horrible.
6. Prefiere los zapatos azules.
7. No necesita pantalones cortos.
8. Prefiere la chaqueta blanca.
9. Le gusta el gorro rojo.
10. Los jeans son feos.

15 | Unos modelos cómicos

Enrique and Maribel are trying on all kinds of clothes at the store. Ask a partner about what they are wearing.

modelo: gorro

A ¿Quién lleva un **gorro verde**?

B Enrique **lo** lleva.

1. zapatos
2. camisa
3. chaqueta
4. pantalones cortos
5. jeans
6. ¿ ?

16 | En la tienda de ropa

Ask a partner about what people are buying or wearing in the picture. Your partner will use direct object pronouns to answer.

A ¿Compra el señor Costa un sombrero rojo?

B Sí, el señor Costa lo compra.

17 | ¿Cuándo lo usas?

Hablar

Work with a partner to name as many situations as you can in which you use the following items.

modelo: un lápiz

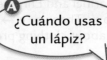

A ¿Cuándo usas un lápiz?

B Lo uso cuando hago la tarea y cuando escribo.

1. una chaqueta
2. el dinero
3. los pantalones cortos
4. un sombrero
5. una computadora

6. un gorro
7. el teléfono
8. un libro
9. una calculadora
10. un cuaderno

18 | ¿Qué llevas en julio?

Hablar

Comparación cultural

Climas diferentes

How does geography affect a country's climate? Countries near the equator have rainy and dry seasons, but have warm temperatures year-round. Countries in the northern and southern hemispheres have opposite seasons. For example, in **Spain,** July is a summer month and the weather is often hot, but in **Chile** it is a winter month. Chile's varied terrain, from beaches to mountains, and length (over 2,600 miles) create many different climates.

Barcelona, España

Los Andes en Chile

Compara con tu mundo *How does the geography of your area affect the climate? Is there a large body of water or a mountain range that influences the weather?*

Ask a partner about the clothing items he or she wears in the following places in July: Chile, Mexico, Spain, Puerto Rico, Argentina, and New York.

A ¿Llevas una camiseta en Chile en julio?

B No, no la llevo. Llevo una chaqueta y...

Más práctica Cuaderno *pp. 157–159* Cuaderno para hispanohablantes *pp. 158–161*

PARA Y PIENSA

Did you get it? In each sentence, use the correct direct object pronoun.
1. Luisa quiere los pantalones blancos. Ella _____ compra.
2. No quiero la blusa nueva. ¿ _____ quieres tú?
3. Nosotros preferimos las camisas azules. _____ compramos.

Get Help Online
ClassZone.com

Todo junto

¡AVANZA!

Goal: *Show what you know* Listen to Maribel and Enrique talk to the salesclerk about what Enrique wants to buy. Then use **e → ie** stem-changing verbs and direct object pronouns to talk about clothing preferences. *Actividades 19–23*

Telehistoria completa

@**HomeTutor** VideoPlus
ClassZone.com

STRATEGIES

Cuando lees

Discover what's forgotten Enrique forgets something in this scene. Find out what he forgot. How does this create a problem?

Cuando escuchas

Take the "emotional temperature" Find out who has the greatest intensity of feeling by listening to voices. Who is the most upset and why?

Escena 1 *Resumen*
Maribel tiene que ir al centro comercial porque necesita el autógrafo de Trini. Pero Enrique quiere ir de compras en una tienda.

Escena 2 *Resumen*
Enrique y Maribel están en una tienda, y Enrique quiere comprar mucha ropa. Maribel prefiere ir al centro comercial.

Escena 3

VIDEO
DVD

AUDIO

Enrique: Tienes razón. La chaqueta... la necesito. *(to the salesclerk)* ¿Vende chaquetas?

Vendedora: ¿En verano? No. Las vendo en el otoño.

Enrique: ¿Cuánto cuesta todo?

Vendedora: Los pantalones cuestan treinta euros, la camisa cuesta veinticinco, y el gorro, quince. Son setenta euros.

Enrique: ¡Mi dinero! ¡No lo tengo!

Maribel: Enrique, tienes que pagar. Son las once y media.

Enrique: Un gorro verde. ¡Lo quiero comprar! ¡Tengo que comprarlo!

Maribel: Enrique, ¡pero tú ya tienes un gorro verde!

Enrique: Sí, pero nunca lo llevo.

Maribel: Quieres una chaqueta, ¿no?

Maribel: ¡No te entiendo! ¿Quieres ir de compras y no tienes dinero?

Enrique: Está en mi mochila. ¿Dónde está mi mochila? ¿Tienes dinero? En el centro comercial yo compro la comida.

Maribel: ¿Con qué piensas pagar? No tienes dinero.

19 | ¿Cierto o falso? *Comprensión de los episodios*

Escuchar
Leer

Read the sentences and say whether they are true or false. Correct the false statements.

1. Enrique piensa que los precios son buenos en el centro comercial.
2. Maribel prefiere llegar al centro comercial a las doce.
3. Maribel necesita comprar una chaqueta.
4. Enrique tiene setenta euros para comprar su ropa.
5. A Maribel le gusta ser diferente.
6. Enrique prefiere llevar una chaqueta en el invierno.
7. Enrique compra una chaqueta en la tienda de ropa.

20 | Analizar la historia *Comprensión de los episodios*

Escuchar
Leer

Answer the questions about the episodes in complete sentences.

1. ¿Qué estación es?
2. ¿Dónde quiere comprar ropa Enrique?
3. ¿De qué color es el gorro?
4. ¿Cuánto cuestan los pantalones? ¿La camisa? ¿El gorro?
5. ¿Qué problema tiene Enrique?

21 | ¡A jugar! Un juego de quién

Hablar

> **STRATEGY Hablar**
>
> **Prepare and don't stress out** Create a list of useful questions and possible answers. Include various types of clothes. Review your verb endings. Then just talk!

Work in a group of three. Give a clue about someone in your Spanish class. The other members of your group will ask you yes/no questions to identify who it is. Follow the model.

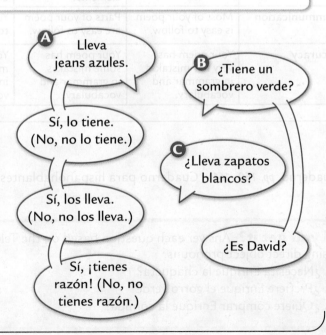

A Lleva jeans azules.

Sí, lo tiene. (No, no lo tiene.)

B ¿Tiene un sombrero verde?

C ¿Lleva zapatos blancos?

Sí, los lleva. (No, no los lleva.)

¿Es David?

Sí, ¡tienes razón! (No, no tienes razón.)

22 | Integración

Leer
Escuchar
Hablar

Read the discount coupon and listen to the store ad. Describe four items you want to buy for your friends and how much each item costs.

Fuente 1 Cupón

ALTA MODA
¡Descuentos de otoño!

Ropa de chicos	Ropa de chicas
• pantalones • chaquetas • jeans	Descuento de **5€**	• zapatos • blusas • vestidos	Descuento de **10€**

Calle Toro, 38 • Avenida de las Américas, 440 Madrid

Fuente 2 Anuncio

Listen and take notes
• ¿Qué venden en la tienda?
• ¿Cuánto cuesta la ropa?

modelo: Quiero comprar un vestido verde para Emily. Cuesta...

23 | Un poema de la estación

Escribir

Write a poem about one of the seasons. Include the following elements.

Para organizarte:
• *el nombre de la estación* ———————→ verano
• *dos colores que describen la estación* ——→ verde, azul
• *tres cosas que quieres* ————————→ quiero zapatos, helado, camisetas
• *cuatro actividades que prefieres hacer* —→ prefiero jugar, pasear, leer, descansar
• *una descripción de cómo estás* ————→ tengo calor

modelo:

Writing Criteria	Excellent	Good	Needs Work
Content	Your poem includes all of the elements.	Your poem includes some of the elements.	Your poem includes a few of the elements.
Communication	Most of your poem is easy to follow.	Parts of your poem are easy to follow.	Your poem is hard to follow.
Accuracy	Your poem has very few mistakes in grammar and vocabulary.	Your poem has some mistakes in grammar and vocabulary.	Your poem has many mistakes in grammar and vocabulary.

Más práctica Cuaderno *pp. 160–161* Cuaderno para hispanohablantes *pp. 162–163*

PARA Y PIENSA

Did you get it? Answer each question based on the Telehistoria with **sí,** using direct object pronouns.
1. ¿Necesita Enrique la chaqueta?
2. ¿Prefiere Enrique el gorro verde?
3. ¿Quiere comprar Enrique la comida?

Get Help Online
ClassZone.com

Juegos y diversiones

Review vocabulary by playing a game.

Pasa la bola

The Setup

Everyone should stand up and form a circle.

Materials

• small foam ball
• stopwatch or clock

Playing the Game

First: One of you will start by saying a vocabulary word from this lesson and tossing a small foam ball to another player. The player catching the ball will have five seconds to think of a word in the same category as the one just said (another color, clothing item, shopping word, or season). Your teacher will be the timekeeper and judge.

Then: Once the player has thought of a word and said it correctly, he or she will toss the ball to another player. That player then has to come up with another word in the same category as the first player's word. Players who cannot think of a valid answer in the allotted time must sit down.

The Winner!

The winner is the last person standing.

dinero

precio

Lectura

¡AVANZA! **Goal:** Read a poem by a Spanish poet. Then talk about what you have read and describe winter in your region.

AUDIO

Las memorias del invierno

Antonio Colinas is a poet and novelist from León, in northern Spain. He published the following poem in 1988.

STRATEGY Leer

Find the feelings Find phrases that show the poet's feelings and write them in a chart like the one below. Write the feeling after each phrase.

- Emotions in *Invierno tardío* by Colinas
  - **Phrase:** es como primavera temprana
    Feeling: happiness
  - **Phrase:**
    Feeling:
  - **Phrase:**
    Feeling:

Antonio Colinas nació[1] en 1946 en La Bañeza, en la provincia de León, España. Escribe poesía, novelas, ensayos[2] y crítica. También estudia literatura italiana y la adapta al español. Su poesía ha ganado[3] muchos premios[4] en España, como el Premio Nacional de Literatura, en 1982. Ahora vive en Salamanca, España.

---

[1] was born   [2] essays   [3] has won   [4] awards

Invierno tardío

No es increíble cuanto ven mis ojos [5]:
nieva sobre el almendro florido [6],
nieva sobre la nieve.
Este invierno mi ánimo [7]
es como primavera temprana,
es como almendro florido
bajo la nieve.

Hay demasiado [8] frío
esta tarde en el mundo [9].
Pero abro la puerta a mi perro
y con él entra en casa [10] calor,
entra la humanidad.

---

[5] **ven...** my eyes see
[6] **sobre...** on the flowery almond tree
[7] spirit   [8] too much   [9] world   [10] house

~56~

PARA Y PIENSA

¿Comprendiste?

1. ¿De dónde es Antonio Colinas? ¿Qué escribe? ¿Dónde vive ahora?
2. ¿Dónde está la persona en el poema? ¿Qué mira? En tu opinión, ¿está triste o contenta la persona?
3. ¿Piensas que el perro es un buen amigo? ¿Por qué?

¿Y tú?
¿Cómo es el invierno en tu región? ¿Qué te gusta hacer?

Conexiones *El arte*

Los árabes en España

For almost 800 years, from 711 to 1492, the Moors, Arab Muslims from northern Africa, occupied an area in southern Spain called **Al-Andalus,** now known as **Andalucía.** This was a period of rich cultural exchange in the arts, sciences, mathematics, agriculture, and architecture.

The Alhambra palace in Granada is a notable example of Moorish architecture in Spain. The interior is exquisitely detailed, bright, and airy. Ornately carved pillars and arches open onto sunny courtyards. The walls and ceilings are decorated with intricate geometric designs.

Design a courtyard based on the architectural styles illustrated in these pictures of the Alhambra. Create a drawing or model to show your design.

El patio de los leones

La Alhambra

Un arco musulmán

Los jardines del Generalife

Proyecto 1 *La música*

Moorish civilization had a lasting influence on the music of Spain. The guitar may be derived from the oud, a type of lute and a classic Arab instrument. The word **guitarra** comes from the Arabic *qithara*. Some contemporary music is similar to the music played during the Moorish rule. Research and write about the musical group *Al-Andalus*. Include the members of the group, the places where they perform, and a description of their music.

Proyecto 2 *La salud*

Olives have always been a part of Spanish tradition. Olive seeds that date back 8,000 years have been found in Spain. The majority of olive trees grown in the country are found in **Andalucía.** Spain is also one of the world's foremost producers of olive oil. Research and write about the health and beauty benefits of olives and olive oil. Describe how they are used on a daily basis.

Proyecto 3 *El lenguaje*

The Moors brought many concepts and inventions to Spain. The Arabic words for many of these things still exist in Spanish. Often these words begin with **al-** or **a-.** Some examples are **almohada, álgebra, algodón,** and **ajedrez.** Using a Spanish-English dictionary, write the meanings of these words. Then find three more Spanish words that begin with **al-,** write their English definitions, and use the Internet or the library to find out if they have Arabic origin.

Vocabulario

Talk About Shopping

el centro comercial	shopping center, mall	el dólar	dollar
¿Cuánto cuesta(n)?	How much does it (do they) cost?	el euro	euro
		ir de compras	to go shopping
Cuesta(n)...	It costs . . . (They cost . . .)	pagar	to pay
		el precio	price
el dinero	money	la tienda	store

Describe Clothing

la blusa	blouse	nuevo(a)	new
los calcetines	socks	los pantalones	pants
la camisa	shirt	los pantalones cortos	shorts
la camiseta	T-shirt		
la chaqueta	jacket	la ropa	clothing
feo(a)	ugly	el sombrero	hat
el gorro	winter hat	el vestido	dress
los jeans	jeans	los zapatos	shoes
llevar	to wear		

Colors

amarillo(a)	yellow	marrón (pl. marrones)	brown
anaranjado(a)	orange		
azul	blue	negro(a)	black
blanco(a)	white	rojo(a)	red
		verde	green

Expressions with *tener*

tener calor	to be hot
tener frío	to be cold
tener razón	to be right
tener suerte	to be lucky

Discuss Seasons

la estación (pl. las estaciones)	season
el invierno	winter
el otoño	autumn, fall
la primavera	spring
el verano	summer

Other Words and Phrases

durante	during
cerrar (ie)	to close
empezar (ie)	to begin
entender (ie)	to understand
pensar (ie)	to think, to plan
preferir (ie)	to prefer
querer (ie)	to want

Gramática

Nota gramatical: tener expressions *p. 223*

Stem-Changing Verbs: e → ie

For **e → ie** stem-changing verbs, the **e** of the stem changes to **ie** in all forms except **nosotros(as)** and **vosotros(as)**.

querer *to want*	
quiero	queremos
quieres	queréis
quiere	quieren

Direct Object Pronouns

Direct object pronouns can be used to replace **direct object nouns.**

Singular		Plural	
me	me	**nos**	us
te	you (familiar)	**os**	you (familiar)
lo	you (formal), him, it	**los**	you, them
la	you (formal), her, it	**las**	you, them

Repaso de la lección

¡LLEGADA!

@HomeTutor
ClassZone.com

Now you can
- talk about what clothes you want to buy
- say what you wear in different seasons

Using
- **tener** expressions
- stem-changing verbs: **e → ie**
- direct object pronouns

To review
- stem-changing verbs: **e → ie** p. 224
- direct object pronouns p. 230

1 Listen and understand

AUDIO

Listen to Paula talk about clothes. Tell whether she wants to buy each article of clothing or not. Use direct object pronouns.

1.

2.

3.

4.

5.

6.

To review
- stem-changing verbs: **e → ie** p. 224

2 Talk about what clothes you want to buy

Fernando is going shopping with his parents. What does he say?

preferir	cerrar	entender
empezar	pensar	querer

Las clases __1.__ el lunes y necesito ropa. Yo __2.__ comprar unas camisetas y unos pantalones pero no tengo mucho dinero. Yo __3.__ las camisetas a las camisas. Yo no __4.__ por qué una camiseta cuesta más en el centro comercial que en otras tiendas. Mi amiga Carla __5.__ que hay ropa más bonita y menos cara en la tienda Moda Zaragoza. Necesito ir hoy porque la tienda __6.__ los domingos.

3 | Talk about what clothes you want to buy

To review
- **tener** expressions p. 223
- stem-changing verbs: **e → ie** p. 224

Tell whether these people are hot or cold, based on what they are thinking about buying.

> **modelo:** Ana / blusa de verano
> Ana piensa comprar una blusa de verano porque tiene calor.

1. Juan y yo / gorros
2. yo / pantalones cortos
3. tú / chaqueta
4. Laura y Carlos / camisetas de verano
5. ustedes / calcetines de invierno
6. Pilar / vestido de primavera

4 | Say what you wear in different seasons

To review
- direct object pronouns p. 230

Write sentences telling who prefers to wear these clothing items.

> **modelo:** los zapatos negros (Juan)
> Juan los prefiere llevar. (Juan prefiere llevarlos.)

1. los pantalones cortos (Rosa)
2. las camisas azules (ellas)
3. el sombrero rojo (yo)
4. la camiseta anaranjada (Carlos)
5. el gorro negro (ellos)
6. la blusa amarilla (nosotras)
7. los calcetines blancos (ustedes)
8. la chaqueta marrón (tú)
9. los zapatos marrones (usted)
10. el vestido verde (Amanda)

5 | Spain and Chile

To review
- **Sevillanas** p. 215
- Comparación cultural pp. 229, 233
- Lectura pp. 238–239

Comparación cultural

Answer these culture questions.

1. What are the characteristics of **sevillanas**?
2. How do the climates of Spain and Chile differ in July and why?
3. What are some characteristics of surrealist art?
4. What season is represented in Antonio Colinas' poem? How does the speaker of the poem feel and why?

Más práctica Cuaderno *pp. 162–173* Cuaderno para hispanohablantes *pp. 164–173*

 Get Help Online ClassZone.com

Lección 1
doscientos cuarenta y tres **243**

España

Tema:

¿Qué hacemos esta noche?

¡AVANZA!

In this lesson you will learn to
- describe places and events in town
- talk about types of transportation
- say what you are going to do
- order from a menu

using
- the verb **ver, ir a** + infinitive
- stem-changing verbs: **o → ue**
- stem-changing verbs: **e → i**

♻ *¿Recuerdas?*
- present tense of **-er** verbs
- the verb **ir, tener** expressions
- direct object pronouns

Comparación cultural

In this lesson you will learn about
- local markets
- art from Spain and Chile
- weekend activities in Spain, Guatemala, and Chile

Compara con tu mundo

Maribel and Enrique are near the Teatro de la Comedia, where many traditional Spanish plays are performed. *What do you and your friends like to do on weekends?*

¿Qué ves?

Mira la foto

¿Es viejo el teatro?

¿Lleva pantalones o un vestido Maribel?

¿De qué color es la camisa de Enrique?

Online SPANISH CLASSZONE.COM

Featuring...

Cultura INTERACTIVA

Animated Grammar

@HomeTutor

And more...
- Get Help Online
- Interactive Flashcards
- Review Games
- WebQuest
- Self-Check Quiz

**El Teatro de la Comedia
en la calle Príncipe**
Madrid, España

Presentación de VOCABULARIO

Goal: Learn about what Enrique and Maribel do when they go out. Then practice what you have learned to describe places and events in town. *Actividades 1–2*

♻ *¿Recuerdas?* Present tense of **-er** verbs p. 168

VIDEO
DVD

AUDIO

A En **el centro** de Madrid hay muchos **lugares** para comer. Maribel y yo queremos ir a **la calle** de Alcalá para **encontrar** un buen **restaurante**. ¿Vamos **a pie, en coche** o **en autobús**?

a pie

en coche

en autobús

B En **el menú** hay muchos **platos principales**. Si te gusta **la carne**, hay **bistec**. Si no, también hay **pescado**.

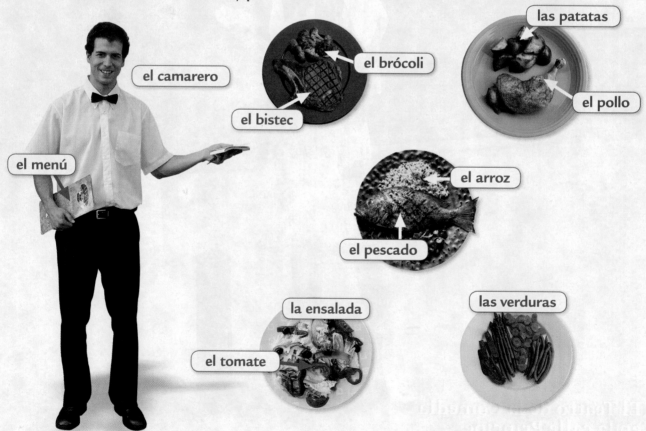

el camarero

el brócoli

las patatas

el bistec

el pollo

el menú

el arroz

el pescado

la ensalada

las verduras

el tomate

C La cuenta es veinticinco euros. ¿Cuánto dinero necesitamos para la propina?

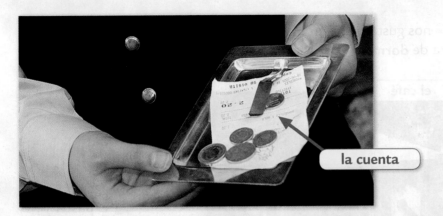

la cuenta

D Tomamos el autobús para ir al cine. Vamos al Cine Ideal para ver una película.

el cine

la ventanilla

las entradas

E Aquí en Madrid también hay teatros y parques pero yo prefiero ir a un concierto para escuchar música.

el teatro

el parque

el concierto

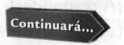
Continuará...

Presentación de VOCABULARIO
(continuación)

F Vamos a **un café. De postre** nos gusta **pedir un pastel.** Después, Maribel está muy cansada. Es la hora de **dormir.**

el café

la mesa

el pastel

En España se dice...

In Spain the word for *cake* is **la tarta.** The word for *beans* is **las alubias.**

dormir

Más vocabulario

allí *there*

almorzar *to eat lunch*

costar *to cost*

los frijoles *beans*

la música rock *rock music*

poder *to be able, can*

servir *to serve*

tal vez *perhaps, maybe*

volver *to return, to come back*

Expansión de vocabulario p. R5

¡A responder! Escuchar

Listen to the waiter. Point to the photo with the food that he mentions.

@HomeTutor VideoPlus
Interactive Flashcards
ClassZone.com

Práctica de VOCABULARIO

1 | Diversiones en el centro

Leer | Read each description and look for the matching word.

1. Es una persona que trabaja en un café.
2. Es el lugar adonde vas para comer.
3. Vas aquí para ver una película.
4. La necesitas para ir a un concierto.
5. Lo comes después del plato principal.
6. Compras entradas aquí.

a. la ventanilla
b. el restaurante
c. la camarera
d. la entrada
e. el cine
f. el postre

Nota gramatical **¿Recuerdas?** Present tense of **-er** verbs p. 168

Ver has an irregular **yo** form in the present tense: **veo.**

Veo muchos autobuses en el centro.   *I see a lot of buses downtown.*

---

2 | ¿Qué ves en el restaurante?

 Hablar | Señor and Señora Ortiz are at the restaurant Los Reyes. Ask a partner what he or she sees.

A ¿Qué ves en el restaurante?
B Allí veo una silla.

Más práctica   Cuaderno *pp. 174–176*   Cuaderno para hispanohablantes *pp. 174–177*

PARA Y PIENSA

Did you get it?
1. Name three things you would find in a restaurant.
2. Name three places where you and your friends might go to have fun.

Get Help Online
ClassZone.com

VOCABULARIO *en contexto*

Goal: Focus on how Maribel and Enrique talk about where they go and how they get there. Then practice these words and **ir a** + infinitive to talk about types of transportation and what you are going to do. *Actividades 3–4*

 ¿Recuerdas? The verb **ir** p. 134

Telehistoria escena 1

@HomeTutor VideoPlus
ClassZone.com

STRATEGIES

Cuando lees

Think about timing Consider timing while reading. How long will Enrique's plan take? Will they see Trini? Why or why not?

Cuando escuchas

Enter the scene As you listen to Enrique's travel plan, enter the scene. If you were Maribel, would you feel calm or nervous about Enrique's ideas? Why?

Enrique

Maribel

Enrique: ¿Trini Salgado está en el centro comercial del Parque de las Avenidas a las doce?

Maribel: Sí. Y ya es tarde. Enrique, ¡por favor!

Enrique: ¡Vale! ¿Y cómo vamos a llegar allí? ¿En autobús?

Enrique puts the T-shirt in his bag so that Maribel can open the map.

Maribel: Podemos empezar aquí en el parque. El centro comercial está allí. ¿Cuál es la calle?

Enrique: Calle Poveda. ¡Es fácil! Tomamos el autobús al centro. Vamos a pie a la biblioteca —aquí. Mi madre está allí. Ella tiene coche. ¡Llegamos al centro comercial en coche!

Maribel: ¡Pero, Enrique! Son las once y cuarenta y cinco. Vamos a llegar tarde. ¿Qué voy a hacer?

Enrique: ¡Ah! El autobús setenta y cuatro va al centro comercial. Llega aquí a las doce y llega al centro comercial a las doce y media.

Maribel: ¡Vale!

Continuará... p. 256

También se dice

España Enrique says **el autobús** to talk about taking the bus. In other Spanish-speaking countries you might hear:
- **Puerto Rico, República Dominicana, Cuba** la guagua
- **México** el camión
- **muchos países** el colectivo, el micro

3 | ¿Cómo piensan llegar? *Comprensión del episodio*

Escuchar
Leer

Read the sentences and tell whether they are true or false.

1. Maribel y Enrique no tienen mapa.
2. La madre de Enrique está en la biblioteca.
3. El centro comercial está en la calle Poveda.
4. Enrique quiere ir a pie al centro comercial.
5. El autobús llega al centro comercial a las doce.

Nota gramatical   *¿Recuerdas?* The verb **ir** p. 134

To talk about what you are going to do, use a form of **ir a** + **infinitive**.

¿Qué **van a hacer** ustedes?   **Vamos a mirar** una película.
*What **are you going to do**?*   ***We're going to watch** a movie.*

Vamos a can also mean *Let's.*

---

4 | ¿Qué vas a comer?

Hablar

Ask a partner what he or she is going to eat this week. Your partner should explain his or her answers.

A ¿Vas a comer carne?

B Sí, voy a comer carne. Es rica. (No, no voy a comer carne. Es horrible.)

1.    2.    3.    4.

5.    6.    7.    8.

PARA Y PIENSA

Did you get it? Complete each sentence with the correct phrase to tell what form of transportation is used.

1. Maribel va a la escuela _____ ; va a tomar el cuarenta y dos.
2. Enrique y su hermano van a ir _____ al parque; les gusta pasear.
3. Maribel y su mamá van al concierto _____ porque no quieren llegar tarde.

Get Help Online
ClassZone.com

Presentación de GRAMÁTICA

¡AVANZA! **Goal:** Learn how to form **o → ue** stem-changing verbs. Then practice using these verbs to talk about going out with friends. *Actividades 5–10*

English Grammar Connection: Remember that there are no stem-changing verbs in the present tense of English (see p. 224). In Spanish, **o → ue** stem changes happen in all three classes of verbs: **-ar, -er,** and **-ir.**

Stem-Changing Verbs: o → ue

Animated Grammar
ClassZone.com

Some verbs have an **o → ue** stem change in the present tense. How do you form the present tense of these verbs?

Here's how:

Remember that stem-changing verbs have regular **-ar, -er,** and **-ir** endings. For **o → ue** stem-changing verbs, the last **o** of the stem changes to **ue** in all forms except **nosotros(as)** and **vosotros(as).**

poder *to be able, can*	
puedo	**podemos**
puedes	**podéis**
puede	**pueden**

Carmen **puede** ir al concierto.
*Carmen **can** go to the concert.*

Other verbs you know that have this stem change are **almorzar, costar, dormir, encontrar,** and **volver.**

Almuerzo a la una.
*I **eat lunch** at one o'clock.*

Antonio, ¿cuándo **vuelves**?
*Antonio, when **are you coming back**?*

Más práctica
Cuaderno *pp. 177–179*
Cuaderno para hispanohablantes *pp. 178–180*

@HomeTutor
Leveled Grammar Practice
ClassZone.com

Práctica de GRAMÁTICA

5 | Un concierto de música rock

Leer
Escribir

Maribel is talking with her friend Toni about when they can go to a concert. Complete what she says with forms of **poder,** and use the poster to answer her question.

Presenta **Los Rebeldes**

en el Centro Cívico, Madrid
Entrada: 18€ en la ventanilla
Fecha: 22–23 de abril
Hora: el viernes por la tarde
(19:00) y por la noche (22:00)
el sábado por la tarde
(14:00) y por la noche (21:00)

Nosotros queremos ir a un concierto el viernes o el sábado, pero ¿cuándo? Yo no __1.__ ir el viernes en la noche porque tengo que trabajar. Manolo no __2.__ ir el sábado en la noche. Ana y Miguel no __3.__ ir el viernes en la noche y el sábado en la tarde no van a estar aquí. Enrique y su hermano no __4.__ ir el sábado en la tarde porque van a un restaurante con su primo. Y Toni, tú no __5.__ ir el sábado en la noche. ¿Cuándo __6.__ ir todos nosotros?

6 | ¿Quieres ir?

Leer
Escribir

Complete the conversation between Enrique and Maribel by choosing the correct verb and conjugating it in the appropriate form.

Enrique: Yo __1.__ (dormir / almorzar) en el café Mariposa hoy. La comida es muy rica y no __2.__ (volver / costar) mucho. ¿Quieres ir?

Maribel: Gracias, pero yo no __3.__ (encontrar / poder) comer ahora. Mis padres __4.__ (volver / dormir) de sus vacaciones en México. Necesito ir a la tienda ahora para comprar comida.

Enrique: Tú __5.__ (poder / dormir) ir a pie porque la tienda está cerca de aquí.

Maribel: Mis padres quieren comer unas verduras y nosotros siempre __6.__ (costar / encontrar) buenas verduras allí.

Enrique: ¿Tú y tus padres __7.__ (poder / volver) ir al cine esta noche? Yo voy a las siete y media.

Maribel: Gracias, Enrique, pero mis padres siempre están muy cansados después de sus vacaciones y __8.__ (dormir / almorzar) mucho.

7 | Las actividades en el centro

Escribir

Combine phrases from the three puzzle pieces to describe activities downtown. Use the correct verb forms to write your sentences.

modelo: el camarero / no poder trabajar / en el restaurante
El camarero no puede trabajar en el restaurante.

las entradas para el concierto

yo

vosotros

tú

usted

nosotros

almorzar

costar

encontrar la calle

poder jugar al fútbol

dormir bien

volver al centro

en el mapa

con amigos en el parque

después de comer mucho

quince euros

en el café con mi familia

en autobús

8 | Todos tienen excusas

Hablar

Talk with another student about the activities that you can't do this weekend. Say that you can't do something and make up an excuse.

modelo: ir a un concierto

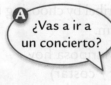

A ¿Vas a ir a un concierto?

B No, no puedo ir a un concierto. Voy a ir al cine con mi hermano.

1. ir al teatro
2. dormir diez horas
3. practicar deportes
4. almorzar en un café
5. pasar un rato con los amigos
6. ver una película en el cine
7. ir al centro
8. comprar ropa
9. montar en bicicleta
10. preparar la comida

9 ¡Vamos a ir de compras!

Comparación cultural

Chichicastenango, Guatemala

Los mercados

How do local markets reflect the culture of an area? Every Sunday, tourists and locals head to El Rastro, one of the oldest flea markets in Madrid, **Spain,** to search for bargains amid the hundreds of stalls. Vendors offer a wide variety of items such as antiques, secondhand clothing, CDs, books, maps, and art.

In **Guatemala,** the town of Chichicastenango hosts a popular market in which you can find handicrafts from the Maya-Quiché culture. Many vendors wear the traditional dress of their region and sell colorful textiles including Mayan blouses called *huipiles.* Other common items include fruits and vegetables, masks, baskets, candles, and flowers.

El Rastro en Madrid, España

Compara con tu mundo *What type of souvenir might a visitor to your community purchase? Why is it popular?*

Ask a partner where you can find books, CDs, fruit, art, vegetables, maps, and **huipiles.**

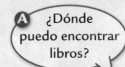

A ¿Dónde puedo encontrar libros?

B Encuentras libros en El Rastro.

10 ¿Y tú?

Hablar
Escribir

Answer the following questions in complete sentences.

1. ¿A qué hora almuerzas?
2. ¿Cuánto cuesta el almuerzo en la cafetería de tu escuela?
3. ¿A qué hora vuelves de la escuela?
4. ¿Cuándo puedes pasar un rato con los amigos?
5. ¿Cuántas horas duermes los sábados?
6. ¿En qué tiendas encuentras tu ropa?

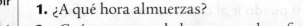
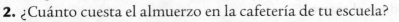

Más práctica   Cuaderno *pp. 177–179*   Cuaderno para hispanohablantes *pp. 178–180*

PARA Y PIENSA

Did you get it? Complete each sentence with the correct form of the appropriate verb: **poder, costar, almorzar,** or **dormir.**

1. El pescado _____ diez dólares.
2. Nosotros _____ a la una en el café.
3. Yo _____ ocho horas.
4. Ellos no _____ contestar.

Get Help Online
ClassZone.com

Lección 2
doscientos cincuenta y cinco   **255**

GRAMÁTICA *en contexto*

Goal: Identify the **o → ue** stem-changing verbs Enrique and Maribel use to talk about things to do in the city. Then practice using these verbs to talk about where you go. *Actividades 11–12*

Telehistoria escena 2

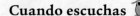

@HomeTutor VideoPlus
ClassZone.com

STRATEGIES

Cuando lees

Compare scenes As you read this scene, compare it to Scene 1. How are these scenes alike in terms of Enrique's promises and his behavior? What trends do you find?

Cuando escuchas

Identify causes A negative feeling can have more than one cause. Listen for the causes of Maribel's anxiety and concerns. How many causes are there? What are they?

VIDEO
DVD

AUDIO

Enrique: ¿Qué vas a hacer hoy por la tarde?

Maribel: Después de ir de compras, quiero volver al centro. Hay un concierto de música rock, o puedo ir al cine a ver una película... ¡o puedo ir al teatro!

Enrique: ¡Un concierto de rock! ¿Puedo ir?

Maribel: Mmm... ¡quiero ir al teatro! Vamos al teatro.

Enrique: ¿Al teatro? Pero las entradas cuestan mucho, y...

After the trouble he caused, Enrique decides to go along with Maribel's idea.

Enrique: ¡Vale! Vamos al teatro.

Maribel: *(amused)* No, vamos al concierto.

Enrique: ¡Muy bien! Voy a comprar las entradas.

Maribel: ¡Pero, Enrique! El autobús...

Enrique: La ventanilla está allí, cerca del café. Vuelvo en dos minutos.

As he runs to buy the tickets, Maribel sees the bus approaching. She decides to go alone, but realizes she no longer has the T-shirt.

Maribel: ¡La camiseta! ¡No encuentro la camiseta! ¡Enrique!

Continuará... p. 262

11 | Planes para la tarde Comprensión del episodio

Escuchar
Leer

Match phrases to complete the sentences.

1. Después de ir de compras, Maribel quiere...
2. Enrique no quiere ir al teatro porque...
3. Maribel y Enrique van...
4. El autobús llega...
5. Enrique va a comprar las entradas...

a. cuando Enrique va a comprar las entradas.
b. volver al centro.
c. a un concierto de música rock en la tarde.
d. y tiene la camiseta.
e. las entradas cuestan mucho.

12 | ¿Qué encuentras?

Hablar

Talk with a partner about what you find in these places.

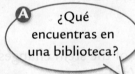

A ¿Qué encuentras en una biblioteca?

B Encuentro libros y computadoras allí.

1.

2.

3.

4.

5.

6.

PARA Y PIENSA

Did you get it? Complete each sentence based on the Telehistoria with the correct form of the verb in parentheses.
1. Maribel _____ ir al cine o al teatro. (poder)
2. Maribel no _____ la camiseta. (encontrar)
3. Enrique _____ tarde y los dos no van al centro comercial. (volver)

Get Help Online
ClassZone.com

Presentación de GRAMÁTICA

Goal: Learn how to form **e → i** stem-changing verbs. Then practice using these verbs to order from a menu. *Actividades 13–18*

♻ *¿Recuerdas?* Direct object pronouns p. 230, **tener** expressions p. 223

English Grammar Connection: Remember that there are no stem-changing verbs in the present tense of English (see p. 224). There are, however, a number of stem-changing verbs in Spanish.

Stem-Changing Verbs: e → i

Animated Grammar
ClassZone.com

Some **-ir** verbs have an **e → i** stem change in the present tense. How do you form the present tense of these verbs?

Here's how:

For **e → i** stem-changing verbs, the last **e** of the stem changes to **i** in all forms except **nosotros(as)** and **vosotros(as).**

s**e**rvir	*to serve*
s**i**rvo	s**e**rvimos
s**i**rves	s**e**rvís
s**i**rve	s**i**rven

El camarero **si**rve la comida.
*The waiter **serves** the food.*

Another verb you know with this stem change is **pedir.**

¿**Pi**des una ensalada?
***Are you ordering** a salad?*

Siempre **pe**dimos pollo.
***We** always **order** chicken.*

Más práctica
Cuaderno *pp. 180–182*
Cuaderno para hispanohablantes *pp. 181–184*

@HomeTutor
Leveled Grammar Practice
ClassZone.com

Práctica de GRAMÁTICA

13 | ¿Qué piden?

Hablar
Escribir

Tell what these people are ordering.

modelo: yo
Yo pido carne.

1. tú

2. mis amigas

3. yo

4. vosotros

5. mi madre

6. Maribel

7. mis abuelos y yo

8. ustedes

14 | ¿Quién sirve la comida? ♻ *¿Recuerdas?* Direct object pronouns p. 230

Hablar
Escribir

Tell what these people ask for and who serves it.

modelo: Maribel: bebida (la camarera)
Maribel pide una bebida y la camarera la sirve.

1. yo: ensalada (Enrique)

2. mi amigo: pollo (sus padres)

3. tú: pescado (yo)

4. mis amigas y yo: verduras (vosotros)

5. usted: patatas (nosotros)

6. vosotros: postre (el camarero)

AUDIO

Pronunciación **La letra c con e, i**

Before **e** and **i**, the Spanish **c** is pronounced like the *c* in *city*.

Listen and repeat.

ce → cero   centro
       cerrar   quince

ci → cien   cine
       precio   estación

In many regions of Spain, the **c** before **e** and **i** is pronounced like the *th* of the English word *think*.

Necesitamos cinco lápices para hacer la tarea de ciencias.

15 | Una cena especial

Hablar
Escribir

Enrique and his family are going out to dinner. Complete what he says with the correct form of **servir** or **pedir**.

> Mi familia __1.__ una mesa cerca de la ventana. Mis padres __2.__ ensaladas y pollo con arroz. Yo __3.__ bistec. Los camareros __4.__ las ensaladas y los platos principales. Todos nosotros __5.__ helado. El camarero __6.__ los postres.

16 | ¿Qué sirven en el café?

Escuchar
Escribir

Enrique is in a café and is talking to the waiters and waitresses. Write sentences to tell what these people are serving.

1. los camareros   **3.** el camarero   **5.** Luis y José
2. el señor Fuentes   **4.** la camarera   **6.** Ana

17 | En el restaurante

Hablar
Escribir

Look at the restaurant scene below. Tell what the people are ordering or serving.

18 | **¿Qué pides del menú?** *¿Recuerdas?* **tener** expressions p. 223

Hablar

Ask a partner what he or she orders in a restaurant in the following situations.

modelo: bebida / en el almuerzo

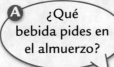

A ¿Qué bebida pides en el almuerzo?

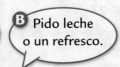

B Pido leche o un refresco.

1. comida / en el almuerzo
2. bebida / cuando tienes frío
3. bebida / en el desayuno
4. comida / cuando tienes calor
5. comida / cuando tienes hambre
6. bebida / cuando tienes mucha sed

Comparación cultural

Las meninas

Why might an artist create a version of another artist's masterpiece? Diego Velázquez served as the official painter for King Philip IV of **Spain** and painted many portraits of the royal family. *Las meninas* shows the *Infanta* (princess) and her attendants. Velázquez included himself in the painting. Three centuries later, Pablo Picasso, also from Spain, completed 58 interpretations of this painting. What similarities and differences do you notice?

Las meninas *(1656), Diego Velázquez*

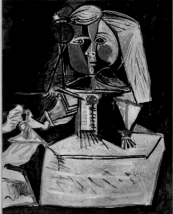

Las meninas (Infanta Margarita) *(1957), Pablo Picasso*

Compara con tu mundo

What famous artwork would you like to try to re-create and why? How would your version be different from the original?

Más práctica Cuaderno *pp. 180–182* Cuaderno para hispanohablantes *pp. 181–184*

 PARA Y PIENSA

Did you get it? Complete each sentence with the correct form of **pedir** or **servir**.

1. En la cena los camareros _____ arroz con pollo.
2. Mi madre hace un pastel y lo _____ de postre.
3. Nosotros no _____ mucho porque no tenemos mucha hambre.

Get Help Online
ClassZone.com

Todo junto

Goal: *Show what you know* Pay attention to how Maribel and Enrique tell the waiter what they would like to eat. Then practice using **o → ue** and **e → i** stem-changing verbs to order food and give your opinion on restaurants. *Actividades 19–23*

Telehistoria completa

@HomeTutor VideoPlus
ClassZone.com

STRATEGIES

Cuando lees

Analyze the communication Analyze this scene's communication by answering these questions: Why does Maribel order so much food? What is the effect?

Cuando escuchar

Listen for contrasts Listen for contrasts during the scene. Examples: What do Maribel and Enrique order? Who promises to pay, and who actually pays?

Escena 1 *Resumen*

Enrique y Maribel pueden tomar el autobús setenta y cuatro al centro comercial. Piensan llegar a las doce y media.

Escena 2 *Resumen*

Enrique va a comprar las entradas para un concierto. El autobús llega pero Enrique no está. Maribel no tiene la camiseta.

Escena 3

VIDEO DVD

AUDIO

They arrive at an outdoor restaurant.

Enrique: Es un restaurante muy bonito.

Maribel: Pero no tengo el autógrafo de Trini.

Enrique: Vamos a pedir la comida. ¡Yo pago!

Maribel: Ah, ¿pagas tú? Ahora pido toda la comida del menú.

The waiter arrives.

Maribel: Señor, ¿sirven pescado hoy?

Camarero: No, hoy no tenemos pescado.

Maribel: Quiero empezar con una ensalada. De plato principal quiero el pollo con verduras y... Sí, y filete con patatas.

Camarero: ¿Dos platos principales? ¿Filete y pollo?

Enrique: Es mucho, ¿no?

Maribel: Sí. Y de postre quiero un arroz con leche.

Enrique: *(nervously)* Pan y agua, por favor.

Maribel: Él va a pagar la cuenta.

Enrique: *(nods, then remembers)* ¡Maribel! ¡Mi mochila! ¡No tengo dinero!

Maribel: *(smiling)* Ay, Enrique, yo sí tengo dinero.

19 | ¿Quién lo hace? *Comprensión de los episodios*

Escuchar
Leer

Read these sentences and tell whether they are about Enrique or Maribel.

1. Quiere volver al centro después de ir de compras.
2. Piensa que las entradas cuestan mucho.
3. No encuentra la camiseta.
4. Piensa que el restaurante es muy bonito.
5. Pide mucha comida.

20 | Problemas en el centro *Comprensión de los episodios*

Escuchar
Leer

Answer the questions according to the episodes.

1. ¿Cómo quieren ir Maribel y Enrique al centro comercial?
2. ¿Adónde va el autobús setenta y cuatro?
3. ¿Por qué no quiere ir al teatro Enrique?
4. ¿Por qué está enojada Maribel?
5. ¿Qué pide Maribel en el restaurante?

21 | Clientes y camareros

Hablar

STRATEGY

Plan the whole scene Plan the whole scene from start to finish. What would the waiter or waitress say before, during, and after the meal? What would the customers say at each stage?

Work in a group of three. Prepare a scene in a café with customers and a waiter or waitress. Present your scene to the class.

Para organizarte:
- qué comidas y bebidas piden
- qué sirve el (la) camarero(a)
- cuánto cuesta la comida (la cuenta y la propina)

Camarero(a) Buenas tardes. ¿Quieren ver el menú?

Cliente 1 Buenas tardes. Sí, por favor. Tenemos mucha hambre.

Ustedes pueden pedir el pollo con patatas. Es mucha comida.

Cliente 2 Tal vez, pero hoy tengo ganas de comer...

22 | Integración

Leer
Escuchar
Hablar

Read the pamphlet and listen to the guide. Describe five activities you are going to do, where, and how you can get there.

Fuente 1 Folleto del hotel

	TRANSPORTE		
	🚶	🚗	🚌
Biblioteca Nacional	■		45
Café Almagro			7
Centro Comercial ABC Serrano		■	19
Cine Ábaco		■	
Parque del Buen Retiro	■		
Plaza de la Moncloa			133
Restaurante Oberón	■	■	
Teatro Marquina	■		

PUERTA DEL SOL, 2   MADRID

Fuente 2 Anuncio del guía turístico

Listen and take notes

• ¿Qué actividades menciona el guía?
• ¿En qué lugares puedes hacer las actividades?

modelo: Voy a comer pescado. Voy al Restaurante Oberón. Puedo ir a pie o en coche...

23 | Una crítica culinaria

Escribir

You are a newspaper food critic. Write a short review of your favorite restaurant. Explain what the waiters are like, what they serve, what you order, what the food is like, and how much it costs.

modelo: El restaurante Salazar es muy bueno. Los camareros son trabajadores. De plato principal sirven...

Writing Criteria	Excellent	Good	Needs Work
Content	Your review includes a lot of information.	Your review includes some information.	Your review includes little information.
Communication	Most of your review is organized and easy to follow.	Parts of your review are organized and easy to follow.	Your review is disorganized and hard to follow.
Accuracy	Your review has few mistakes in grammar and vocabulary.	Your review has some mistakes in grammar and vocabulary.	Your review has many mistakes in grammar and vocabulary.

Más práctica   Cuaderno *pp. 183–184*   Cuaderno para hispanohablantes *pp. 185–186*

PARA Y PIENSA

Did you get it? Choose the correct verb to make each sentence logical according to the Telehistoria.
1. Maribel y Enrique (almuerzan / encuentran) en un restaurante bonito.
2. Maribel (sirve / pide) mucha comida.
3. Enrique no (puede / vuelve) pagar.

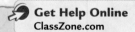

Get Help Online
ClassZone.com

Juegos y diversiones

Review vocabulary by playing a game.

CUATRO RINCONES

The Setup

Your teacher will label a poster for each corner of the room: **el restaurante, el cine, el parque,** and **el centro.** Form two teams.

Materials

- index cards with Spanish words and phrases
- four posters representing places in a city

Playing the Game

Your teacher will give each of you in turn an index card with a Spanish word or phrase on it. Go to the corner of the room for the place related to the word or phrase on your card. Then use the word(s) on your card and the location name in a sentence.

Your team will receive one point for each player who goes to the correct corner and a second point for each player to use the words correctly in a sentence.

The Winner!

The team with the most points at the end wins.

Hay tiendas en el centro.

EL CENTRO

Lectura cultural

AUDIO

¡AVANZA! **Goal:** Read about weekend activities in Spain and Chile. Then talk about what each city offers and compare these activities with what you do on weekends.

Comparación cultural

El fin de semana en España y Chile

STRATEGY Leer

List attractions and places
Use a table like the one below to list attractions and the places where they can be found.

	conciertos	zoológico	botes
Madrid	Parque del Buen Retiro		
Santiago de Chile			

España

Los habitantes de Madrid, España, y Santiago de Chile hacen muchas actividades en el fin de semana. Van a parques, restaurantes, teatros, cines y otros lugares divertidos. También van de compras.

En Madrid hay muchos lugares interesantes para pasar los fines de semana. La Plaza Mayor tiene muchos cafés y restaurantes. Hay un mercado de sellos[1] los domingos. El Parque del Buen Retiro es un lugar perfecto para descansar y pasear. En este parque hay jardines[2], cafés y un lago[3] donde las personas pueden alquilar botes. Hay conciertos allí en el verano. Otro parque popular es la Casa de Campo. Hay un zoológico, una piscina[4], un parque de diversiones[5] y un lago para botes.

Hay muchas tiendas en el centro. El almacén[6] más grande es El Corte Inglés: allí los madrileños[7] pueden comprar ropa, comida y mucho más.

---

[1] **mercado...** stamp market   [2] gardens   [3] lake
[4] swimming pool   [5] **parque...** amusement park
[6] department store   [7] people of Madrid

El Parque del Buen Retiro en Madrid

En Santiago de Chile las personas pasan los fines de semana en muchos lugares. Siempre hay mucha actividad en la Plaza de Armas, la parte histórica de Santiago. Hay conciertos allí los domingos.

El parque del Cerro Santa Lucía es perfecto para pasear. Los santiaguinos[8] pueden ver jardines y el panorama de Santiago. El Cerro San Cristóbal en el Parque Metropolitano es un lugar favorito para comer, correr y montar en bicicleta. Hay jardines, piscinas, un zoológico, cafés y restaurantes en el parque.

Los santiaguinos van a tiendas en el centro y a centros comerciales como Alto Las Condes. En el Mercado Central pueden comprar pescado y frutas y comer en restaurantes con precios baratos[9].

---

[8] people of Santiago, Chile   [9] inexpensive

La Plaza de Armas

Chile

Cerro San Cristóbal

PARA Y PIENSA

¿Comprendiste?
1. ¿Qué hay en la Plaza Mayor y la Plaza de Armas los domingos?
2. ¿A qué parques van los madrileños y los santiaguinos?
3. ¿Dónde pueden ir de compras los habitantes de Madrid y Santiago?

¿Y tú?
¿Cuál(es) de estos lugares en Madrid y Santiago quieres visitar? ¿Adónde vas los fines de semana donde vives? ¿Qué haces allí?

Proyectos culturales

Pinturas de España y Chile

What messages can an artist communicate through a painting? When you look at a painting, you might see something different than what the artist originally intended when he or she painted it. In fact, a single work of art can have a number of different interpretations.

España *Landscape near El Escorial (1932), Ignacio Zuloaga y Zabaleta*

Chile Calle de Melipilla *(sin fecha),*
Juan Francisco González

Proyecto 1 *Interpret and investigate*

Interpreting the two paintings above from **Spain** and **Chile.**

Instructions
1. After looking at each painting, describe it to yourself. What message do you get from it? As you scan the painting, does any particular point draw your attention?
2. Use the Internet or your school's library to learn more about the two paintings. You might look up information about the artists and whether the paintings reflect personal events in their lives.

Proyecto 2 *Your own painting*

Now try your hand at being an artist.

Materials for your own painting
Construction paper
Charcoal pencil, colored pencils or pens, watercolor paint, paintbrushes

Instructions
Create a landscape scene on construction paper. Use the paintings above as an inspiration.

En tu comunidad

Visit a museum in your community or area that contains works of art from a Spanish-speaking country. What can you learn about that country by examining the artwork? Record your impressions in a journal.

En resumen
Vocabulario y gramática

Animated Grammar
Interactive Flashcards
ClassZone.com

Vocabulario

Describe Places in Town

el café	café
el centro	center, downtown
el cine	movie theater; the movies
el parque	park
el restaurante	restaurant
el teatro	theater

Describe Events in Town

el concierto	concert
las entradas	tickets
la música rock	rock music
la película	movie
la ventanilla	ticket window

Getting Around Town

a pie	by foot
la calle	street
en autobús	by bus
en coche	by car
encontrar (ue)	to find
tomar	to take

In a Restaurant

el (la) camarero(a)	(food) server
costar (ue)	to cost
la cuenta	bill
de postre	for dessert
el menú	menu
la mesa	table
el plato principal	main course
la propina	tip

For Dinner

el arroz	rice
el bistec	beef
el brócoli	broccoli
la carne	meat
la ensalada	salad
los frijoles	beans
el pastel	cake
la patata	potato
el pescado	fish
el pollo	chicken
el tomate	tomato
las verduras	vegetables

Ordering from a Menu

pedir (i)	to order, to ask for
servir (i)	to serve

Other Words and Phrases

allí	there
almorzar (ue)	to eat lunch
aquí	here
dormir (ue)	to sleep
el lugar	place
poder (ue)	to be able, can
tal vez	perhaps, maybe
ver	to see
volver (ue)	to return, to come back

Gramática

Notas gramaticales: The verb **ver** *p. 249*, **ir a** + infinitive *p. 251*

Stem-Changing Verbs: o → ue

For **o → ue** stem-changing verbs, the last **o** of the stem changes to **ue** in all forms except **nosotros(as)** and **vosotros(as)**.

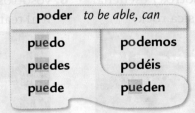

poder *to be able, can*	
puedo	**po**demos
puedes	**po**déis
puede	**pue**den

Stem-Changing Verbs: e → i

For **e → i** stem-changing verbs, the last **e** of the stem changes to **i** in all forms except **nosotros(as)** and **vosotros(as)**.

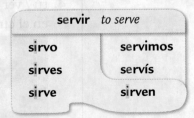

servir *to serve*	
sirvo	**ser**vimos
sirves	**ser**vís
sirve	**sir**ven

Repaso de la lección

¡LLEGADA!

Now you can
- describe places and events in town
- talk about types of transportation
- say what you are going to do
- order from a menu

Using
- ir a + infinitive
- stem-changing verbs: o → ue
- stem-changing verbs: e → i

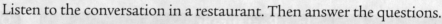

To review
- stem-changing verbs: o → ue p. 252
- ir a + infinitive p. 251
- stem-changing verbs: e → i p. 258

1 | Listen and understand

Listen to the conversation in a restaurant. Then answer the questions.

1. ¿Cuántas personas van a comer?
2. ¿Cómo son los platos principales?
3. ¿Qué pide Raúl con el bistec?
4. ¿Qué pide Raúl para beber?
5. ¿Qué pide Tere de plato principal?
6. ¿Quién pide el pastel de postre?

To review
- ir a + infinitive p. 251

2 | Say what you are going to do

Tell what people are going to do on Saturday and how they plan to get there.

modelo: Angélica / almorzar en un restaurante
Angélica va a almorzar en un restaurante.
Va a ir en autobús.

1. Gilberto / correr en el parque

2. yo / volver al centro

3. las chicas / beber refrescos en un café

4. tú / ver una película en el cine

5. nosotros / escuchar música rock

6. vosotros / ir al teatro

To review
• stem-changing
  verbs: **o → ue**
  p. 252

3 | Describe places and events in town

Tomás is describing his activities. Complete his e-mail message with the correct form of the appropriate verb.

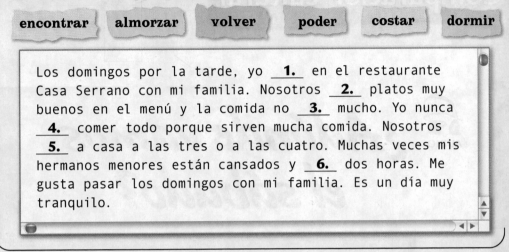

| encontrar | almorzar | volver | poder | costar | dormir |

Los domingos por la tarde, yo __1.__ en el restaurante Casa Serrano con mi familia. Nosotros __2.__ platos muy buenos en el menú y la comida no __3.__ mucho. Yo nunca __4.__ comer todo porque sirven mucha comida. Nosotros __5.__ a casa a las tres o a las cuatro. Muchas veces mis hermanos menores están cansados y __6.__ dos horas. Me gusta pasar los domingos con mi familia. Es un día muy tranquilo.

To review
• stem-changing
  verbs: **e → i**
  p. 258

4 | Order from a menu

Describe the problems in the restaurant.

> **modelo:** Leonor: carne / el camarero: pescado
> Leonor pide carne, pero el camarero sirve pescado.

1. tú: agua / la camarera: leche
2. yo: brócoli / el camarero: patatas
3. ustedes: bistec / los camareros: pollo
4. Nicolás: ensalada / el camarero: tomates
5. nosotros: arroz / los camareros: verduras
6. vosotros: pastel / la camarera: helado

To review
• Comparación
  cultural pp. 244,
  255, 261
• Lectura cultural
  pp. 266–267

5 | Spain, Guatemala, and Chile

Comparación cultural

Answer these culture questions.

1. What is featured at Madrid's Teatro de la Comedia?
2. What can you find at Madrid's Rastro and Chichicastenango's market?
3. Who is depicted in *Las meninas*?
4. What can you see and do in Madrid's Parque del Buen Retiro and Santiago's Parque Metropolitano?

Más práctica Cuaderno *pp. 185–196*   Cuaderno para hispanohablantes *pp. 187–196*

Get Help Online
ClassZone.com

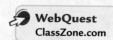

Comparación cultural

Guatemala

España

Chile

AUDIO

¿Adónde vamos el sábado?

Lectura y escritura

WebQuest
ClassZone.com

① Leer Activities that young people do vary around the world. Read what Anita, Rodrigo, and Armando do for fun on Saturdays.

② Escribir Using the three descriptions as models, write a short paragraph about what you like to do on Saturdays.

STRATEGY Escribir

Create an activity chart
To write about what you do for fun on Saturdays, use an activity chart like the one shown.

Categoría	Detalles
lugares	
ropa	
actividades	

Step 1 Complete the chart with details about where you go, what you wear, and what you do for fun on Saturdays.

Step 2 Write your paragraph. Make sure to include all the information from your chart. Check your writing by yourself or with help from a friend. Make final corrections.

Compara con tu mundo

Use the paragraph you wrote to compare the activities you do for fun to the activities described by *one* of the three students. How are the activities similar? How are they different?

Cuaderno *pp. 197–199*   Cuaderno para hispanohablantes *pp. 197–199*

Guatemala

Anita

¿Qué tal? Soy Anita y me gusta escuchar música folklórica. El sábado mis amigos y yo pensamos ir a un concierto de marimba[1] en el centro. Las entradas no cuestan mucho y los conciertos son muy buenos. ¿Qué ropa voy a llevar? Quiero llevar un vestido porque es primavera y hace calor. Mis amigos prefieren llevar camisetas y jeans.

_____
[1] musical instrument resembling a xylophone

España

Rodrigo

¡Hola! Me llamo Rodrigo y vivo en Madrid. El sábado quiero ir de compras con mi hermano. Siempre necesito comprar camisetas y calcetines. Muchas veces los encuentro en el centro comercial. Se llama Xanadú y tiene tiendas, restaurantes y ¡un parque de nieve! Allí puedes practicar deportes de invierno durante todo el año. A mi hermano le gusta la nieve en el verano, pero a mí no. En el verano ¡prefiero tener calor!

Chile

Armando

¡Hola! Me llamo Armando y soy de Santiago, Chile. En septiembre puedes ir a muchos rodeos porque hay muchas fiestas nacionales en Chile. El sábado voy a ir a un rodeo con mis amigos para ver a los huasos[2]. Pienso llevar unos jeans nuevos y una chaqueta porque no quiero tener frío. Quiero llevar un sombrero de vaquero[3], pero no puedo. ¡Cuestan mucho!

_____
[2] Chilean cowboys   [3] cowboy

Repaso inclusivo
♻ Options for Review

1 | Listen, understand, and compare

Escuchar

Listen to Mrs. Estrada and her son, Carlitos, order a meal at a restaurant. Then answer the questions.

1. ¿Qué tiene ganas de comer Carlitos?
2. ¿Qué pide para empezar? ¿Y de plato principal?
3. ¿Qué plato pide la señora Estrada para empezar?
4. ¿Qué no sirven hoy en el restaurante?
5. ¿Qué van a beber ellos?

Which order most resembles what you like to eat? What foods and drinks do you order when you go to restaurants?

2 | Present a family outing

Hablar

Prepare a presentation about a family outing to a restaurant. Bring in a photo of your own or one from a magazine. Talk about the clothes each person is wearing, what food the restaurant serves, what each person orders, and how much it costs. You should talk for at least two minutes.

3 | Compare school days

Hablar

Interview a partner about his or her day at school. Ask about the classes your partner prefers, what he or she eats for lunch and at what time, and what he or she is going to do after school today. Finish by comparing your days. Your conversation should be at least three minutes long.

¿A qué hora almuerzas?

Almuerzo a las doce.

4 | Help find a lost child

Hablar

Role-play a situation in which you are a mall employee in customer service. Your partner is at the mall with a younger cousin, but can't find him or her. Ask your partner about age, physical characteristics, and clothing. Copy this chart on a piece of paper and use it to organize your information. Your conversation should be at least two minutes long.

Edad	
Características físicas	
Ropa	

5 | Create a fashion show

Hablar
Escribir

Work in a group of five. Individually, write a description of the clothes you are wearing. Include color, where you can buy each item, how much they cost, and in what season(s) you can wear them. Your description should have at least eight sentences. Then perform the fashion show for the class, reading each other's descriptions as each "model" walks down the runway.

6 | Plan a weekend with family

Leer
Escribir

You are studying in Barcelona, Spain, for the summer and your parents are coming to visit. Read this newspaper supplement to find out about the weekend's events. Then write an e-mail to your parents, and suggest what you can do and where you can go together or separately during the weekend. Keep in mind everyone's likes and dislikes. Your e-mail should have at least six suggestions.

Suplemento especial – fin de semana

GUÍA DEL OCIO - BARCELONA

VIERNES

Cena especial
Comida española típica, con música de flamenco.
Restaurante Casals (de las 21.30 a las 23.30 h)

Concierto
Los hermanos Pujols tocan música rock.
Plaza Cataluña (a las 14.30 h)

SÁBADO

Películas
Terror en el centro
Hollywood. Película de terror. Dos chicos de Nueva York van en autobús cuando llegan unos extraterrestres horribles.
Cines Maremagnum (a las 16.00 y 18.30 h)

Mi tía loca
España. Película cómica. La historia de una chica y su tía favorita.
Cine Diagonal Mar (a las 13.30 y 21.00 h)

Comprar y pasear
La calle que lo tiene todo: libros, ropa, comida ¡y más!
Las Ramblas (todo el día)

DOMINGO

Eliminar el cáncer
Puedes pasear y donar dinero para combatir el cáncer.
Parque Güell (a las 10.00 h)

Compras
Los mejores precios del verano en las tiendas de ropa.
Centro Comercial Barcelona Glorias (de las 10.30 a las 20.30 h)

Concierto de Beethoven
La orquesta de Barcelona toca música clásica. Un concierto para toda la familia.
Teatro Liceu (a las 20.00 h)

4 Help find a lost child

Role-play a situation in which you are a mall employee in customer service. Your partner is at the mall with a younger cousin, but can't find him or her. Ask your partner about age, physical characteristics, and clothing. Copy this chart on a piece of paper and use it to organize your information. Your conversation should be at least two minutes long.

Edad	
Características físicas	
Ropa	

5 Create a fashion show

Work in a group of five, individually write a description of the clothes you are wearing. Include color, where you can buy each item, how much they cost, and in what season(s) you can wear them. Your description should have at least eight sentences. Then perform the fashion show for the class, reading each other's descriptions as each "model" walks down the runway.

6 Plan a weekend with family

You are studying in Barcelona, Spain, for the summer and your parents are coming to visit. Read this newspaper supplement to find out about the weekend's events. Then write an e-mail to your parents and suggest what you can do and where you can go together or separately during the weekend. Keep in mind everyone's likes and dislikes. Your e-mail should have at least six suggestions.

Recursos

Lección 1
¿Qué te gusta hacer?

Talk About Activities

cuidar niños	to baby-sit
pintar	to paint
la reunión	meeting
el club	club
manejar	to drive
trabajar a tiempo parcial	to work part-time
trabajar de voluntario	to volunteer
tocar un instrumento	to play an instrument

Instruments

el piano	piano
el clarinete	clarinet
la flauta	flute
el saxofón	saxophone
el tambor	drum
la trompeta	trumpet
la viola	viola
el violín	violin

Snack Foods and Beverages

la merienda	snack
las papitas	chips
las galletas saladas	crackers
las galletitas	cookies
el chicle	chewing gum
los dulces	candy
la limonada	lemonade

Lección 2
Mis amigos y yo

Describe Yourself and Others

Personality

listo(a)	clever / smart
callado(a)	quiet
extrovertido(a)	outgoing
tímido(a)	shy
sincero(a)	sincere
tonto(a)	silly
travieso(a)	mischievous
paciente	patient
talentoso(a)	talented
creativo(a)	creative
ambicioso(a)	ambitious

Appearance

el pelo oscuro	dark hair
el pelo rizado	curly hair
el pelo lacio	straight hair
calvo(a)	bald
los frenillos	braces

People

el (la) policía	police officer
el actor	actor
la actriz	actress
el (la) compañero(a) de clase	classmate
el (la) bombero(a)	firefighter
el (la) secretario(a)	secretary
el jefe, la jefa	boss

Unidad 2

Expansión de vocabulario

Lección 1
Somos estudiantes

Tell Time and Discuss Daily Schedules

la medianoche	midnight
el mediodía	noon

Describing Classes

School Subjects

la asignatura	school subject
la educación física	physical education
las ciencias sociales	social studies
la geometría	geometry
la geografía	geography
el álgebra	algebra
la lengua, el idioma	language
la literatura	literature
la biología	biology
la química	chemistry
la banda	band
el coro	choir
la orquesta	orchestra
la hora de estudio	study hall

In School

la asamblea	assembly
el recreo	recess, break

Classroom Activities

preguntar	to ask
la respuesta	answer
la prueba	test, quiz

Describe Frequency

cada	each
a veces	sometimes
¿Con qué frecuencia...?	How often. . . ?
rara vez	rarely

Other Words and Phrases

terminar	to finish
esperar	to wait (for)
mientras	while
otra vez	again

Lección 2
En la escuela

Describe Classroom Objects

la carpeta	folder
las tijeras	scissors
la regla	ruler
el diccionario	dictionary
la impresora	printer
la bandera	flag
el globo	globe

Places in School

la sala de clase	classroom
el casillero	locker
el auditorio	auditorium

Say Where Things Are Located

entre	between
fuera (de)	out / outside (of)
(a la) derecha (de)	(to the) right (of)
(a la) izquierda (de)	(to the) left (of)
aquí	here
allí	there
enfrente (de)	across from, facing

Talk About How You Feel

feliz, alegre	happy
preocupado(a)	worried
listo(a)	ready
Estoy de acuerdo.	I agree.

Other Words and Phrases

mismo(a)	same
según	according to
creer	to think, to believe
especialmente	especially
olvidar	to forget
sobre	about
además	besides, further
suficiente, bastante	enough
sin	without

Lección 1
Mi comida favorita

Talk About Foods and Beverages

For Breakfast	
desayunar	to have breakfast
la mantequilla	butter
la miel	honey
el pan tostado	toast
el batido	milkshake, smoothie

For Lunch	
la bolsa	bag
la mantequilla de cacahuate	peanut butter
la jalea	jelly
el atún	tuna
la ensalada	salad

Fruit	
el plátano	banana; plantain
la toronja	grapefruit
la piña	pineapple
el durazno	peach
el limón	lemon
la sandía	watermelon

Lección 2
En mi familia

Talk About Family

el esposo	husband
la esposa	wife
la hermanastra	stepsister
el hermanastro	stepbrother
la media hermana	half-sister
el medio hermano	half-brother
el nieto	grandson
la nieta	granddaughter
el sobrino	nephew
la sobrina	niece
el (la) bebé	baby

Pets

el pájaro	bird
el pez (pl. los peces)	fish
el conejo	rabbit
el lagarto	lizard
la rana	frog
el hámster	hamster

Unidad 4 — Expansión de vocabulario

Lección 1
¡Vamos de compras!

Describe Clothing

las botas	boots
el impermeable	raincoat
la falda	skirt
el suéter	sweater
la sudadera (con capucha)	(hooded) sweatshirt
los pantalones deportivos	sweatpants
el abrigo	coat
los zapatos de tenis	tennis shoes, sneakers
el pijama	pajamas
las sandalias	sandals
la gorra	baseball cap
las gafas de sol	sunglasses
los guantes	gloves
la bufanda	scarf
el paraguas	umbrella
la bolsa	bag, purse

Colors

morado(a)	purple
rosado(a)	pink
gris	gray

Discuss Seasons

el norte	north
el sur	south
el este	east
el oeste	west

Lección 2
¿Qué hacemos esta noche?

Describe Places In Town

la iglesia	church
el edificio	building
el centro de videojuegos	arcade
la piscina	pool
la acera	sidewalk
el correo	post office
la librería	bookstore
la zapatería	shoe store
el templo	temple
la tienda de discos	music store

Music

el rap	rap
alternativa	alternative
la música electrónica	electronic music, techno
la canción	song
la letra	lyrics

In a Restaurant

la cuchara	spoon
el cuchillo	knife
el tenedor	fork
el vaso	glass
la servilleta	napkin
el tazón	bowl
la taza	cup

For Dinner

el puerco	pork
el pavo	turkey
los fideos	noodles
la salsa	sauce
la pimienta	pepper
la sal	salt
los mariscos	seafood

Vegetables

la zanahoria	carrot
la lechuga	lettuce
el maíz	corn

Para y piensa
Self-Check Answers

 Lección preliminar

p. 5
1. Buenos días.
2. ¿Cómo estás?
Answers may vary but can include:
3. Adiós, hasta mañana, hasta luego.

p. 9
1. c.
2. a.
3. b.

p. 11
1. See p. 10

p. 15
1. b.
2. a.
3. c.

p. 17
1. seis - dos - cinco - uno - cuatro - dos - cero - nueve
2. tres - siete - cero - ocho - nueve - dos - seis - tres
3. cuatro - uno - ocho - cinco - dos - siete - seis - cero

p. 19
1. lunes
2. mañana

p. 21
1. b.
2. a.
3. c.

p. 24
1. ¿Cómo se dice *please*?
2. ¿Comprendes?

Unidad 1 Estados Unidos

Lección 1
p. 35 Práctica de vocabulario
1. escuchar música
2. hacer la tarea

p. 37 Vocabulario en contexto
1. jugar
2. música
3. comer

p. 41 Práctica de gramática
1. Cristóbal y yo somos de Honduras.
2. Tomás es de la República Dominicana.
3. Yo soy de México.

p. 43 Gramática en contexto
1. El Sr. Costas es de la Florida.
2. Alicia es de Miami.
3. Teresa y Miguel son de Honduras y Cuba.

p. 47 Práctica de gramática
1. Le gusta
2. Te gusta
3. Nos gusta

p. 50 Todo junto
1. Teresa es de Honduras. Le gusta tocar la guitarra.
2. Alicia es de Miami. Le gusta comer.
3. Miguel es de Cuba. Le gusta mirar la televisión.

Lección 2
p. 63 Práctica de vocabulario
1. Juan es bajo.
2. David es artístico.
3. Carlos es serio.

p. 65 Vocabulario en contexto
1. perezoso
2. atlético
3. estudioso

p. 69 Práctica de gramática
1. la televisión
2. unas frutas
3. el libro
4. unos hombres

p. 71 Gramática en contexto
1. Ricardo es un amigo de Alberto.
2. Marta y Carla son unas chicas de una clase de Juan.
3. Ana es una chica muy inteligente.

p. 75 Práctica de gramática
1. una estudiante desorganizada
2. unos chicos simpáticos
3. unas mujeres trabajadoras
4. un hombre grande

p. 78 Todo junto
1. Alberto es un chico simpático.
2. Ricardo es un estudiante trabajador.
3. Sandra es una persona organizada.

Unidad 2 México

Lección 1

p. 97 Práctica de vocabulario
1. Me gusta dibujar en la clase de arte.
2. Hay veintitrés chicos en la clase de matemáticas.

p. 99 Vocabulario en contexto
1. a las diez y cuarto
   (a las diez y quince)
2. las ocho y veinte
3. a las siete

p. 103 Práctica de gramática
1. Juan nunca tiene que preparar la comida.
2. Tenemos la clase de inglés todos los días.
3. Siempre tengo que usar la computadora.

p. 105 Gramática en contexto
1. tienen
2. tiene que
3. tienen

p. 109 Práctica de gramática
1. usamos
2. preparo
3. dibujan
4. Necesitas

p. 112 Todo junto
1. toma
2. practicar
3. estudian

Lección 2

p. 125 Práctica de vocabulario
Answers may vary but can include:
1. el baño, el gimnasio, la cafetería, la biblioteca, etc.
2. el mapa, el escritorio, la silla, el reloj, etc.

p. 127 Vocabulario en contexto
1. la biblioteca
2. el gimnasio
3. la biblioteca

p. 131 Práctica de gramática
1. Estoy cerca de las ventanas.
2. Pablo, ¿estás nervioso?

p. 133 Gramática en contexto
Answers may vary but can include:
1. Pablo y Claudia están en la biblioteca.
2. Pablo está nervioso.
3. Pablo tiene que estar en el gimnasio a las cinco.

p. 137 Práctica de gramática
1. Teresa va a la cafetería.
2. Los estudiantes van a la oficina del director.
3. Nosotros vamos al gimnasio.
4. Yo voy a la clase de matemáticas.

p. 140 Todo junto
1. está; va a
2. están; van a
3. está; va a

Unidad 3 Puerto Rico

Lección 1

p. 159 Práctica de vocabulario
Answers may vary but can include:
1. los huevos, el cereal, el yogur, la fruta
2. el sándwich, la sopa, la hamburguesa

p. 161 Vocabulario en contexto
1. Quiénes
2. Cuándo
3. Por qué

p. 165 Práctica de gramática
1. Me gustan los huevos en el desayuno.
2. A José le gusta la pizza con jamón.
3. ¿Por qué no te gusta la fruta?

p. 167 Gramática en contexto
1. gusta
2. gusta
3. gustan

p. 171 Práctica de gramática
1. hacen; comen   3. hace; bebe
2. haces; leo

p. 174 Todo junto
1. gusta; come
2. gustan; comparten

Lección 2

p. 187 Práctica de vocabulario
1. hijo   3. hermanas
2. padres

p. 189 Vocabulario en contexto
1. Marisol tiene catorce años.
2. El gato de la familia Vélez tiene ocho años.
3. Los padres de Marisol tienen cincuenta y dos años.

p. 193 Práctica de gramática
1. mi; el seis de septiembre
2. nuestros; el veinticinco de enero.
3. su; el diecisiete de abril.

p. 195 Gramática en contexto
1. El cumpleaños de Camila es el doce de junio.
2. El cumpleaños de Ester es el primero de octubre.
3. El cumpleaños de Tito es el veintiocho de marzo.
4. El cumpleaños de Celia es el diecisiete de enero.

p. 199 Práctica de gramática
1. Mi hermano es más alto que mi padre.
2. Me gustan las manzanas tanto como las bananas.
3. La clase de matemáticas es mejor que la clase de arte.

p. 202 Todo junto
1. Sus perros son tan grandes como Marisol.
2. Su primo es menor que él.
3. Sus perros son más perezosos que los gatos.

Unidad 4 España

Lección 1

p. 221 Práctica de vocabulario
1. ¿Cuánto cuestan los calcetines blancos?
2. ¿Cuánto cuesta el vestido azul?
3. ¿Cuánto cuesta la chaqueta anaranjada?
4. ¿Cuánto cuestan los pantalones cortos rojos?

p. 223 Vocabulario en contexto
1. tiene frío
2. tiene calor
3. tiene frío

p. 227 Práctica de gramática
1. pienso
2. empieza
3. cierra

p. 229 Gramática en contexto
1. entiende
2. prefiere
3. quiere

p. 233 Práctica de gramática
1. los
2. La
3. Las

p. 236 Todo junto
1. Sí, Enrique la necesita.
2. Sí, Enrique lo prefiere.
3. Sí, Enrique la quiere comprar.
   (Sí, Enrique quiere comprarla.)

Lección 2

p. 249 Práctica de vocabulario
Answers may vary but can include:
1. El menú, el (la) camarero(a), la cuenta, los platos principales, etc.
2. El teatro, el parque, el cine, etc.

p. 251 Vocabulario en contexto
1. en autobús
2. a pie
3. en coche

p. 255 Práctica de gramática
1. cuesta
2. almorzamos
3. duermo
4. pueden

p. 257 Gramática en contexto
1. puede
2. encuentra
3. vuelve

p. 261 Práctica de gramática
1. sirven
2. sirve
3. pedimos

p. 264 Todo junto
1. almuerzan
2. pide
3. puede

Resumen de gramática

Nouns, Articles, and Pronouns

Nouns

Nouns identify people, animals, places, and things. All Spanish nouns, even if they refer to objects, are either **masculine** or **feminine.** They are also either **singular** or **plural.**

Nouns ending in **-o** are usually masculine; nouns ending in **-a** are usually feminine.

To form the **plural** of a noun, add **-s** if the noun ends in a vowel; add **-es** if it ends in a consonant.

Singular Nouns		Plural Nouns	
Masculine	**Feminine**	**Masculine**	**Feminine**
abuelo	abuela	abuelos	abuelas
chico	chica	chicos	chicas
hombre	mujer	hombres	mujeres
papel	pluma	papeles	plumas
zapato	blusa	zapatos	blusas

Articles

Articles identify the class of a noun: masculine or feminine, singular or plural. **Definite articles** are the equivalent of the English word *the*. **Indefinite articles** are the equivalent of *a, an,* or *some*.

Definite Articles	Masculine	Feminine
Singular	**el** chico	**la** chica
Plural	**los** chicos	**las** chicas

Indefinite Articles	Masculine	Feminine
Singular	**un** chico	**una** chica
Plural	**unos** chicos	**unas** chicas

Pronouns

Pronouns take the place of nouns. The pronoun used is determined by its function or purpose in a sentence.

Subject Pronouns		Direct Object Pronouns	
yo	nosotros(as)	me	nos
tú	vosotros(as)	te	os
usted	ustedes	lo, la	los, las
él, ella	ellos(as)		

Adjectives

Adjectives describe nouns. In Spanish, adjectives match the **gender** and **number** of the nouns they describe. To make an adjective plural, add **-s** if it ends in a vowel; add **-es** if it ends in a consonant. The adjective usually comes after the noun in Spanish.

Adjectives

	Masculine	Feminine
Singular	el chico alt**o**	la chica alt**a**
	el chico inteligente	la chica inteligente
	el chico joven	la chica joven
	el chico trabajador	la chica trabajado**ra**
Plural	los chicos alto**s**	las chicas alta**s**
	los chicos inteligente**s**	las chicas inteligente**s**
	los chicos jóven**es**	las chicas jóven**es**
	los chicos trabajador**es**	las chicas trabajador**as**

Sometimes adjectives are shortened when they are placed in front of a masculine singular noun.

Shortened Forms

bueno	**buen** chico
malo	**mal** chico

Possessive adjectives indicate who owns something or describe a relationship between people or things. They agree in number with the nouns they describe. **Nuestro(a)** and **vuestro(a)** must also agree in gender with the nouns they describe.

Possessive Adjectives

	Masculine		Feminine	
Singular	**mi** amigo	**nuestro** amigo	**mi** amiga	**nuestra** amiga
	tu amigo	**vuestro** amigo	**tu** amiga	**vuestra** amiga
	su amigo	**su** amigo	**su** amiga	**su** amiga
Plural	**mis** amigos	**nuestros** amigos	**mis** amigas	**nuestras** amigas
	tus amigos	**vuestros** amigos	**tus** amigas	**vuestras** amigas
	sus amigos	**sus** amigos	**sus** amigas	**sus** amigas

Comparatives

Comparatives are used to compare two people or things.

Comparatives

más (+)	menos (–)	tan, tanto (=)
más serio **que...**	**menos** serio **que...**	**tan** serio **como...**
Me gusta leer **más que** pasear.	Me gusta pasear **menos que** leer.	Me gusta hablar **tanto como** escuchar.

There are a few irregular comparative words. When talking about the age of people, use **mayor** and **menor**. When talking about qualities, use **mejor** and **peor**.

Age	Quality
mayor	mejor
menor	peor

Verbs: Present Tense

Regular Verbs

Regular verbs ending in **-ar, -er,** or **-ir** always have regular endings in the present tense.

-ar Verbs		-er Verbs		-ir Verbs	
habl**o**	habl**amos**	vend**o**	vend**emos**	compart**o**	compart**imos**
habl**as**	habl**áis**	vend**es**	vend**éis**	compart**es**	compart**ís**
habl**a**	habl**an**	vend**e**	vend**en**	compart**e**	compart**en**

Verbs with Irregular yo Forms

Some verbs have regular forms in the present tense except for the **yo** form.

hacer

ha**go**	hacemos
haces	hacéis
hace	hacen

ver

v**eo**	vemos
ves	veis
ve	ven

Stem-Changing Verbs

e → ie

qu**ie**ro	queremos
qu**ie**res	queréis
qu**ie**re	qu**ie**ren

Other **e → ie** stem-changing verbs are **cerrar, comenzar, despertarse, empezar, entender, pensar,** and **preferir.**

e → i

s**i**rvo	servimos
s**i**rves	servís
s**i**rve	s**i**rven

Another **e → i** stem-changing verb is **pedir.**

o → ue

puedo	podemos
puedes	podéis
puede	**pue**den

Other **o → ue** stem-changing verbs are **almorzar, costar, dormir, encontrar,** and **volver.**

Irregular Verbs

The following verbs are irregular in the present tense.

estar

estoy	estamos
estás	estáis
está	están

ir

voy	vamos
vas	vais
va	van

ser

soy	somos
eres	sois
es	son

tener

tengo	tenemos
tienes	tenéis
tiene	tienen

Glosario
español-inglés

This Spanish-English glossary contains all the active vocabulary words that appear in the text as well as passive vocabulary lists. **LP** refers to the Lección preliminar.

a to, at
  A la(s)... At... o'clock. **2.1**
  a pie on foot **4.2**
  ¿A qué hora es/son...? At what time is/are...? **2.1**
abril April **3.2**
la abuela grandmother **3.2**
el abuelo grandfather **3.2**
los abuelos grandparents **3.2**
aburrido(a) boring **2.2**
acabar de... to have just... **5.2**
la actividad activity **1.1**
Adiós. Goodbye. **LP**
adónde (to) where **2.2**
  ¿Adónde vas? Where are you going? **2.2**
agosto August **3.2**
el agua (fem.) water **1.1**
ahora now **3.1**
al to the **2.2**
  al lado (de) next to **2.2**
allí there **4.2**
el almacén (pl. **los almacenes**) department store
almorzar (ue) to eat lunch **4.2**
el almuerzo lunch **3.1**
alquilar to rent **1.1**
  alquilar un DVD to rent a DVD **1.1**
alto(a) tall **1.2**
amarillo(a) yellow **4.1**
el (la) amigo(a) friend **1.2**
anaranjado(a) orange (color) **4.1**
andar en patineta to skateboard **1.1**
el ánimo spirit
antes (de) before **1.1**
la antorcha torch
el anuncio advertisement; announcement

el año year **3.2**
  el Año Nuevo New Year
  ¿Cuántos años tienes? How old are you? **3.2**
  tener... años to be... years old **3.2**
aprender to learn **1.1**
  aprender el español to learn Spanish **1.1**
los apuntes notes **2.1**
  tomar apuntes to take notes **2.1**
aquí here **4.2**
el arrecife de coral coral reef
el arroz rice **4.2**
el arte art **2.1**
el artículo article
artístico(a) artistic **1.2**
atlético(a) athletic **1.2**
el autobús (pl. **los autobuses**) bus **4.2**
  en autobús by bus **4.2**
avanzar to advance, to move ahead
  ¡Avanza! Advance!, Move ahead!
  avancemos let's advance, let's move ahead
el aymara indigenous language of Bolivia and Peru
azul blue **4.1**

bailar to dance
el (la) bailarín(ina) (pl. **los bailarines**) dancer
el baile dance
bajo(a) short (height) **1.2**
la banana banana **3.1**
la banda musical band
el baño bathroom **2.2**
la batalla battle
beber to drink **1.1**
la bebida beverage, drink **3.1**
la biblioteca library **2.2**
la bicicleta bicycle **1.1**

bien well, fine **LP**
  Bien. ¿Y tú/usted? Fine. And you? (familiar/formal) **LP**
  Muy bien. ¿Y tú/usted? Very well. And you? (familiar/formal) **LP**
el bistec beef **4.2**
blanco(a) white **4.1**
la blusa blouse **4.1**
bonito(a) pretty **1.2**
el borrador eraser **2.2**
el brindis celebratory toast
el brócoli broccoli **4.2**
bueno(a) good **1.2**
  Buenos días. Good morning. **LP**
  Buenas noches. Good evening; Good night. **LP**
  Buenas tardes. Good afternoon. **LP**

cada each; every
el café coffee; café **3.1, 4.2**
la cafetería cafeteria **2.2**
la calavera skull
el calcetín (pl. **los calcetines**) sock **4.1**
la calculadora calculator **2.2**
caliente hot
la calle street **4.2**
el (la) camarero(a) (food) server **4.2**
el cambio change
la camisa shirt **4.1**
la camiseta T-shirt **4.1**
cansado(a) tired **2.2**
Carnaval Carnival
la carne meat **4.2**
la carreta horse-drawn carriage
la casa house
el cascarón (pl. **los cascarones**) confetti-filled egg

la caseta small house or tent

casi almost **2.1**

castaño(a) brown (hair) **1.2**

catorce fourteen **2.1**

el cementerio cemetery

la cena dinner **3.1**

el centro center, downtown **4.2**

   el centro comercial shopping center, mall **4.1**

cerca (de) near (to) **2.2**

el cereal cereal **3.1**

cero zero **LP**

cerrar (ie) to close **4.1**

la chaqueta jacket **4.1**

la chica girl **1.2**

el chico boy **1.2**

cien one hundred **2.1**

las ciencias science **2.1**

cierto(a) true

cinco five **LP**

cincuenta fifty **2.1**

el cine movie theater; the movies **4.2**

la clase class, classroom **LP**; kind, type

el coche car **4.2**

   en coche by car **4.2**

el colegio high school

comer to eat **1.1**

cómico(a) funny **1.2**

la comida meal; food **1.1, 3.1**

como as, like

¿Cómo...? How...? **3.1**

   ¿Cómo eres? What are you like? **1.2**

   ¿Cómo estás? How are you? (familiar) **LP**

   ¿Cómo está usted? How are you? (formal) **LP**

   ¿Cómo se llama? What's his/her/your (formal) name? **LP**

   ¿Cómo te llamas? What's your name? (familiar) **LP**

comparar to compare

compartir to share **3.1**

comprar to buy **1.1**

¿Comprendiste? Did you understand?

la computadora computer **2.1**

común common

el concierto concert **4.2**

contento(a) happy **2.2**

contestar to answer **2.1**

el correo electrónico e-mail **1.1**

correr to run **1.1**

costar (ue) to cost **4.2**

   ¿Cuánto cuesta(n)? How much does it (do they) cost? **4.1**

   Cuesta(n)... It (They) cost... **4.1**

la Cremà burning of papier-mâché figures during Las Fallas

el cuaderno notebook **2.2**

el cuadro painting

¿Cuál(es)? Which?; What? **3.1**

   ¿Cuál es la fecha? What is the date? **3.2**

   ¿Cuál es tu/su número de teléfono? What is your phone number? (familiar/formal) **LP**

cuando when **2.2**

¿Cuándo? When? **2.2**

cuánto(a) how much **3.2**

   ¿Cuánto cuesta(n)? How much does it (do they) cost? **4.1**

cuántos(as) how many **3.2**

   ¿Cuántos(as)...? How many...? **2.1**

   ¿Cuántos años tienes? How old are you? **3.2**

cuarenta forty **2.1**

cuatro four **LP**

cuatrocientos(as) four hundred **3.2**

la cuenta bill (in a restaurant) **4.2**

el cumpleaños birthday **3.2**

   ¡Feliz cumpleaños! Happy birthday! **3.2**

de of, from **1.1**

   de la mañana in the morning (with a time) **2.1**

   De nada. You're welcome. **LP**

   de la noche at night (with a time) **2.1**

   ¿De qué color es/son...? What color is/are...?

   de la tarde in the afternoon (with a time) **2.1**

   de vez en cuando once in a while **2.1**

debajo (de) underneath, under **2.2**

del (de la) of *or* from the **2.2**

delante (de) in front (of) **2.2**

demasiado too much

dentro (de) inside (of) **2.2**

los deportes sports **1.1**

deprimido(a) depressed **2.2**

el desayuno breakfast **3.1**

descansar to rest **1.1**

desear to wish, to want

el desfile parade

después (de) afterward; after **1.1**

detrás (de) behind **2.2**

el día day **LP**

   Buenos días. Good morning. **LP**

   ¿Qué día es hoy? What day is today? **LP**

   todos los días every day **2.1**

dibujar to draw **1.1**

el dibujo drawing

diciembre December **3.2**

diecinueve nineteen **2.1**

dieciocho eighteen **2.1**

dieciséis sixteen **2.1**

diecisiete seventeen **2.1**

diez ten **LP**

diferente different

difícil difficult **2.1**

el difunto deceased

el dinero money **4.1**

el (la) director(a) principal **2.2**

el disfraz (*pl.* **los disfraces**) costume

divertido(a) fun **2.2**

doce twelve **2.1**

el dólar dollar **4.1**

domingo Sunday **LP**

donde where

¿Dónde? Where? **2.2**

   ¿De dónde eres? Where are you from? (familiar) **LP**

   ¿De dónde es? Where is he/she from? **LP**

   ¿De dónde es usted? Where are you from? (formal) **LP**

dormir (ue) to sleep **4.2**

dos two **LP**

doscientos(as) two hundred **3.2**

durante during **4.1**

el DVD DVD **1.1**

el ejército army

él he **1.1**

ella she **1.1**

ellos(as) they **1.1**

emocionado(a) excited **2.2**

empezar (ie) to begin **4.1**

en in **2.1**; on

   en autobús by bus **4.2**

   en coche by car **4.2**

Encantado(a). Delighted; Pleased to meet you. **LP**

encima (de) on top (of) **2.2**

encontrar (ue) to find **4.2**

la encuesta survey

enero January **3.2**

enojado(a) angry **2.2**

la ensalada salad **4.2**

enseñar to teach **2.1**

entender (ie) to understand **4.1**

la entrada ticket **4.2**

entrar to enter

el equipo team

la escena scene

escribir to write **1.1**

  escribir correos electrónicos to write e-mails **1.1**

el escritorio desk **2.2**

la escritura writing

escuchar to listen (to) **1.1**

  escuchar música to listen to music **1.1**

la escuela school **1.1**

  la escuela secundaria high school

el español Spanish **2.1**

especial special

el esqueleto skeleton

la estación (*pl.* **las estaciones**) season **4.1**

estar to be **2.2**

  ¿Está bien? OK?

el (la) estudiante student **1.2**

estudiar to study **1.1**

estudioso(a) studious **1.2**

el euro euro **4.1**

el examen (*pl.* **los exámenes**) test, exam **2.1**

fácil easy **2.1**

las fallas displays of large papier-mâché figures

el (la) fallero(a) celebrant of Las Fallas

falso(a) false

la familia family **3.2**

febrero February **3.2**

la fecha date **3.2**

  ¿Cuál es la fecha? What is the date? **3.2**

  la fecha de nacimiento birth date **3.2**

feo(a) ugly **4.1**

la fiesta party; holiday

  la fiesta nacional national holiday

  la fiesta patria patriotic holiday

el fin de semana weekend

el (la) francés(esa) (*pl.* **los franceses**) French

los frijoles beans **4.2**

la fruta fruit **1.1**

los fuegos artificiales fireworks

la fuente source; fountain

el fútbol soccer (the sport) **1.1**

la galleta cookie **1.1**

el (la) gato(a) cat **3.2**

el gimnasio gymnasium **2.2**

el gorro winter hat **4.1**

Gracias. Thank you. **LP**

  Muchas gracias. Thank you very much. **LP**

la gramática grammar

grande big, large; great **1.2**

el grito shout

guapo(a) good-looking **1.2**

la guitarra guitar **1.1**

gustar

  Me gusta... I like... **1.1**

  No me gusta... I don't like... **1.1**

  ¿Qué te gusta hacer? What do you like to do? **1.1**

  ¿Te gusta...? Do you like...? **1.1**

el gusto pleasure

  El gusto es mío. The pleasure is mine. **LP**

  Mucho gusto. Nice to meet you. **LP**

hablar to talk, to speak **1.1**

  hablar por teléfono to talk on the phone **1.1**

hacer (hago) to make, to do **3.1**

  Hace calor. It is hot. **LP**

  Hace frío. It is cold. **LP**

  Hace sol. It is sunny. **LP**

  Hace viento. It is windy. **LP**

  hacer la tarea to do homework **1.1**

¿Qué tiempo hace? What is the weather like? **LP**

la hamburguesa hamburger **3.1**

hasta until

  Hasta luego. See you later. **LP**

  Hasta mañana. See you tomorrow. **LP**

hay... there is/are... **2.1**

el helado ice cream **1.1**

la hermana sister **3.2**

el hermano brother **3.2**

los hermanos brothers, brother(s) and sister(s) **3.2**

la hija daughter **3.2**

el hijo son **3.2**

los hijos children, son(s) and daughter(s) **3.2**

la hispanidad cultural community of Spanish speakers

la historia history **2.1**

Hola. Hello; Hi. **LP**

el hombre man **1.2**

la hora hour; time **2.1**

  ¿A qué hora es/son...? At what time is/are...? **2.1**

  ¿Qué hora es? What time is it? **2.1**

el horario schedule **2.1**

horrible horrible **3.1**

hoy today **LP**

  ¿Qué día es hoy? What day is today? **LP**

  Hoy es... Today is... **LP**

el huevo egg **3.1**

el idioma language

Igualmente. Same here; Likewise. **LP**

importante important **3.1**

  Es importante. It's important. **3.1**

los incas Incas, an indigenous South American people

la independencia independence

la información information

el inglés English **2.1**

inteligente intelligent **1.2**

interesante interesting **2.2**

el invierno winter **4.1**

ir to go **2.2**
  ir a... to be going to... **4.2**
  ir de compras to go shopping **4.1**
  Vamos a... Let's... **4.2**

el jamón (*pl.* **los jamones**) ham **3.1**
el jardín (*pl.* **los jardines**) garden
los jeans jeans **4.1**
joven (*pl.* **jóvenes**) young **1.2**
jueves Thursday **LP**
jugar (ue) to play (sports or games)
  jugar al fútbol to play soccer **1.1**
el jugo juice **1.1**
  el jugo de naranja orange
  juice **3.1**
julio July **3.2**
junio June **3.2**

el lado side
  al lado (de) next to **2.2**
el lago lake
el lápiz (*pl.* **los lápices**) pencil **2.2**
la lección (*pl.* **las lecciones**) lesson
la leche milk **3.1**
la lectura reading
leer to read **1.1**
  leer un libro to read a book **1.1**
lejos (de) far (from) **2.2**
las lentejas lentils
el libertador liberator
el libro book **1.1**
llamarse to be called
  ¿Cómo se llama? What's his/her/
  your (formal) name? **LP**
  ¿Cómo te llamas? What's your
  name? (familiar) **LP**
  Me llamo... My name is... **LP**
  Se llama... His/Her name is... **LP**
la llegada arrival
llegar to arrive **2.1**
llevar to wear **4.1**
llover (ue) to rain
  Llueve. It is raining. **LP**
el lugar place **4.2**
lunes Monday **LP**

la madrastra stepmother **3.2**
la madre mother **3.2**
el (la) maestro(a) teacher **LP**
malo(a) bad **1.2**
  Mal. ¿Y tú/usted? Bad. And you?
  (familiar/formal) **LP**
la manzana apple **3.1**
mañana tomorrow **LP**
  Hasta mañana. See you
  tomorrow. **LP**
  Mañana es... Tomorrow is... **LP**
la mañana morning **2.1**
  de la mañana in the morning
  (with a time) **2.1**
el mapa map **2.2**
marrón (*pl.* **marrones**) brown **4.1**
martes Tuesday **LP**
marzo March **3.2**
más more **1.1**
  Más o menos. ¿Y tú/usted? So-
  so. And you? (familiar/
  formal) **LP**
  más que... more than... **3.2**
  más... que more... than **3.2**
la máscara mask
la mascleta firecracker explosions
  during Las Fallas
las matemáticas math **2.1**
mayo May **3.2**
mayor older **3.2**
la medianoche midnight
medio(a) half
  ...y media half past... (the
  hour) **2.1**
mejor better **3.2**
menor younger **3.2**
menos less
  ...menos (diez) (ten) to/before...
  (the hour) **2.1**
  menos que... less than... **3.2**
  menos... que less... than **3.2**
el mensaje instantáneo instant
  message
el menú menu **4.2**
el mercado market
  el mercado al aire libre open-air
  market
el mes month **3.2**
la mesa table **4.2**
mi my **3.2**
miércoles Wednesday **LP**
mil thousand, one thousand **3.2**

un millón (de) million, one
  million **3.2**
el minuto minute **2.1**
mirar to watch **1.1**; to look at
  mirar la televisión to watch
  television **1.1**
mismo(a) same
la mochila backpack **2.2**
montar to ride **1.1**
  montar en bicicleta to ride a
  bike **1.1**
mucho a lot **2.1**
  Mucho gusto. Nice to meet
  you. **LP**
muchos(as) many **2.1**
  muchas veces often, many
  times **2.1**
la mujer woman **1.2**
el mundo world
el museo museum
la música music **1.1**
  la música folklórica folk music
  la música rock rock music **4.2**
el (la) músico(a) musician
muy very **1.2**
  Muy bien. ¿Y tú/usted? Very well.
  And you? (familiar/formal) **LP**

nacer to be born
nada nothing
  De nada. You're welcome. **LP**
la naranja orange (fruit) **3.1**
necesitar to need **2.1**
negro(a) black **4.1**
nervioso(a) nervous **2.2**
nevar (ie) to snow
  Nieva. It is snowing. **LP**
la nieve snow
el ninot (*pl.* **los ninots**) large papier-
  mâché figure
no no **LP**
la noche night **2.1**; evening **LP**
  Buenas noches. Good evening;
  Good night. **LP**
  de la noche at night (with a
  time) **2.1**
la Nochebuena Christmas Eve
la Nochevieja New Year's Eve
el nombre name
nosotros(as) we **1.1**

la nota grade (on a test) **2.1**

   sacar una buena/mala nota to get a good/bad grade **2.1**

novecientos(as) nine hundred **3.2**

noventa ninety **2.1**

noviembre November **3.2**

nuestro(a) our **3.2**

nueve nine **LP**

nuevo(a) new **4.1**

el número number **LP**

   el número de teléfono phone number **LP**

nunca never **2.1**

nutritivo(a) nutritious **3.1**

o or **1.1**

ocho eight **LP**

ochocientos(as) eight hundred **3.2**

octubre October **3.2**

ocupado(a) busy **2.2**

la oficina office **2.2**

   la oficina del (de la) director(a) principal's office **2.2**

el ojo eye

once eleven **2.1**

la oración (*pl.* **las oraciones**) sentence

organizado(a) organized **1.2**

el otoño autumn, fall **4.1**

otro(a) other **3.1**

el padrastro stepfather **3.2**

el padre father **3.2**

los padres parents **3.2**

pagar to pay **4.1**

la página page

el país country, nation **LP**

el pan bread **3.1**

   el pan de muertos special bread made for Día de los Muertos

los pantalones pants **4.1**

   los pantalones cortos shorts **4.1**

la papa potato **1.1**

   las papas fritas French fries **1.1**

el papel paper **2.2**

   el papel picado paper cutouts

para for; in order to **3.1**

parar to stop

   Para y piensa. Stop and think.

la pareja pair

el párrafo paragraph

el parque park **4.2**

   el parque de diversiones amusement park

la parte part

el pasado the past

pasar to happen

   pasar un rato con los amigos to spend time with friends **1.1**

   ¿Qué pasa? What's happening? **LP**

   ¿Qué te pasa (a ti)? What's the matter (with you)?

pasear to go for a walk **1.1**

el paseo walk, stroll; ride

el pasillo hall **2.2**

el pastel cake **4.2**

la patata potato **4.2**

pedir (i) to order, to ask for **4.2**

la película movie **4.2**

pelirrojo(a) red-haired **1.2**

el pelo hair **1.2**

   el pelo castaño/rubio brown/ blond hair **1.2**

pensar (ie) to think; to plan **4.1**

peor worse **3.2**

pequeño(a) little, small **1.2**

Perdón. Excuse me. **LP**

perezoso(a) lazy **1.2**

el periódico newspaper

   el periódico escolar student newspaper

pero but **1.1**

el (la) perro(a) dog **3.2**

la persona person **1.2**

el pescado fish (as food) **4.2**

el pie foot

   a pie on foot **4.2**

la piscina swimming pool

la pista clue

el pizarrón (*pl.* **los pizarrones**) chalkboard, board **2.2**

la pizza pizza **1.1**

la planta plant

el plato plate; dish; course

   el plato principal main course **4.2**

la playa beach

la pluma pen **2.2**

un poco a little **1.2**

pocos(as) few

poder (ue) to be able, can **4.2**

el pollo chicken **4.2**

por for, per

   Por favor. Please. **LP**

   ¿Por qué? Why? **3.1**

porque because **1.2**

el postre dessert **4.2**

   de postre for dessert **4.2**

practicar to practice **1.1**

   practicar deportes to play or practice sports **1.1**

el precio price **4.1**

preferir (ie) to prefer **4.1**

la pregunta question

el premio award

preparar to prepare **1.1**

   preparar la comida to prepare food, to make a meal **1.1**

presentar to introduce **LP**

   Te/Le presento a... Let me introduce you to... (familiar/ formal) **LP**

la primavera spring **4.1**

primero(a) first

   el primero de... the first of... (date) **3.2**

el (la) primo(a) cousin **3.2**

los primos cousins **3.2**

el problema problem **2.2**

la procesión (*pl.* **las procesiones**) procession

proclamar to declare

la propina tip (in a restaurant) **4.2**

el pueblo town

la puerta door **2.2**

¿Qué? What? **3.1**

   ¿De qué color es/son...? What color is/are...?

   ¿Qué día es hoy? What day is today? **LP**

   ¿Qué hora es? What time is it? **2.1**

   ¿Qué pasa? What's happening? **LP**

   ¿Qué tal? How's it going? **LP**

   ¿Qué te gusta hacer? What do you like to do? **1.1**

   ¿Qué tiempo hace? What is the weather like? **LP**

el quechua indigenous language from South America

querer (ie) to want **4.1**

el queso cheese **3.1**
    el queso crema cream cheese
¿Quién(es)? Who? **3.1**
    ¿Quién es? Who is he/she/it? **LP**
quince fifteen **2.1**
quinientos(as) five hundred **3.2**

un rato a while, a short time
la raza (human) race
la razón (*pl.* **las razones**) reason
    tener razón to be right **4.1**
la reconstrucción (*pl.* **las
    reconstrucciones**) reenactment
recordar (ue) to remember
    ¿Recuerdas? Do you remember?
el recorrido run, journey
el recreo recess
el refresco soft drink **1.1**
regular OK **LP**
    Regular. ¿Y tú/usted? OK. And
    you? (familiar/formal) **LP**
el reloj watch; clock **2.2**
el repaso review
responder to reply
el restaurante restaurant **4.2**
el resultado result
el resumen summary
    en resumen in summary
los Reyes Magos Three Kings
rico(a) tasty, delicious **3.1**
rojo(a) red **4.1**
la rosca de reyes sweet bread eaten
    on January 6
la ropa clothing **4.1**
rubio(a) blond **1.2**

sábado Saturday **LP**
sacar una buena/mala nota to get a
    good/bad grade **2.1**
¡Saludos! Greetings!
    Saludos desde... Greetings from...
el sándwich sandwich **3.1**
    el sándwich de jamón y queso
    ham and cheese sandwich **3.1**
el santo saint
seis six **LP**
seiscientos(as) six hundred **3.2**

la semana week **LP**
    el fin de semana weekend
    Semana Santa Holy Week
Señor (Sr.) Mr. **LP**
Señora (Sra.) Mrs. **LP**
Señorita (Srta.) Miss **LP**
septiembre September **3.2**
ser to be **1.1**
    Es de... He/She is from... **LP**
    Es el... de... It's the... of... (day and
    month) **3.2**
    Es la.../Son las... It is...
    o'clock. **2.1**
    Soy de... I'm from... **LP**
serio(a) serious **1.2**
servir (i) to serve **4.2**
sesenta sixty **2.1**
setecientos(as) seven hundred **3.2**
setenta seventy **2.1**
si if
sí yes **LP**
siempre always **2.1**
siete seven **LP**
la silla chair **2.2**
simpático(a) nice, friendly **1.2**
sobre about; on
el sombrero hat **4.1**
la sopa soup **3.1**
su his, her, its, their, your
    (formal) **3.2**
el supermercado supermarket

tal vez perhaps, maybe **4.2**
también also, too **1.1**
    también se dice... you can
    also say...
tan... como as... as **3.2**
tanto como... as much as... **3.2**
tanto(a) so much
tantos(as) so many
tarde late **2.1**
la tarde afternoon **2.1**
    Buenas tardes. Good
    afternoon. **LP**
    de la tarde in the afternoon
    (with a time) **2.1**
la tarea homework **1.1**
la tarjeta postal postcard
el teatro theater **4.2**

el teléfono telephone
    **¿Cuál es tu/su número de
    teléfono?** What is your phone
    number? (familiar/formal) **LP**
    Mi número de teléfono es... My
    phone number is... **LP**
el tema theme
temprano early **2.1**
tener to have **2.1**
    ¿Cuántos años tienes? How old
    are you? **3.2**
    tener... años to be... years old **3.2**
    tener calor to be hot **4.1**
    tener frío to be cold **4.1**
    tener ganas de... to to feel
    like... **3.1**
    tener hambre to be hungry **3.1**
    tener que... to have to... **2.1**
    tener razón to be right **4.1**
    tener sed to be thirsty **3.1**
    tener suerte to be lucky **4.1**
la tía aunt **3.2**
el tiempo weather **LP**
    ¿Qué tiempo hace? What is the
    weather like? **LP**
la tienda store **4.1**
el tío uncle **3.2**
los tíos uncles, uncle(s) and
    aunt(s) **3.2**
típico(a) typical
el tipo type
la tiza chalk **2.2**
tocar to play (an instrument) **1.1**
    tocar la guitarra to play the
    guitar **1.1**
todo junto all together
todos(as) all **1.2**
    todos los días every day **2.1**
tomar to take **4.2**
    tomar apuntes to take notes **2.1**
el tomate tomato **4.2**
trabajador(a) hard-working **1.2**
trabajar to work **1.1**
tranquilo(a) calm **2.2**
trece thirteen **2.1**
treinta thirty **2.1**
treinta y uno thirty-one **2.1**
tres three **LP**
trescientos(as) three hundred **3.2**
triste sad **2.2**
tu your (sing., familiar) **3.2**
tú you (sing., familiar) **1.1**
el turismo tourism
el turrón (*pl.* **los turrones**) almond
    nougat candy

último(a) last
la unidad unit
uno one **LP**
usar to use **2.1**
   usar la computadora to use the
     computer **2.1**
usted you (sing., formal) **1.1**
ustedes you (pl.) **1.1**
la uva grape **3.1**
   las doce uvas twelve grapes
     eaten on New Year's Eve

¡Vale! OK!
varios(as) various
veinte twenty **2.1**
veintiuno twenty-one **2.1**
el (la) vendedor(a) salesclerk
vender to sell **3.1**
la ventana window **2.2**
la ventanilla ticket window **4.2**
ver (veo) to see **4.2**

el verano summer **4.1**
la verdad truth
   ¿Verdad? Really?; Right? **LP**
verde green **4.1**
las verduras vegetables **4.2**
el vestido dress **4.1**
la vez (*pl.* **las veces**) time
   a veces sometimes
   de vez en cuando once in a
     while **2.1**
   muchas veces often, many
     times **2.1**
   tal vez maybe **4.2**
la vida life
el videojuego video game
viejo(a) old **1.2**
el viento wind
   Hace viento. It is windy. **LP**
viernes Friday **LP**
el villancico seasonal children's
   song
visitar to visit
vivir to live **3.2**
el vocabulario vocabulary
volver (ue) to return, to come
   back **4.2**
vosotros(as) you (pl. familiar) **1.1**
vuestro(a) your (pl. familiar) **3.2**

y and
   ...y (diez) (ten) past... (the
     hour) **2.1**
   ...y cuarto quarter past... (the
     hour) **2.1**
   ...y media half past... (the
     hour) **2.1**
   ¿Y tú? And you? (familiar) **LP**
   ¿Y usted? And you? (formal) **LP**
ya already **3.2**
yo I **1.1**
el yogur yogurt **3.1**

el zapato shoe **4.1**

Glosario
inglés-español

This English-Spanish glossary contains all the active vocabulary words that appear in the text as well as passive vocabulary lists. **LP** refers to Lección preliminar.

A

about sobre
activity la actividad **1.1**
to advance avanzar
advertisement el anuncio
after después (de) **1.1**
afternoon la tarde **2.1**
   Good afternoon. Buenas tardes. **LP**
   in the afternoon de la tarde **2.1**
afterward después **1.1**
all todos(as) **1.2**
all together todo junto
almost casi **2.1**
already ya **3.2**
also también **1.1**
always siempre **2.1**
and y
angry enojado(a) **2.2**
announcement el anuncio
answer la respuesta
to answer contestar **2.1**
apple la manzana **3.1**
April abril **3.2**
arrival la llegada
to arrive llegar **2.1**
art el arte **2.1**
article el artículo
artistic artístico(a) **1.2**
as como
   as... as tan... como **3.2**
   as much as... tanto como... **3.2**
to ask for pedir (i) **4.2**
at a
   at night de la noche **2.1**
   At... o'clock. A la(s)... **2.1**
   At what time is/are...? ¿A qué hora es/son...? **2.1**
athletic atlético(a) **1.2**
August agosto **3.2**
aunt la tía **3.2**
autumn el otoño **4.1**
award el premio

B

backpack la mochila **2.2**
bad malo(a) **1.2**
   Bad. And you? (familiar/formal) Mal. ¿Y tú/usted? **LP**
banana la banana **3.1**
bathroom el baño **2.2**
to be ser **1.1**; estar **2.2**
   to be able poder (ue) **4.2**
   to be called llamarse
   to be cold tener frío **4.1**
   to be hot tener calor **4.1**
   to be hungry tener hambre **3.1**
   to be lucky tener suerte **4.1**
   to be right tener razón **4.1**
   to be thirsty tener sed **3.1**
   to be... years old tener... años **3.2**
beach la playa
beans los frijoles **4.2**
because porque **1.2**
beef el bistec **4.2**
before antes (de) **1.1**; menos (with a time) **2.1**
to begin empezar (ie) **4.1**
behind detrás (de) **2.2**
better mejor **3.2**
beverage la bebida **3.1**
bicycle la bicicleta **1.1**
big grande **1.2**
bill (in a restaurant) la cuenta **4.2**
birth date la fecha de nacimiento **3.2**
birthday el cumpleaños **3.2**
   Happy birthday! ¡Feliz cumpleaños! **3.2**
black negro(a) **4.1**
blond rubio(a) **1.2**
blouse la blusa **4.1**
blue azul **4.1**
board el pizarrón (*pl.* los pizarrones) **2.2**
boat el bote
book el libro **1.1**
boring aburrido(a) **2.2**

boy el chico **1.2**
bread el pan **3.1**
breakfast el desayuno **3.1**
broccoli el brócoli **4.2**
brother el hermano **3.2**
brown marrón (*pl.* marrones) **4.1**
   brown hair el pelo castaño **1.2**
bus el autobús (*pl.* los autobuses) **4.2**
   by bus en autobús **4.2**
busy ocupado(a) **2.2**
but pero **1.1**
to buy comprar **1.1**

C

café el café **4.2**
cafeteria la cafetería **2.2**
cake el pastel **4.2**
calculator la calculadora **2.2**
calm tranquilo(a) **2.2**
can (to be able) poder (ue) **4.2**
car el coche **4.2**
   by car en coche **4.2**
cat el (la) gato(a) **3.2**
center el centro **4.2**
cereal el cereal **3.1**
chair la silla **2.2**
chalk la tiza **2.2**
chalkboard el pizarrón (*pl.* los pizarrones) **2.2**
change el cambio
cheese el queso **3.1**
   cream cheese el queso crema
chicken el pollo **4.2**
children los hijos **3.2**
class la clase **LP**
classroom la clase **LP**
clock el reloj **2.2**
to close cerrar (ie) **4.1**
clothing la ropa **4.1**
clue la pista
coffee el café **3.1**

cold el frío
   It is cold. Hace frío. **LP**
   to be cold tener frío **4.1**
color el color
   What color is/are...? ¿De qué color es/son...?
to come back volver (ue) **4.2**
common común
to compare comparar
computer la computadora **2.1**
concert el concierto **4.2**
cookie la galleta **1.1**
coral reef el arrecife de coral
to correct corregir
to cost costar (ue) **4.2**
   How much does it (do they) cost? ¿Cuánto cuesta(n)? **4.1**
   It (They) cost... Cuesta(n)... **4.1**
costume el disfraz (*pl.* los disfraces)
country el país **LP**
course el plato
   main course el plato principal **4.2**
cousin el (la) primo(a) **3.2**

dance el baile
to dance bailar
date la fecha **3.2**
   birth date la fecha de nacimiento **3.2**
   What is the date? ¿Cuál es la fecha? **3.2**
daughter la hija **3.2**
day el día **LP**
   every day todos los días **2.1**
   What day is today? ¿Qué día es hoy? **LP**
December diciembre **3.2**
delicious rico(a) **3.1**
Delighted. Encantado(a). **LP**
department store el almacén (*pl.* los almacenes)
depressed deprimido(a) **2.2**
desk el escritorio **2.2**
dessert el postre **4.2**
   for dessert de postre **4.2**
different diferente
difficult difícil **2.1**
dinner la cena **3.1**
dish el plato
   main dish el plato principal **4.2**

disorganized desorganizado(a) **1.2**
to do hacer (hago) **3.1**
dog el (la) perro(a) **3.2**
dollar el dólar **4.1**
door la puerta **2.2**
downtown el centro **4.2**
to draw dibujar **1.1**
drawing el dibujo
dress el vestido **4.1**
drink la bebida **3.1**
to drink beber **1.1**
during durante **4.1**
DVD el DVD **1.1**

each cada
early temprano **2.1**
easy fácil **2.1**
to eat comer **1.1**
   to eat lunch almorzar (ue) **4.2**
egg el huevo **3.1**
eight ocho **LP**
eight hundred ochocientos(as) **3.2**
eighteen dieciocho **2.1**
eleven once **2.1**
e-mail el correo electrónico **1.1**
English el inglés **2.1**
to enter entrar
eraser el borrador **2.2**
euro el euro **4.1**
evening la noche **LP**
   Good evening. Buenas noches. **LP**
every cada
   every day todos los días **2.1**
exam el examen (*pl.* los exámenes) **2.1**
excited emocionado(a) **2.2**
Excuse me. Perdón. **LP**
eye el ojo

fall el otoño **4.1**
false falso(a)
family la familia **3.2**
far (from) lejos (de) **2.2**
father el padre **3.2**
February febrero **3.2**
to feel like... tener ganas de... **3.1**

few pocos(as)
fifteen quince **2.1**
fifty cincuenta **2.1**
to find encontrar (ue) **4.2**
fine bien **LP**
   Fine. And you? (familiar/ Bien. ¿Y tú/usted? formal) **LP**
fireworks los fuegos artificiales
first primero(a)
   the first of... el primero de... **3.2**
fish el pescado **4.2**
five cinco **LP**
five hundred quinientos(as) **3.2**
food la comida **1.1, 3.1**
food server el (la) camarero(a) **4.2**
foot el pie
   on foot a pie **4.2**
for para **3.1**; por
forty cuarenta **2.1**
fountain la fuente
four cuatro **LP**
four hundred cuatrocientos(as) **3.2**
fourteen catorce **2.1**
French fries las papas fritas **1.1**
Friday viernes **LP**
friend el (la) amigo(a) **1.2**
   to spend time with friends pasar un rato con los amigos **1.1**
from de **1.1**
fruit la fruta **1.1**
fun divertido(a) **2.2**
funny cómico(a) **1.2**

garden el jardín (*pl.* los jardines)
girl la chica **1.2**
to go ir **2.2**
   to be going to... ir a... **4.2**
   to go for a walk pasear **1.1**
   to go shopping ir de compras **4.1**
good bueno(a) **1.2**
   Good afternoon. Buenas tardes. **LP**
   Good evening. Buenas noches. **LP**
   Good morning. Buenos días. **LP**
   Good night. Buenas noches. **LP**
Goodbye. Adiós. **LP**
good-looking guapo(a) **1.2**

grade la nota **2.1**
   to get a good/bad grade sacar una buena/mala nota **2.1**
grammar la grámatica
grandfather el abuelo **3.2**
grandmother la abuela **3.2**
grandparents los abuelos **3.2**
grape la uva **3.1**
green verde **4.1**
Greetings! ¡Saludos!
   Greetings from... Saludos desde...
guitar la guitarra **1.1**
gymnasium el gimnasio **2.2**

hair el pelo **1.2**
   blond hair pelo rubio **1.2**
   brown hair pelo castaño **1.2**
half medio(a)
   half past... ... y media **2.1**
hall el pasillo **2.2**
ham el jamón (*pl.* los jamones) **3.1**
hamburger la hamburguesa **3.1**
to happen pasar
   What's happening? ¿Qué pasa? **LP**
happy contento(a) **2.2**
hard-working trabajador(a) **1.2**
hat el sombrero **4.1**
   winter hat el gorro **4.1**
to have tener **2.1**
   to have to... tener que... **2.1**
he él **1.1**
Hello. Hola. **LP**
her su **3.2**
here aquí **4.2**
Hi. Hola. **LP**
high school el colegio, la escuela secundaria
his su **3.2**
history la historia **2.1**
homework la tarea **1.1**
   to do homework hacer la tarea **1.1**
horrible horrible **3.1**
hot caliente
   It is hot. Hace calor. **LP**
   to be hot tener calor **4.1**
hour la hora **2.1**

How...? ¿Cómo...? **3.1**
   How are you? ¿Cómo estás? (familiar); ¿Cómo está usted? (formal) **LP**
   How many...? ¿Cuántos(as)...? **2.1**
   How old are you? ¿Cuántos años tienes? **3.2**
   How's it going? ¿Qué tal? **LP**
how many cuántos(as) **3.2**
how much cuánto(a) **3.2**
   How much does it (do they) cost? ¿Cuánto cuesta(n)? **4.1**
hungry: to be hungry tener hambre **3.1**

I yo **1.1**
ice cream el helado **1.1**
if si
important importante **3.1**
   It's important. Es importante. **3.1**
in en **2.1**
   in front (of) delante (de) **2.2**
   in order to para **3.1**
   in the afternoon de la tarde **2.1**
   in the morning de la mañana **2.1**
inexpensive barato(a)
information la información
inside (of) dentro (de) **2.2**
intelligent inteligente **1.2**
interesting interesante **2.2**
to introduce presentar **LP**
   Let me introduce you to... Te/Le presento a... (familiar/formal) **LP**
its su **3.2**

jacket la chaqueta **4.1**
January enero **3.2**
jeans los jeans **4.1**
juice el jugo **1.1**
   orange juice el jugo de naranja **3.1**
July julio **3.2**
June junio **3.2**

kind la clase

lake el lago
language el idioma, el lenguaje
large grande **1.2**
late tarde **2.1**
later
   See you later. Hasta luego. **LP**
lazy perezoso(a) **1.2**
to learn aprender **1.1**
   to learn Spanish aprender el español **1.1**
less menos
   less than... menos que... **3.2**
   less... than menos... que **3.2**
lesson la lección
Let's... Vamos a... **4.2**
library la biblioteca **2.2**
life la vida
like como
to like
   Do you like...? ¿Te gusta...? **1.1**
   I don't like... No me gusta... **1.1**
   I like... Me gusta... **1.1**
   What do you like to do? ¿Qué te gusta hacer? **1.1**
Likewise. Igualmente. **LP**
to listen (to) escuchar **1.1**
   to listen to music escuchar música **1.1**
little pequeño(a) **1.2**
   a little un poco **1.2**
to live vivir **3.2**
to look (at) mirar
a lot mucho **2.1**
lunch el almuerzo **3.1**
   to eat lunch almorzar (ue) **4.2**

to make hacer (hago) **3.1**
mall el centro comercial **4.1**
man el hombre **1.2**
many muchos(as) **2.1**
   many times muchas veces **2.1**
map el mapa **2.2**

March marzo **3.2**
market el mercado
  open-air market el mercado al
    aire libre
math las matemáticas **2.1**
May mayo **3.2**
maybe tal vez **4.2**
meal la comida **1.1, 3.1**
meat la carne **4.2**
to meet
  Nice to meet you. Mucho
    gusto. **LP**
menu el menú **4.2**
milk la leche **3.1**
million un millón (de) **3.2**
minute el minuto **2.1**
Miss Señorita (Srta.) **LP**
Monday lunes **LP**
money el dinero **4.1**
month el mes **3.2**
more más **1.1**
  more than... más que... **3.2**
  more... than más... que **3.2**
morning la mañana **2.1**
  Good morning. Buenos
    días. **LP**
  in the morning de la
    mañana **2.1**
mother la madre **3.2**
movie la película **4.2**
movie theater el cine **4.2**
the movies el cine **4.2**
Mr. Señor (Sr.) **LP**
Mrs. Señora (Sra.) **LP**
museum el museo
music la música **1.1**
  folk music la música folklórica
  rock music la música rock **4.2**
my mi **3.2**

name el nombre
  His/Her name is... Se
    llama... **LP**
  My name is... Me llamo... **LP**
  What's his/her/your (formal)
    name? ¿Cómo se llama? **LP**
  What's your (familiar)
    name? ¿Cómo te llamas? **LP**
near (to) cerca (de) **2.2**
to need necesitar **2.1**
nervous nervioso(a) **2.2**
never nunca **2.1**

new nuevo(a) **4.1**
  New Year el Año Nuevo
newspaper el periódico
  student newspaper el periódico
    escolar
next to al lado (de) **2.2**
nice simpático(a) **1.2**
  Nice to meet you. Mucho
    gusto. **LP**
night la noche **2.1**
  at night de la noche **2.1**
  Good night. Buenas noches. **LP**
nine nueve **LP**
nine hundred novecientos(as) **3.2**
nineteen diecinueve **2.1**
ninety noventa **2.1**
no no **LP**
notebook el cuaderno **2.2**
notes los apuntes **2.1**
  to take notes tomar apuntes **2.1**
November noviembre **3.2**
now ahora **3.1**
number el número **LP**
  phone number el número de
    teléfono **LP**
nutritious nutritivo(a) **3.1**

o'clock: It is... o'clock. Es la.../Son
  las... **2.1**
October octubre **3.2**
of de **1.1**
office la oficina **2.2**
  principal's office la oficina del
    (de la) director(a) **2.2**
often muchas veces **2.1**
OK
  OK! ¡Vale!
  OK? ¿Está bien?
  OK. And you? Regular. ¿Y tú/
    usted? (familiar/formal) **LP**
old viejo(a) **1.2**
  How old are you? ¿Cuántos
    años tienes? **3.2**
  to be... years old tener...
    años **3.2**
older mayor **3.2**
on en; sobre
  on foot a pie **4.2**
  on top (of) encima (de) **2.2**
once: once in a while de vez en
  cuando **2.1**
one uno **LP**
one hundred cien **2.1**

one thousand mil **3.2**
or o **1.1**
orange (color) anaranjado(a) **4.1**
orange (fruit) la naranja **3.1**
to order pedir (i) **4.2**
organized organizado(a) **1.2**
other otro(a) **3.1**
our nuestro(a) **3.2**

page la página
painting el cuadro
pair la pareja
pants los pantalones **4.1**
paper el papel **2.2**
parade el desfile
paragraph el párrafo
parents los padres **3.2**
park el parque **4.2**
  amusement park el parque de
    diversiones
part la parte
party la fiesta
past
  half past... ...y media **2.1**
  quarter past... ...y cuarto **2.1**
the past el pasado
to pay pagar **4.1**
pen la pluma **2.2**
pencil el lápiz (*pl.* los lápices) **2.2**
perhaps tal vez **4.2**
person la persona **1.2**
phone el teléfono **LP**
  What is your phone number?
    ¿Cuál es tu/su número de
    teléfono? (familiar/formal) **LP**
  My phone number is... Mi
    número de teléfono es... **LP**
pizza la pizza **1.1**
place el lugar **4.2**
to plan pensar (ie) **4.1**
plant la planta
plate el plato
to play
  (an instrument) tocar **1.1**
  (games) jugar (ue) **1.1**
  (sports) jugar (ue), practicar **1.1**
Please. Por favor. **LP**
  Pleased to meet you.
    Encantado(a). **LP**
pleasure el gusto
  The pleasure is mine. El gusto
    es mío. **LP**
postcard la tarjeta postal

potato la papa **1.1**; la patata **4.2**
to practice practicar **1.1**
to prefer preferir (ie) **4.1**
to prepare preparar **1.1**
   to prepare food/a meal
    preparar la comida **1.1**
pretty bonito(a) **1.2**
price el precio **4.1**
principal el (la) director(a) **2.2**
problem el problema **2.2**

quarter (to) (menos) cuarto **2.1**
quarter past ...y cuarto **2.1**

to rain llover (ue)
   It is raining. Llueve. **LP**
to read leer **1.1**
   to read a book leer un libro **1.1**
reading la lectura
Really? ¿Verdad?
recess el recreo
red rojo(a) **4.1**
red-haired pelirrojo(a) **1.2**
to rent alquilar **1.1**
   to rent a DVD alquilar un
    DVD **1.1**
to reply responder
to rest descansar **1.1**
restaurant el restaurante **4.2**
result el resultado
to return volver (ue) **4.2**
review el repaso
rice el arroz **4.2**
to ride a bike montar en
   bicicleta **1.1**
right derecho(a)
   Right? ¿Verdad? **LP**
   to be right tener razón **4.1**
to run correr **1.1**

sad triste **2.2**
salad la ensalada **4.2**
salesclerk el (la) vendedor(a)
same mismo(a)
   Same here. Igualmente. **LP**

sandwich el sándwich **3.1**
   ham and cheese sandwich el
    sándwich de jamón y queso **3.1**
Saturday sábado **LP**
scene la escena
schedule el horario **2.1**
school la escuela **1.1**
   high school el colegio, la escuela
    secundaria
science las ciencias **2.1**
season la estación (*pl.* las
   estaciones) **4.1**
to see ver (veo) **4.2**
   See you later. Hasta luego. **LP**
   See you tomorrow. Hasta
    mañana. **LP**
to sell vender **3.1**
sentence la oración (*pl.* las oraciones)
September septiembre **3.2**
serious serio(a) **1.2**
to serve servir (i) **4.2**
seven siete **LP**
seven hundred setecientos(as) **3.2**
seventeen diecisiete **2.1**
seventy setenta **2.1**
to share compartir **3.1**
she ella **1.1**
shirt la camisa **4.1**
shoe el zapato **4.1**
shop: to go shopping ir de
   compras **4.1**
shopping center el centro
   comercial **4.1**
short (height) bajo(a) **1.2**
shorts los pantalones cortos **4.1**
sister la hermana **3.2**
six seis **LP**
six hundred seiscientos(as) **3.2**
sixteen dieciséis **2.1**
sixty sesenta **2.1**
to skateboard andar en patineta **1.1**
to sleep dormir (ue) **4.2**
small pequeño(a) **1.2**
snow la nieve
to snow nevar (ie)
   It is snowing. Nieva. **LP**
so
   so many tantos(as)
   so much tanto(a)
soccer el fútbol **1.1**
sock el calcetín (*pl.* los calcetines) **4.1**
soft drink el refresco **1.1**
sometimes a veces
son el hijo **3.2**
So-so. And you? Más o menos. ¿Y
   tú/usted? (familiar/formal) **LP**

soup la sopa **3.1**
source la fuente
Spanish el español **2.1**
to speak hablar **1.1**
special especial
to spend: to spend time with
   friends pasar un rato con los
    amigos **1.1**
spirit el ánimo
sports los deportes **1.1**
spring la primavera **4.1**
stepfather el padrastro **3.2**
stepmother la madrastra **3.2**
to stop parar
store la tienda **4.1**
street la calle **4.2**
student el (la) estudiante **1.2**
studious estudioso(a) **1.2**
to study estudiar **1.1**
summary el resumen
   in summary en resumen
summer el verano **4.1**
sun el sol
   It is sunny. Hace sol. **LP**
Sunday domingo **LP**
supermarket el supermercado
survey la encuesta
swimming pool la piscina

table la mesa **4.2**
to take tomar **4.2**
   to take notes tomar apuntes **2.1**
to talk hablar **1.1**
   to talk on the phone hablar por
    teléfono **1.1**
tall alto(a) **1.2**
tasty rico(a) **3.1**
to teach enseñar **2.1**
teacher el (la) maestro(a) **LP**
team el equipo
ten diez **LP**
test el examen (*pl.* los exámenes) **2.1**
Thank you. Gracias. **LP**
   Thank you very much. Muchas
    gracias. **LP**
theater el teatro **4.2**
their su **3.2**
them ellos(as) **7.2**
theme el tema
there allí **4.2**
   there is/are... hay... **2.1**
they ellos(as) **1.1**

to think pensar (ie) **4.1**
thirst la sed
   to be thirsty tener sed **3.1**
thirteen trece **2.1**
thirty treinta **2.1**
thirty-one treinta y uno **2.1**
thousand mil **3.2**
three tres **LP**
three hundred trescientos(as) **3.2**
Thursday jueves **LP**
ticket la entrada **4.2**
time la hora **2.1**; la vez
   At what time is/are...? ¿A qué
     hora es/son...? **2.1**
   What time is it? ¿Qué hora
     es? **2.1**
tip la propina **4.2**
tired cansado(a) **2.2**
to menos (with a time) **2.1**; a
today hoy **LP**
   Today is... Hoy es... **LP**
   What day is today? ¿Qué día es
     hoy? **LP**
tomato el tomate **4.2**
tomorrow mañana **LP**
   See you tomorrow. Hasta
     mañana. **LP**
   Tomorrow is... Mañana es... **LP**
too también **1.1**
too much demasiado
tourism el turismo
town el pueblo
true cierto(a)
T-shirt la camiseta **4.1**
Tuesday martes **LP**
twelve doce **2.1**
twenty veinte **2.1**
twenty-one veintiuno **2.1**
two dos **LP**
two hundred doscientos(as) **3.2**
type el tipo; la clase
typical típico(a)

ugly feo(a) **4.1**
uncle el tío **3.2**
under debajo (de) **2.2**
underneath debajo (de) **2.2**
to understand entender (ie) **4.1**
   Did you understand?
     ¿Comprendiste?
unit la unidad

to use usar **2.1**
   to use the computer usar la
     computadora **2.1**

various varios(as)
vegetables las verduras **4.2**
very muy **1.2**
   Very well. And you? Muy bien.
     ¿Y tú/usted? (familiar/formal)
     LP
video game el videojuego
to visit visitar
vocabulary vocabulario

waiter el camarero **4.2**
waitress la camarera **4.2**
to walk caminar **6.2**
   to go for a walk pasear **1.1**
to want querer (ie) **4.1**; desear
watch el reloj **2.2**
to watch mirar **1.1**
   to watch television mirar la
     televisión **1.1**
water el agua (fem.) **1.1**
we nosotros(as) **1.1**
to wear llevar **4.1**
weather el tiempo **LP**
   What is the weather like? ¿Qué
     tiempo hace? **LP**
Wednesday miércoles **LP**
week la semana **LP**
welcome: You're welcome. De
   nada. **LP**
well bien **LP**
   Very well. And you? Muy bien.
     ¿Y tú/usted? (familiar/formal)
     LP
what qué
   What? ¿Qué?; ¿Cuál? **3.1**
   What are you like? ¿Cómo
     eres? **1.2**
   What color is/are...? ¿De qué
     color es/son...?
   What day is today? ¿Qué día es
     hoy? **LP**
   What do you like to do? ¿Qué
     te gusta hacer? **1.1**
   What is the date? ¿Cuál es la
     fecha? **3.2**

   What is the weather like? ¿Qué
     tiempo hace? **LP**
   What is your phone number?
     ¿Cuál es tu/su número de
     teléfono? (familiar/formal) **LP**
   What time is it? ¿Qué hora
     es? **2.1**
   What's happening? ¿Qué
     pasa? **LP**
   What's his/her/your (formal)
     name? ¿Cómo se llama? **LP**
   What's your (familiar)
     name? ¿Cómo te llamas? **LP**
when cuando **2.2**
   When? ¿Cuándo? **2.2**
where donde
   Where? ¿Dónde? **2.2**
   (To) Where? ¿Adónde? **2.2**
   Where are you from? ¿De
     dónde eres es usted
     (familiar)/(formal)? **LP**
   Where are you going? ¿Adónde
     vas? **2.2**
   Where is he/she from? ¿De
     dónde es? **LP**
Which? ¿Cuál(es)? **3.1**
a while un rato
   once in a while de vez en
     cuando **2.1**
white blanco(a) **4.1**
Who? ¿Quién(es)? **3.1**
   Who is he/she/it?
     ¿Quién es? **LP**
Why? ¿Por qué? **3.1**
wind el viento
   It is windy. Hace viento. **LP**
window la ventana **2.2**
   ticket window la ventanilla **4.2**
winter el invierno **4.1**
to wish desear
woman la mujer **1.2**
to work trabajar **1.1**
world el mundo
worse peor **3.2**
to write escribir **1.1**
   to write e-mails escribir correos
     electrónicos **1.1**
writing la escritura

year el año **3.2**
   New Year el Año Nuevo
   to be... years old tener...
     años **3.2**

yellow amarillo(a) **4.1**

yes sí **LP**

yogurt el yogur **3.1**

you

  (sing., familiar) tú **1.1**

  (sing., formal) usted **1.1**

  (pl., familiar) vosotros(as) **1.1**

  (pl.) ustedes **1.1**

young joven (*pl.* jóvenes) **1.2**

younger menor **3.2**

your

  (sing., familiar) tu **3.2**

  (pl., familiar) vuestro(a) **3.2**

  (formal) su **3.2**

zero cero **LP**

GLOSARIO
inglés-español

❋ Índice

Índice

M

Madrid (Spain), 266
mamama, 188
maps
    de Soto expedition, 54
    hurricane route, 178
    Mexico, 90
    Puerto Rico, 152
    Spain, 214
    Spanish-speaking world, 12, 13
    United States, 28
    Zempoala (Mexico), 116
masculine. See gender
masculine adjectives, 66
masculine nouns, 66
    form of numbers before, 97
Maya ruins, 91
meals
    restaurants, 246, 248, 269
    sobremesa, 182–183
    vocabulary, 158–159, 179
    See also food
Las meninas (Velázquez), 261
menu, ordering from, 246, 248, 269
Mexico, 90–91
    art of, 109, 137, 144
    bilingual school, 114–115
    celebrations of, C4–C5, C6–C7,
        C8–C9, C10–C11, C14–C15,
        C18–C19, C20–C21
    cooking and foods of, 65, 82, 90
    famous persons from, 90
    indigenous cultures, 130, 137
    location on map, 12, 13, 90
    map of, 90
    Mexican-American culture, 75
    murals, 91, 109
    scenes of, 91, 93, 121, 142
    school uniforms, 102
    statistics, 90
    student life, 87, 102, 149
    televised secondary school, 116
    Tex-Mex food, 65
    traditional foods of, 65
    Universidad Nacional
        Autónoma de México
        (UNAM), 91
    vocabulary variations by country,
        70, 104, 122, 132, 160, 222, 250
    yarn painting, 144
    Zempoala (town), 116

Miami
    beach, 31
    Cuban-American art, 45
    Little Havana (**Calle Ocho**), 29
    Los Premios Juventud, 43
    recreation, 36, 81
    scenes of, 29, 31, 81
micro, 250
money
    of Mexico, 90
    of Puerto Rico, 152
    of Spain, 214
    of Venezuela, C24
montar en bicicleta, 36
months, 185
Moors, 240
murals, 9, 91, 109
Music (Cortada), 45
music
    Andean, 206
    instruments of Puerto Rico and
        Peru, 206
    Los Premios Juventud, 43
    of Puerto Rico, 205
    sevillanas, 215
    of Spain, 215, 240
    Tex-Mex music, 54
musical instruments
    in celebrations, C2
    of Puerto Rico and Peru, 206
musical stars, **Los Premios
    Juventud,** 43

N

ñ (letter), 71
names, 4
National Museum of Anthropology
    (Mexico City), 130
native cultures, C6, C7, C8, C9, C22,
    C23, 130, 137, 255
Las Navidades, C10–C11
New York City, 1, 9
Nicaragua
    celebrations of C4–C5
    location on map, 12, 13
Niña campesina sonriente (Sayán Polo),
    199
nouns
    definite articles for, 66, 83
    gender, 66
    gustar +, 162, 179
    indefinite articles for, 66, 83
    noun-adjective agreement, 72, 83

possession, expressing, 184
    singular/plural, 66
number
    agreement of possessive
        adjectives, 190, 194
    noun-adjective agreement, 72, 83
numbers
    from 1 to 10, 16
    from 11 to 100, 94
    from 200 to 1,000,000, 186
    before masculine and feminine
        nouns, 97
    date of birth, 192, 195
    expressing age, 189
    telephone numbers, 16, 25

O

o→ue stem-changing verbs, present
    tense, 252, 269
olives, 240
opposites, 63
órale, 222
origin, expressing, 14, 25, 38, 39

P

Panama
    celebrations of, C10–C11
    location on map, 12, 13
papas fritas, 70
papitas, 70
Paraguay
    celebrations of, C14–C15
    indigenous cultures, 130
    location on map, 12, 13
Parque del Buen Retiro (Spain),
    266
**Partido Independista
    Puertorriqueño,** 193
Partido Nuevo Progresista, 193
Partido Popular Democrático, 193
Paseo del Río (San Antonio), 58,
    59, 80
patatas fritas, 70
pedir, 258
pensar, 224
performers, **Los Premios Juventud,**
    43
La persistencia de la memoria (Dalí),
    229
personal description, 60–63, 65, 67,
    68, 71, 75, 76, 83
personality, vocabulary, 83

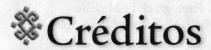

Créditos

Acknowledgment

"Invierno tardío" by Antonio Colinas. Reprinted by permission of the author.

Photography

Cover *center* Steve Dunwell/The Image Bank/Getty Images; *inset* Marc Bacon/LatinFocus.com; **i** *Title Page* Steve Dunwell/The Image Bank/Getty Images; *Half Title Page* Marc Bacon/LatinFocus.com; **iii** Marc Bacon/LatinFocus.com; **Back Cover** *top left* Steve Dunwell/The Image Bank/Getty Images; *top center* Rodriguez Joseph/Gallery Stock Limited; *top right* Panoramic Images/Getty Images; *bottom left* Doug Armand/Getty Images; *bottom center* David Noton/Masterfile; *bottom right* P. Pet/zefa/Corbis; **iv** *top* Guy Jarvis/School Division/Houghton Mifflin Co.; *bottom left* Jaime Puebla/AP Images; *bottom right* Alberto Martin/Agencia EFE; **v** *bottom left* Gregory Bull/AP Images; *bottom right* Jennifer Szymaszek/AP Images; **vi** Ann Summa/McDougal Littell/Houghton Mifflin Co.; **vii** *left, right* Ann Summa/McDougal Littell/Houghton Mifflin Co.; **xxii** *top* Erich Lessing/Art Resource, New York; **xxiii** *top* Ann Summa/McDougal Littell/Houghton Mifflin Co.; *center, bottom* Ken Karp/McDougal Littell/Houghton Mifflin Co.; **xxv** *top* Jay Penni/McDougal Littell/Houghton Mifflin Co.; **xxvii** *left, right* Michael Goss/McDougal Littell/Houghton Mifflin Co.; **xxviii** *top left* Robert Galbraith/Reuters Pictures; *top right* McDougal Littell/Houghton Mifflin Co.; **xxix** *top left* Richard Wareham Fotografie/Alamy; *top right* Ann Summa Stock; *center* Edward Hernandez/Edward H. Photos; *bottom* Philip Coblentz/Brand X Pictures/Getty Images; **C2** *banner, left to right 1* Jesus Dominguez/Agencia EFE; *2-4* Rafael Diaz/Agencia EFE; *all others* Rafael Diaz/Agencia EFE; **C3** *top left, top right* Rafael Diaz/Agencia EFE; *bottom right* Jesus Dominguez/Agencia EFE; **C4** *banner, left to right* Juan Carlos Ulate/Reuters Pictures; The Brownsville Herald/Anthony Padilla/AP Images; Jose Luis Magana/AP Images; Agencia EFE; *bottom left* Hector Lopez/Agencia EFE; *bottom right* Marco Ugarte/AP Images; **C5** *top right* Kent Gilbert/AP Images; *top left* Daniel LeClair/Reuters Pictures; *bottom right* Juan Carlos Ulate/Reuters Pictures; **C6** *banner, left to right* Greg Smith/Corbis; Eduardo Verdugo/AP Images; Claudia Daut/Landov/Reuters Pictures; Les Stone/NewsCom/Zuma Press; *left* Laura Cano/NewsCom/Agence France Presse; *bottom right* Jacqueline Castellon/NewsCom/Notimex; **C7** *center left* Dennis Callahan/NewsCom/Notimex; *bottom right* Susana Vera/Reuters Pictures; *top right* Claudia Daut/Reuters/Landov LLC; **C8** *banner, left to right* Ann Summa; © 2007 Robert Frerck/Odyssey/Chicago; Denis Defibaugh; Rodrigo Abd/AP Images; *bottom left* Juan Barreto/Getty Images; *bottom left, inset* Ann Summa; *center left* Charles Bennett/AP Images; *top right* Marco Ugarte/AP Images; **C9** *top left* Glen Allison/Alamy; *top right* Eduardo Verdugo/AP Images; *bottom left* Jaime Puebla/AP Images; **C10** *banner, left to right* Marcelo Del Pozo/NewsCom/Reuters; Enrique Marcarian/Reuters Pictures; Juan Martin/Agencia EFE; Blake Sell/NewsCom/Reuters; *top left* Alberto Lowe/NewsCom/Reuters; *bottom left* Viesti Associates, Inc.; *bottom right* Leo La Valle/Agencia EFE; **C11** *top* Silvia Izquierdo/AP Images; *bottom* Desmond Boylan/NewsCom/Reuters; **C12** *banner, left to right* Dolores Ochoa R./AP Images; Marcou/Sipa Press; Denis Doyle/AP Images; Eric L. Weather/Lonely Planet Images; Luis Nereo Bueno Martinez/NewsCom/Reforma; *top left* Silvia Izquierdo/AP Images; *bottom right* Alberto Martin/Agencia EFE; *bottom center* Juanjo Martin/Agencia EFE; *bottom left* Olga Vasilkova/ShutterStock; **C13** *top right* Kryzsztof Dydynki/Lonely Planet Images; *left* Richard I'Anson/Lonely Planet Images; **C14** *banner, left to right* Miguel Vidal/Reuters/Corbis; Pablo Aneli/EPA/Sipa Press; Miguel Menendez V./EPA/Sipa Press; Andres Leighton/AP Images; *left* Elvira Urquijo A./EPA/Sipa Press; *bottom right* Martin Crespo/EPA/Sipa Press; **C15** *top left* Juan Barreto/Staff/Getty Images; *right* David Mercado/Reuters Pictures; *bottom left* Javier Galeano/AP Images; *bottom right* Guy Jarvis/McDougal Littell/Houghton Mifflin Co.; **C16** *banner, left to right 1* Kai Forsterling/Agencia EFE; *2* Hannah Levy/Lonely Planet Images; *3-5* Manuel Bruque/Agencia EFE; *bottom* Hannah Levy/Lonely Planet Images; *left* J.C. Cardenas/Agencia EFE; **C17** *right* Heino Kalis/Reuters/Corbis; *left* Kai Forsterling/Agencia EFE; **C18** *banner, left to right* Jack Kurtz/NewsCom/Zuma Press; Viesti Associates, Inc.; Viesti Associates, Inc.; Jack Kurtz/NewsCom/Zuma Press; *bottom right* Viesti Associates, Inc.; *left* Ann Summa; **C19** *top left* Pilar Olivares/Reuters Pictures; *bottom right* Viesti Associates, Inc.; *right* Brian Doben/BA-REPS.com; **C20** *banner, left to right* Tyler Hicks/New York Times; Joe Raedle/Getty Images; Jorge Uzon/Getty Images; Damian Dovarganes/AP Images; *right, bottom left* Robert Galbraith/Reuters Pictures; **C21** *top right* Jose Luis Magana/AP Images; *center* Michael Springer/Zuma Press; **C22** *banner, left to right 1-2* Paolo Aguilar/Agencia EFE; Paolo Aguilar/Agencia EFE; *bottom right, left* Paolo Aguilar/Agencia EFE; **C23** *right* Guillermo Legaria/Agencia EFE; *left* Christian Lombardi/Agencia EFE; **C24** *banner, left to right* Dado Galdieri/AP Images; Tony Morrison/South American Pictures; Stuart Franklin/Magnum Photos; *left* Daniel Munoz/Reuters/Corbis; *bottom right* Jupiter Images/Comstock; **C25** *bottom* Pablo Corral V/Corbis; *top left* Stuart Franklin/Magnum Photos; *top right* *Simón Bolívar* (1830), José Gil de Castro. Oil on canvas, 237cm x 167cm (93 5/16" x 65 3/4"). Museo Nacional de

Arqueología, Antropología, e Historia del Perú, Instituto Nacional de Cultura, Lima. Photograph by Mireille Vautier/The Art Archive; **1–2** Alan Schein Photography/Corbis; **1** *bottom left* Gregory Bull/AP Images; *bottom right* Jennifer Szymaszek/AP Images; **2** *all* Ken Karp/McDougal Littell/Houghton Mifflin Co.; **3** *all* Ken Karp/McDougal Littell/Houghton Mifflin Co.; **5** *both* Ken Karp/McDougal Littell/Houghton Mifflin Co.; **6** *all* Ken Karp/McDougal Littell/Houghton Mifflin Co.; **7** *all* Ken Karp/McDougal Littell/Houghton Mifflin Co.; **8** *bottom* Ken Karp/ McDougal Littell/Houghton Mifflin Co.; **9** *bottom, Sábado en la Ciento Diez (Saturday on 110th Street)* (1996), Manuel Vega. Located at 110th Street station, #6 line of the New York City subway system. Commissioned and owned by Metropolitan Transportation Authority Arts for Transit. © 1996 Manuel Vega. Photography by Mike Kamber/© Metropolitan Transportation Authority; *top left, top right* Ken Karp/McDougal Littell/Houghton Mifflin Co.; **12** *top* Ann Summa/McDougal Littell/Houghton Mifflin Co.; **14** *both* Ann Summa/McDougal Littell/Houghton Mifflin Co.; **16** *all* Ken Karp/McDougal Littell/Houghton Mifflin Co.; **18** *both* Ken Karp/McDougal Littell/Houghton Mifflin Co.; **20** *all* Jay Penni/McDougal Littell/Houghton Mifflin Co.; **21** *left* Clive Watkins/ShutterStock; *center left* Adam Jones/Getty Images; *center right* WizData, Inc./ShutterStock; *right* Michael Coglianty/Getty Images; **22** *both* Ken Karp/McDougal Littell/Houghton Mifflin Co.; **23** *both* Ken Karp/McDougal Littell/Houghton Mifflin Co.; **27** *top left* David R. Frazier Photolibrary, Inc./Alamy; *top right, bottom right* HIRB/Index Stock Imagery; *bottom left* © 2007 Robert Frerck/Odyssey/Chicago; **28** *teen girls* Ann Summa/McDougal Littell/Houghton Mifflin Co.; *bottom right* McDougal Littell/Houghton Mifflin Co.; *center* Image Club; **29** *bottom center* Richard Cummins/Lonely Planet Images; *bottom left* Eric Gray/AP Images; *center inset* Ann Summa/McDougal Littell/Houghton Mifflin Co.; *center right* AFP/Getty Images; *top left* Jeff Greenberg/PhotoEdit; **30-31** Ann Summa/McDougal Littell/Houghton Mifflin Co.; **32** *all* Ann Summa/McDougal Littell/Houghton Mifflin Co.; **33** *fruit* Tina Rencelj/ShutterStock; *ice cream* Comstock; *fries* Royalty-Free/Corbis; *pizza* SuperStock; *cookies* Michael Newman/PhotoEdit; *water* PhotoDisc/Getty Images; *soda* Guy Jarvis/School Division/Houghton Mifflin Co.; *the rest* Ann Summa/McDougal Littell/Houghton Mifflin Co.; **34** *all* Ann Summa/McDougal Littell/Houghton Mifflin Co.; **35** *modelo* Guy Jarvis/School Division/Houghton Mifflin Co.; *1* Michael Newman/PhotoEdit; *3* Comstock; *4* Royalty-Free/Corbis; *5* PhotoDisc/Getty Images; *6* Tina Rencelj/ ShutterStock; **36** *both* Ann Summa/McDougal Littell/Houghton Mifflin Co.; **40** *1, 4* Ann Summa/McDougal Littell/ Houghton Mifflin Co.; **42** Ann Summa/McDougal Littell/Houghton Mifflin Co.; **43** *left* Rodrigo Varela/WireImage. com; *right* Orlando Garcia/Getty Images; **45** *Music* (2005), Xavier Cortada. Acrylic on canvas, 60 in. x 96 in. Courtesy of the artist.; **46** *all* Ann Summa/McDougal Littell/Houghton Mifflin Co.; **47** PhotoDisc/Getty Images; **48** *all* Ann Summa/McDougal Littell/Houghton Mifflin Co.; **49** *both* Ann Summa/McDougal Littell/Houghton Mifflin Co.; **51** Jay Penni/McDougal Littell/Houghton Mifflin Co.; **52** *left* Michael Newman/PhotoEdit; *clipboard* Guy Jarvis/School Division/Houghton Mifflin Co.; **53** *top right* PhotoDisc/Getty Images; *top left* Tracy Frankel/Getty Images; *bottom right* Stewart Cohen/Getty Images; *clipboard* Guy Jarvis/School Division/Houghton Mifflin Co.; **54** *top* Bettmann/Corbis; *bottom* Vince Bucci /AFP/ Getty Images; **58–59** Ann Summa/McDougal Littell/Houghton Mifflin Co.; **60** *all* Ann Summa/McDougal Littell/Houghton Mifflin Co.; **61** *all* Ann Summa/McDougal Littell/Houghton Mifflin Co.; **62** *all* Ann Summa/McDougal Littell/Houghton Mifflin Co.; **64** Ann Summa/McDougal Littell/Houghton Mifflin Co.; **65** *center* Stockbyte Royalty Free; *bottom right* Jim Scherer Photography Inc./StockFood; *bottom left* Jay Penni/ McDougal Littell/Houghton Mifflin Co.; **67** *modelo* Michael Newman/PhotoEdit; *1* Royalty-Free/Corbis; *2* Guy Jarvis/School Division/Houghton Mifflin Co.; *3, 5* FoodCollection/SuperStock; *4, 6* Comstock; *7* Tina Rencelj/ ShutterStock; **69** *modelo left* Tina Rencelj/ShutterStock; *modelo right* Royalty-Free/Corbis; *1 right, 6 left* PhotoDisc; *2 right, 2 left, 3 left* Ann Summa/McDougal Littell/Houghton Mifflin Co.; *4 left* Michael Newman/PhotoEdit; *4 right* FoodCollection/SuperStock; *5 right* Guy Jarvis/School Division/Houghton Mifflin Co.; *6 right* Jay Penni/McDougal Littell/Houghton Mifflin Co.; **70** *both* Ann Summa/McDougal Littell/Houghton Mifflin Co.; **75** *bottom right* Guy Jarvis/School Division/Houghton Mifflin Co.; *top right,* Eric Gay/AP Images; **76** *all* Ann Summa/McDougal Littell/ Houghton Mifflin Co.; **77** *all* Ann Summa/McDougal Littell/Houghton Mifflin Co.; **79** Jay Penni/McDougal Littell/ Houghton Mifflin Co.; **80** *bottom* Phil Schermeister/Corbis; **81** *background* Royalty-Free/Corbis; *inset* Carl Schneider/ Corbis; **82** *bottom left* ShutterStock; *bottom right* McDougal Littell/Houghton Mifflin Co.; *top* Jay Penni/McDougal Littell/Houghton Mifflin Co.; **86–87** Richard Wareham Fotografie/Alamy; **87** *center* David Young-Wolff/PhotoEdit; *bottom* © 2007 Robert Frerck/Odyssey/Chicago; **88** *teens* Jay Penni/McDougal Littell/Houghton Mifflin Co.; **90** *whisk* Jay Penni/McDougal Littell/Houghton Mifflin Co.; *cup* PhotoObjects/Jupiterimages Corp.; *center* Image Club; *bottom left* Ann Summa/McDougal Littell/Houghton Mifflin Co.; **91** *top left* Ann Summa; *center right* Erich Lessing/Art Resource, New York; *bottom left, The Historical Representation of Culture* (1949), Juan O'Gorman. Mosaic, southeast view of exterior of Biblioteca Central, Universidad Nacional Autónoma de México (UNAM), Mexico City. © 2005 Sandro Landucci, Mexico City/Estate of Juan O'Gorman. Photograph by Ian Pearson/Mexicolore/Bridgeman Art Library; *bottom right* Detail, *The Historical Representation of Culture* (1949), Juan O'Gorman. Exterior of Biblioteca Central, Universidad Nacional Autónoma de México (UNAM), Mexico City. © 2005 Sandro Landucci, Mexico City/Estate of Juan O'Gorman. Photograph by Ian Pearson/Mexicolore/Bridgeman Art Library; **94** *agenda* Jay Penni/McDougal

Littell/Houghton Mifflin Co.; **95** *map inset* Royalty-Free/Corbis; **101** *bottom right* Jay Penni/McDougal Littell/Houghton Mifflin Co.; *6 map inset* Royalty-Free/Corbis; **103** *2, 3, 4, 5 left, 5 right* Ann Summa/McDougal Littell/Houghton Mifflin Co.; **109** *Alfabetización (Learning the ABCs)* (1925), Diego Rivera. Mural, 2.06 m. x 1.33 m., Court of Fiestas, Level 3, West Wall, Secretaría de Educación Pública, Mexico City, DF, Mexico. © 2005 Banco de México Diego Rivera & Frida Kahlo Museums Trust, Av. Cinco de Mayo No. 2, Col. Centro, Del. Cuauhtémoc 06059, México D.F./ Photograph by Schalkwijk/Art Resource, New York; **113** Jay Penni/McDougal Littell/Houghton Mifflin Co.; **114** *both* The American School Foundation of Guadalajara, A.C.; **115** *all* The American School Foundation of Guadalajara, A.C.; **116** *center* Benson Latin American Collection/The University of Texas at Austin; *bottom* Danny Lehman/Corbis; **122** *paper* Jay Penni/McDougal Littell/Houghton Mifflin Co.; *pencil* PhotoDisc; *backpack* Guy Jarvis/School Division/Houghton Mifflin Co.; *clock rim* Willem Bosman/ShutterStock; *clock face* Andres Rodriguez/ShutterStock; **127** *modelo* Gabe Palmer/Corbis; *1* Ira Block/IPNstock; *3 map inset* Royalty-Free/Corbis; **129** *3* HIRB/Index Stock Imagery; **135** Jay Penni/McDougal Littell/Houghton Mifflin Co.; **137** *left, Autorretrato con collar (Self-portrait with Necklace)* (1933), Frida Kahlo. Oil on metal, 35 cm x 29 cm. © 2005 Colección Jacques y Natasha Gelman, Cuernavaca, Mexico. © 2005 Banco de México Diego Rivera & Frida Kahlo Museums Trust, Av. Cinco de Mayo No. 2, Col. Centro, Del. Cuauhtémoc 06059, México D.F./ Photograph by Agencia EFE; *right, Frida Kahlo* (1941), Nickolas Muray. Color photograph, assembly (Carbro) process, 40.1 cm x 29.9 cm. Gift of Mrs. Nickolas Muray. GEH NEG: 40130; 71:0050:0016. George Eastman House; **141** Jay Penni/McDougal Littell/Houghton Mifflin Co.; **142** *bottom left* Robert Fried/Alamy; *bottom right* Guy Jarvis/School Division/Houghton Mifflin Co.; **143** *right* © 2007 Robert Frerck/Odyssey/Chicago; *top left* Guy Jarvis/School Division/Houghton Mifflin Co.; **144** *bottom right* Lynne Guitar, Ph.D.; *bottom left* James Lyon/Lonely Planet Images; *top* Jay Penni/McDougal Littell/Houghton Mifflin Co.; **148–149** © 2007 David Dudenhoefer/Odyssey/Chicago.; **149** *center* HIRB/Index Stock Imagery; *bottom* Dan Gair/index Stock Imagery; **150** Jay Penni/McDougal Littell/Houghton Mifflin Co.; **152** *pasteles* Martha Granger/EDGE Productions/McDougal Littell/Houghton Mifflin Co.; *flag* Image Club; **153** *bottom center inset* Kevin Schafer/Corbis; *center right* Angelo Cavalli/age fotostock; *bottom left* Robert Fried/DDB Stock Photography; **156** *eggs* Comstock; *yogurt* Jay Penni/McDougal Littell/Houghton Mifflin Co.; **157** *bottom right* John A. Rizzo/Getty Images; **158** *apple* Comstock; **159** *modelo right, 4 right* SuperStock; *modelo left* Royalty-Free/Corbis; *5 left* Comstock; *3 left* John A. Rizzo/Getty Images; *6 left* FoodPix/Getty Images; **161** *1* SuperStock; *3* John A. Rizzo/Getty Images; *8* FoodCollection/SuperStock; **163** Jay Penni/McDougal Littell/Houghton Mifflin Co.; **164** *bottom* Renee Comet Photography, Inc./StockFood; **170** *left, La Plaza de Colón* (1986), Manuel Hernández Acevedo. Oil on board. Collection of Arte de la Cooperativa de Seguros Múltiples de Puerto Rico. © 2005 Víctor Manuel Hernández/Estate of Manuel Hernández Acevedo; **174** *all* Comstock; **175** Jay Penni/McDougal Littell/Houghton Mifflin Co.; **176** *grapes* PhotoObjects/Jupiterimages Corp.; *the rest* Guy Jarvis/School Division/Houghton Mifflin Co.; **177** *whole pineapple* Jim Jurica/ShutterStock; *halved pineapple* Rudolf Georg/ShutterStock; *can label* McDougal Littell/Houghton Mifflin Co.; *the rest* Guy Jarvis/School Division/Houghton Mifflin Co.; **178** *top* NOAA; *bottom* Tony Arruza/Corbis; **193** Kim Karpeles/Alamy; **199** *top, Goyita* (1949), Rafael Tufiño. Oil on canvas, 25 1/2 " x 21". Photograph by John Betancourt. Courtesy of Pablo Tufiño; *bottom, Smiling Country Girl* (2005), Fernando Sayán Polo. Oil on canvas, 15" x 21". Courtesy of the artist.; **202** Comstock; **203** Jay Penni/McDougal Littell/Houghton Mifflin Co.; **204** *left* Ed Kashi/Corbis; *right* HIRB/Index Stock Imagery; **205** *gift box* PhotoDisc; *the rest* Edward Hernandez/Edward H. Photos; **206** *top* Jay Penni/McDougal Littell/Houghton Mifflin Co.; *bottom left* PhotoObjects/Jupiterimages Corp.; *bottom right* David Stares/Alamy; **210–211** Jorgrn Schytte/Peter Arnold, Inc.; **211** *bottom* Terry Harris/Alamy; *center* J Marshall-Tribaleye Images/Alamy; **212** Jay Penni/McDougal Littell/Houghton Mifflin Co.; **213** David Sacks/Getty Images; **214** *bottom right* Martha Granger/EDGE Productions/McDougal Littell/Houghton Mifflin Co.; *center* Image Club; **215** *bottom left* Anthony Cassidy/Getty Images; *center right, Don Quixote* (1955), Pablo Picasso. Gouache on paper. Private collection. © 2007 Estate of Pablo Picasso/Artists Rights Society (ARS), New York. Photograph by Bridgeman Art Library; *center* AP Images; *top left* Shizuo Kambayashi/AP Images; **218** *top right* Jon Ivern/age fotostock; **219** *t-shirts* Jay Penni/McDougal Littell/Houghton Mifflin Co.; *shorts* Guy Jarvis/School Division/Houghton Mifflin Co.; *Euros* Gary Conner/PhotoEdit; **220** *spring* Jonelle Weaver/Botanica/Jupiterimages; *summer* José Pascual/age fotostock; *fall* M.A. Otsoa de Alda/age fotostock; *winter* Paco Ayala/age fotostock; **221** *3* Jay Penni/McDougal Littell/Houghton Mifflin Co.; *1, 6* Guy Jarvis/School Division/Houghton Mifflin Co.; *2, 4, 5, 7* C Squared Studios/Getty Images; *8* PhotoObjects/Jupiterimages Corp.; *modelo* Jessica Bethke/ShutterStock; **225** *shirt* PhotoObjects/Jupiterimages Corp.; *blouse* Jay Penni/McDougal Littell/Houghton Mifflin Co.; *socks* Burke/Triolo/Getty Images; *hat* Stockbyte Royalty Free; *shoes* Michael Newman/PhotoEdit; *jeans* C Squared Studios/Getty Images; **226** Jay Penni/McDougal Littell/Houghton Mifflin Co.; **227** *1* Burke/Triolo/Getty Images; *2* Siede Preis/Getty Images; *3* Guy Jarvis/School Division/Houghton Mifflin Co.; *4, 8* Lara Barrett/ShutterStock; *5, 6* C Squared Studios/Getty Images; *7* Michael Newman/PhotoEdit; *hat* Stief & Schnare/SuperStock; **229** *bottom, The Persistence of Memory* (1931), Salvador Dalí. Oil on canvas, 9 1/2" x 13" (24.1 cm x 33 cm). Museum of Modern Art, New York (162.1934). Given anonymously. © 2007 Salvador Dalí, Gala-Salvador Dalí Foundation/Artists Rights Society (ARS), New York. Digital Image © The Museum of Modern Art/Licensed by SCALA/Art Resource, NY; **233** *right* Edward Parker/Alamy; *left*

Michelle Chaplow/Alamy; **236** *right* Getty Images; *left* PhotoSpin; **237** Jay Penni/McDougal Littell/Houghton Mifflin Co.; **238** *inset* Victor Lerena/Agencia EFE; *background* Guy Jarvis/School Division/Houghton Mifflin Co.; **239** *left* Yanik Chauvin/ShutterStock; *right* Guy Jarvis/School Division/Houghton Mifflin Co.; **240** *top left* Frank Vetere/ Alamy; *top center* Royalty-Free/Corbis; *bottom right* F. Damm/Zefa/Corbis; *top right* Victor Kotler/age fotostock; **246** *steak, chicken, veggies* Jay Penni/McDougal Littell/Houghton Mifflin Co.; *fish* Rusty Hill/StockFood; **247** *bottom right* Mauricio-José Schwarz/Alamy; **248** *cake* Comstock; **251** *modelo* Christina Peters/Foodpix/Jupiterimages; *1* Jay Penni/ McDougal Littell/Houghton Mifflin Co.; *2* Rita Maas/Getty Images; *3* Rusty Hill/StockFood; *5, 6, 7* Comstock; *8* J.G. Photography/Alamy; **253** *background* Stockbyte Royalty Free; **255** *top* Bruno Perousse/age fotostock; *bottom* © 2007 Robert Frerck/Odyssey/Chicago; **257** *modelo* Royalty-Free/Corbis; *1* Jon Ivern/age fotostock; *2* Guy Moberly/ Lonely Planet Images; *6* Nigel Francis/Corbis; **259** *modelo* Christina Peters/Foodpix/Jupiterimages; *1* J.G. Photography/Alamy; *2* Jay Penni/McDougal Littell/Houghton Mifflin Co.; *3* Comstock; *5* Rita Maas/Getty Images; *6* James Carrier Photography/StockFood; *7, teen girl* Jay Penni/McDougal Littell/Houghton Mifflin Co.; *8* Rusty Hill/ StockFood; **261** *right, Las Meninas (Infanta Margarita)* (1957), Pablo Picasso. Oil on canvas, 194 cm x 260 cm. Gift of the artist, 1968, Museo Picasso, Barcelona (MPB 70.433)/© 2007 Estate of Pablo Picasso/Artists Rights Society (ARS), New York/Bridgeman Art Library; *left, Las Meninas* (1656), Diego Rodríguez Velázquez. Oil on canvas, 276 cm x 318 cm. Museo del Prado, Madrid, Spain. Photograph by Erich Lessing/Art Resource, New York; **265** Jay Penni/ McDougal Littell/Houghton Mifflin Co.; *downtown Madrid* Nigel Francis/Corbis; **266** *bottom left* Ken Welsh/age fotostock; **267** *both* Yadid Levy/Alamy; **268** *top right, Landscape Near El Escorial* (1932), Ignacio Zuloaga y Zabaleta. Oil on canvas, 71 cm x 96 cm. Photograph by Erich Lessing/Art Resource, New York; *bottom right, Calle de Melipilla* (sin fecha), Juan Francisco González (1853 -1933). Óleo sobre cartón, 30 cm x 41 cm. Colección Museo Nacional de Bellas Artes, Santiago, Chile; Jay Penni/McDougal Littell/Houghton Mifflin Co.; **272–273** © 2007 David Dudenhoefer/ Odyssey/Chicago; **273** *center* Pierre Merimee/Corbis; *bottom* David Noton/Getty Images; **274** *teens* Jay Penni/ McDougal Littell/Houghton Mifflin Co.

All other photography by Jorge Albán/McDougal Littell/Houghton Mifflin Co.

Illustration

4 *top* Anna Veltfort; **10** *all* Vilma Ortiz-Dillon; **12-15** *maps* Mapquest.com; **16** *keypad* Steve McEntee; **20** *map* Mapquest.com; **24** *all* Anna Veltfort; **26** *all* James Yamasaki; **28-29** *map* Mike Reagan; **39** *all* Vilma Ortiz-Dillon; **41** Beth Griffis Johnson; **45** *faces* Steve McEntee; **46** Pablo Torrecilla; **54** *map* Mapquest.com; **65** Steve McEntee; **68** Vilma Ortiz-Dillon; **71** *both* Anna Veltfort; **73** Anna Veltfort; **74** *both* Brie Spangler; **90-91** *map* Mike Reagan; **95** *clocks* Steve McEntee; **97** *digital clocks* Steve McEntee; **99** Steve McEntee; **108** *both* Brie Spangler; **114, 115** *logo* The American School Foundation of Guadalajara, A.C.; **116** *map* Mapquest.com; **124** *faces* Steve McEntee; **125** Steve McEntee; **130** *faces* Steve McEntee; **131** Anna Veltfort; **133** *faces* Steve McEntee; **136** Pablo Torrecilla; **151** Steve McEntee; **152-153** *map* Mike Reagan; **159** Vilma Ortiz-Dillon; **163** *faces* Steve McEntee; **165** Steve McEntee; **169** *all* Anna Veltfort; **171** Vincent Regimbald; **185** *calendar pages* Kenneth Batelman; **192** Steve McEntee; **197** *all* Anna Veltfort; **198** Pablo Torrecilla; **214-215** *map* Mike Reagan; **221** *top* Anna Veltfort; **232** Vincent Regimbald; **249** Vilma Ortiz-Dillon; **260** Tim Jones.

All other illustrations by Robin Storesund or Chris Wilson/McDougal Littell/Houghton Mifflin Co.